𝕮𝖊𝖓𝖙𝖊𝖓𝖆𝖗𝖕 𝕰𝖉𝖎𝖙𝖎𝖔𝖓

THE COMPLETE WORKS OF
RALPH WALDO EMERSON

WITH

A BIOGRAPHICAL

INTRODUCTION AND NOTES

BY EDWARD WALDO EMERSON AND

A GENERAL INDEX

VOLUME

IX

Ralph Waldo Emerson in 1854

POEMS

BY

RALPH WALDO EMERSON

BOSTON AND NEW YORK

HOUGHTON MIFFLIN COMPANY

The Riverside Press Cambridge

PREFACE

IN Mr. Cabot's prefatory note to the Riverside Edition of the Poems, published the
year after Mr. Emerson's death, he said : —

"This volume contains nearly all the pieces
included in the POEMS and MAY-DAY of former
editions. In 1876, Mr. Emerson published a
selection from his Poems, adding six new ones
and omitting many.[1] Of those omitted, several
are now restored, in accordance with the expressed wishes of many readers and lovers of
them. Also some pieces never before published
are here given in an Appendix ; on various
grounds. Some of them appear to have had
Mr. Emerson's approval, but to have been
withheld because they were unfinished. These
it seemed best not to suppress, now that they can
never receive their completion. Others, mostly
of an early date, remained unpublished, doubtless because of their personal and private nature.
Some of these seem to have an autobiographic
interest sufficient to justify their publication.
Others again, often mere fragments, have been

[1] *Selected Poems* : Little Classic Edition.

admitted as characteristic, or as expressing in poetic form thoughts found in the Essays.

" In coming to a decision in these cases it seemed, on the whole, preferable to take the risk of including too much rather than the opposite, and to leave the task of further winnowing to the hands of Time.

" As was stated in the preface to the first volume of this edition of Mr. Emerson's writings, the readings adopted by him in the Selected Poems have not always been followed here, but in some cases preference has been given to corrections made by him when he was in fuller strength than at the time of the last revision.

" A change in the arrangement of the stanzas of ' May-Day,' in the part representative of the march of Spring, received his sanction as bringing them more nearly in accordance with the events in Nature."

In the preparation of the Riverside Edition of the *Poems*, Mr. Cabot very considerately took the present editor into counsel (as representing Mr. Emerson's family), who at that time in turn took counsel with several persons of taste and mature judgment with regard es-

pecially to the admission of poems hitherto
unpublished and of fragments that seemed interesting and pleasing. Mr. Cabot and he were
entirely in accord with regard to the Riverside
Edition. In the Centenary Edition, the substance of the Riverside Edition has been preserved, with hardly an exception, although some
poems and fragments have been added. None of
the poems therein printed have been omitted.
" The House," which appeared in the first volume of *Poems*, and " Nemesis," " Una," " Love
and Thought " and " Merlin's Songs," from the
May-Day volume, have been restored. To the
few mottoes of the Essays, which Mr. Emerson
printed as " Elements " in *May-Day*, most of the
others have been added. Following Mr. Emerson's precedent of giving his brother Edward's
" Last Farewell " a place beside the poem in his
memory, two pleasing poems by Ellen Tucker,
his first wife, which he published in the *Dial*, have
been placed with his own poems relating to her.

The publication in the last edition of some
poems that Mr. Emerson had long kept by
him, but had never quite been ready to print,
and of various fragments on Poetry, Nature
and Life, was not done without advice and care-

ful consideration, and then was felt to be perhaps a rash experiment. The continued interest
which has been shown in the author's thought
and methods and life — for these unfinished
pieces contain much autobiography — has made
the present editor feel it justifiable to keep
almost all of these and to add a few. Their order
has been slightly altered.

A few poems from the verse-books sufficiently complete to have a title are printed in the
Appendix for the first time : " Insight," " September," " October," " Hymn " and " Riches."

After much hesitation the editor has gathered in their order of time, and printed at the
end of the book, some twenty early pieces, a few
of them taken from the Appendix of the last
edition and others never printed before. They
are for the most part journals in verse covering
the period of his school-teaching, study for the
ministry and exercise of that office, his sickness,
bereavement, travel abroad and return to the
new life. This sad period of probation is illu-
minated by the episode of his first love. Not
for their poetical merit, except in flashes, but
for the light they throw on the growth of his
thought and character are they included.

With regard to the notes: the editor has annotated the poems where possible from the journals and the essays, has given various readings where it seemed worth while, and their dates when he knew them, with such circumstances and facts as he thought might be interesting. He has in a few instances given from the note-book the original rhapsody in which Mr. Emerson strove to render on the moment, as best he might, the message which he heard from the woodland Muse.

Where there is any question as to the significance of a poem or passage, the editor has tried to make clear in which cases the explanations he offers are given confidently as based on authority, and in which cases he merely hazards a surmise. He admits responsibility for many titles in the Appendix.

No attempt will be made to estimate Emerson's place among the poets. It was his lot to be

Joy-giver and enjoyer,

as his Saadi says the poet should be, and, though not thinking highly of his own work, he said, " I am more of a poet than anything else." In September, 1839, he wrote to his unseen friend, John Sterling, " I am naturally keenly susceptible to the pleasures of rhythm, and cannot believe but one day I shall attain to that splendid dialect, so ardent is my wish ; and these wishes, I suppose, are ever only the buds of power ; but up to this hour I have never had a true success in such attempts." With an eager patience he waited his appointed hour when his expression should be liberated, for the message came to him listening ; "for poetry," he said, "was all written before time was, and whenever we are so finely organized that we can penetrate into that region where the air is music, we hear those primal warblings and attempt to write them down, but we lose ever and anon a word or a verse, and substitute something of our own and thus miswrite the poem. The men of more delicate ear write down these cadences more faithfully, and these transcripts, though imperfect, become the songs of Nations." He saw the stream of Nature and Spirit always flowing, and he told his friend Dr. Bartol, " The miller, like the poet, is a lazy man, setting his wheel in the Stream ; " and added, " But his watching is work."

Dr. Holmes, in the last years of his life,

studied his friend's poems and tried him by his own test (though he by no means admits this as the only one) : —

"Shall we rank Emerson among the great poets or not?

"'The great poets are judged by the frame of mind which they induce; and to them, of all men, the severest criticism is due.'

"These are Emerson's words in the Preface to *Parnassus*. His own poems will stand the test as well as any in the language."

The case is not closed. In this volume the course of the Muse, as Emerson tells it, is pursued with regard to his own poems.

> I hang my verses in the wind,
> Time and tide their faults will find.

EDWARD W. EMERSON.

March 12, 1904.

xvi   CONTENTS

CONTENTS

The portrait used as a frontispiece to this volume is from a daguerreotype taken by Hawes in 1854, now in the possession of the family, and never before reproduced.

I

POEMS

POEMS

GOOD–BYE

GOOD-BYE, proud world! I 'm going home:
Thou art not my friend, and I 'm not thine.
Long through thy weary crowds I roam;
A river-ark on the ocean brine,
Long I 've been tossed like the driven foam;
But now, proud world! I 'm going home.

Good-bye to Flattery's fawning face;
To Grandeur with his wise grimace;
To upstart Wealth's averted eye;
To supple Office, low and high;
To crowded halls, to court and street;
To frozen hearts and hasting feet;
To those who go, and those who come;
Good-bye, proud world! I 'm going home.

I am going to my own hearth-stone,
Bosomed in yon green hills alone, —
A secret nook in a pleasant land,
Whose groves the frolic fairies planned;
Where arches green, the livelong day,
Echo the blackbird's roundelay,

And vulgar feet have never trod
A spot that is sacred to thought and God.

O, when I am safe in my sylvan home,
I tread on the pride of Greece and Rome;
And when I am stretched beneath the pines,
Where the evening star so holy shines,
I laugh at the lore and the pride of man,
At the sophist schools and the learned clan;
For what are they all, in their high conceit,
When man in the bush with God may meet?

EACH AND ALL

LITTLE thinks, in the field, yon red-cloaked clown
Of thee from the hill-top looking down;
The heifer that lows in the upland farm,
Far-heard, lows not thine ear to charm;
The sexton, tolling his bell at noon,
Deems not that great Napoleon
Stops his horse, and lists with delight,
Whilst his files sweep round yon Alpine height; [1]
Nor knowest thou what argument
Thy life to thy neighbor's creed has lent.
All are needed by each one;
Nothing is fair or good alone.
I thought the sparrow's note from heaven,

Singing at dawn on the alder bough;
I brought him home, in his nest, at even;
He sings the song, but it cheers not now,
For I did not bring home the river and sky; —
He sang to my ear, — they sang to my eye.[1]
The delicate shells lay on the shore;
The bubbles of the latest wave
Fresh pearls to their enamel gave,
And the bellowing of the savage sea
Greeted their safe escape to me.
I wiped away the weeds and foam,
I fetched my sea-born treasures home;
But the poor, unsightly, noisome things
Had left their beauty on the shore
With the sun and the sand and the wild uproar.
The lover watched his graceful maid,
As 'mid the virgin train she strayed,
Nor knew her beauty's best attire
Was woven still by the snow-white choir.
At last she came to his hermitage,
Like the bird from the woodlands to the cage; —
The gay enchantment was undone,
A gentle wife, but fairy none.
Then I said, ' I covet truth;
Beauty is unripe childhood's cheat;
I leave it behind with the games of youth : '—
As I spoke, beneath my feet
The ground-pine curled its pretty wreath,
Running over the club-moss burrs;

I inhaled the violet's breath;
Around me stood the oaks and firs;
Pine-cones and acorns lay on the ground;
Over me soared the eternal sky,
Full of light and of deity;
Again I saw, again I heard,
The rolling river, the morning bird; —
Beauty through my senses stole;
I yielded myself to the perfect whole.

THE PROBLEM

I LIKE a church; I like a cowl;
I love a prophet of the soul;
And on my heart monastic aisles
Fall like sweet strains, or pensive smiles;
Yet not for all his faith can see
Would I that cowlèd churchman be.

Why should the vest on him allure,
Which I could not on me endure?

Not from a vain or shallow thought
His awful Jove young Phidias brought; [1]
Never from lips of cunning fell
The thrilling Delphic oracle;
Out from the heart of nature rolled

The burdens of the Bible old;
The litanies of nations came,
Like the volcano's tongue of flame,
Up from the burning core below,—
The canticles of love and woe:
The hand that rounded Peter's dome
And groined the aisles of Christian Rome
Wrought in a sad sincerity;
Himself from God he could not free;
He builded better than he knew;—
The conscious stone to beauty grew.[1]

Know'st thou what wove yon woodbird's nest
Of leaves, and feathers from her breast?
Or how the fish outbuilt her shell,
Painting with morn each annual cell?
Or how the sacred pine-tree adds
To her old leaves new myriads?
Such and so grew these holy piles,
Whilst love and terror laid the tiles.
Earth proudly wears the Parthenon,
As the best gem upon her zone,
And Morning opes with haste her lids
To gaze upon the Pyramids;
O'er England's abbeys bends the sky,
As on its friends, with kindred eye;
For out of Thought's interior sphere
These wonders rose to upper air;
And Nature gladly gave them place,

Adopted them into her race,
And granted them an equal date
With Andes and with Ararat.

These temples grew as grows the grass;
Art might obey, but not surpass.
The passive Master lent his hand
To the vast soul that o'er him planned;
And the same power that reared the shrine
Bestrode the tribes that knelt within.
Ever the fiery Pentecost
Girds with one flame the countless host,
Trances the heart through chanting choirs,
And through the priest the mind inspires.
The word unto the prophet spoken
Was writ on tables yet unbroken;
The word by seers or sibyls told,
In groves of oak, or fanes of gold,
Still floats upon the morning wind,
Still whispers to the willing mind.
One accent of the Holy Ghost
The heedless world hath never lost.
I know what say the fathers wise, —
The Book itself before me lies,
Old *Chrysostom*, best Augustine,[1]
And he who blent both in his line,
The younger *Golden Lips* or mines,
Taylor, the Shakspeare of divines.
His words are music in my ear,

I see his cowlèd portrait dear;
And yet, for all his faith could see,
I would not the good bishop be.

TO RHEA

THEE, dear friend, a brother soothes,
Not with flatteries, but truths,
Which tarnish not, but purify
To light which dims the morning's eye.
I have come from the spring-woods,
From the fragrant solitudes ; —
Listen what the poplar-tree
And murmuring waters counselled me.

If with love thy heart has burned ;
If thy love is unreturned ;
Hide thy grief within thy breast,
Though it tear thee unexpressed ;
For when love has once departed
From the eyes of the false-hearted,
And one by one has torn off quite
The bandages of purple light ;
Though thou wert the loveliest
Form the soul had ever dressed,
Thou shalt seem, in each reply,
A vixen to his altered eye ;

Thy softest pleadings seem too bold,
Thy praying lute will seem to scold;
Though thou kept the straightest road,
Yet thou errest far and broad.

But thou shalt do as do the gods
In their cloudless periods;
For of this lore be thou sure, —
Though thou forget, the gods, secure,
Forget never their command,
But make the statute of this land.
As they lead, so follow all,
Ever have done, ever shall.
Warning to the blind and deaf,
'T is written on the iron leaf,
Who drinks of Cupid's nectar cup
Loveth downward, and not up;
He who loves, of gods or men,
Shall not by the same be loved again;
His sweetheart's idolatry
Falls, in turn, a new degree.
When a god is once beguiled
By beauty of a mortal child
And by her radiant youth delighted,
He is not fooled, but warily knoweth
His love shall never be requited.
And thus the wise Immortal doeth, —
'T is his study and delight
To bless that creature day and night;

From all evils to defend her;
In her lap to pour all splendor;
To ransack earth for riches rare,
And fetch her stars to deck her hair:
He mixes music with her thoughts,
And saddens her with heavenly doubts:
All grace, all good his great heart knows,
Profuse in love, the king bestows,
Saying, ' Hearken! Earth, Sea, Air!
This monument of my despair
Build I to the All-Good, All-Fair.
Not for a private good,
But I, from my beatitude,
Albeit scorned as none was scorned,
Adorn her as was none adorned.
I make this maiden an ensample
To Nature, through her kingdoms ample,
Whereby to model newer races,
Statelier forms and fairer faces;
To carry man to new degrees
Of power and of comeliness.
These presents be the hostages
Which I pawn for my release.
See to thyself, O Universe!
Thou art better, and not worse.' —
And the god, having given all,
Is freed forever from his thrall.

THE VISIT

Askest, ' How long thou shalt stay ? '
Devastator of the day !
Know, each substance and relation,
Thorough nature's operation,
Hath its unit, bound and metre ;
And every new compound
Is some product and repeater, —
Product of the earlier found.
But the unit of the visit,
The encounter of the wise, —
Say, what other metre is it
Than the meeting of the eyes ?
Nature poureth into nature
Through the channels of that feature,
Riding on the ray of sight,
Fleeter far than whirlwinds go,
Or for service, or delight,
Hearts to hearts their meaning show,
Sum their long experience,
And import intelligence.
Single look has drained the breast ;
Single moment years confessed.
The duration of a glance
Is the term of convenance,

And, though thy rede be church or state,
Frugal multiples of that.
Speeding Saturn cannot halt;
Linger, — thou shalt rue the fault:
If Love his moment overstay,
Hatred's swift repulsions play.

URIEL

It fell in the ancient periods
    Which the brooding soul surveys,
Or ever the wild Time coined itself
    Into calendar months and days.

This was the lapse of Uriel,
Which in Paradise befell.
Once, among the Pleiads walking,
Seyd overheard the young gods talking;
And the treason, too long pent,
To his ears was evident.
The young deities discussed
Laws of form, and metre just,
Orb, quintessence, and sunbeams,
What subsisteth, and what seems.
One, with low tones that decide,
And doubt and reverend use defied,
With a look that solved the sphere,

And stirred the devils everywhere,
Gave his sentiment divine
Against the being of a line.
' Line in nature is not found;
Unit and universe are round;
In vain produced, all rays return;
Evil will bless, and ice will burn.'
As Uriel spoke with piercing eye,
A shudder ran around the sky;
The stern old war-gods shook their heads,
The seraphs frowned from myrtle-beds;
Seemed to the holy festival
The rash word boded ill to all;
The balance-beam of Fate was bent;
The bounds of good and ill were rent;
Strong Hades could not keep his own,
But all slid to confusion.[1]

A sad self-knowledge, withering, fell
On the beauty of Uriel;
In heaven once eminent, the god
Withdrew, that hour, into his cloud;
Whether doomed to long gyration
In the sea of generation,
Or by knowledge grown too bright
To hit the nerve of feebler sight.[2]
Straightway, a forgetting wind
Stole over the celestial kind,
And their lips the secret kept,

If in ashes the fire-seed slept.
But now and then, truth-speaking things
Shamed the angels' veiling wings;
And, shrilling from the solar course,
Or from fruit of chemic force,
Procession of a soul in matter,[1]
Or the speeding change of water,
Or out of the good of evil born,
Came Uriel's voice of cherub scorn,
And a blush tinged the upper sky,
And the gods shook, they knew not why.

THE WORLD-SOUL

THANKS to the morning light,
  Thanks to the foaming sea,
To the uplands of New Hampshire,
  To the green-haired forest free;
Thanks to each man of courage,
  To the maids of holy mind,
To the boy with his games undaunted
  Who never looks behind.[2]

Cities of proud hotels,
  Houses of rich and great,
Vice nestles in your chambers,
  Beneath your roofs of slate.

It cannot conquer folly, —
　　Time-and-space-conquering steam, —
And the light-outspeeding telegraph
　　Bears nothing on its beam.

The politics are base;
　　The letters do not cheer;
And 't is far in the deeps of history,
　　The voice that speaketh clear.
Trade and the streets ensnare us,
　　Our bodies are weak and worn;
We plot and corrupt each other,
　　And we despoil the unborn.

Yet there in the parlor sits
　　Some figure of noble guise, —
Our angel, in a stranger's form,
　　Or woman's pleading eyes;
Or only a flashing sunbeam
　　In at the window-pane;
Or Music pours on mortals
　　Its beautiful disdain.[1]

The inevitable morning
　　Finds them who in cellars be;
And be sure the all-loving Nature
　　Will smile in a factory.
Yon ridge of purple landscape,
　　Yon sky between the walls,

Hold all the hidden wonders
  In scanty intervals.

Alas! the Sprite that haunts us
  Deceives our rash desire;
It whispers of the glorious gods,
  And leaves us in the mire.
We cannot learn the cipher
  That 's writ upon our cell;
Stars taunt us by a mystery
  Which we could never spell.[1]

If but one hero knew it,
  The world would blush in flame;
The sage, till he hit the secret,
  Would hang his head for shame.
Our brothers have not read it,
  Not one has found the key;
And henceforth we are comforted, —
  We are but such as they.[2]

Still, still the secret presses;
  The nearing clouds draw down;
The crimson morning flames into
  The fopperies of the town.
Within, without the idle earth,
  Stars weave eternal rings;
The sun himself shines heartily,
  And shares the joy he brings.

And what if Trade sow cities
    Like shells along the shore,
And thatch with towns the prairie broad
    With railways ironed o'er ? —
They are but sailing foam-bells
    Along Thought's causing stream,
And take their shape and sun-color
    From him that sends the dream.

For Destiny never swerves
    Nor yields to men the helm ;
He shoots his thought, by hidden nerves,
    Throughout the solid realm.
The patient Dæmon sits,
    With roses and a shroud ;
He has his way, and deals his gifts, —
    But ours is not allowed.[1]

He is no churl nor trifler,
    And his viceroy is none, —
Love-without-weakness, —
    Of Genius sire and son.
And his will is not thwarted ;
    The seeds of land and sea
Are the atoms of his body bright,
    And his behest obey.

He serveth the servant,
    The brave he loves amain ;

He kills the cripple and the sick,
  And straight begins again;
For gods delight in gods,
  And thrust the weak aside;
To him who scorns their charities
  Their arms fly open wide.

When the old world is sterile
  And the ages are effete,
He will from wrecks and sediment
  The fairer world complete.
He forbids to despair;
  His cheeks mantle with mirth;
And the unimagined good of men
  Is yeaning at the birth.

Spring still makes spring in the mind
  When sixty years are told;
Love wakes anew this throbbing heart,
  And we are never old;
Over the winter glaciers
  I see the summer glow,
And through the wild-piled snow-drift
  The warm rosebuds below.

THE SPHINX

THE Sphinx is drowsy,
  Her wings are furled:
Her ear is heavy,
  She broods on the world.
"Who'll tell me my secret,
  The ages have kept? —
I awaited the seer
  While they slumbered and slept: —

"The fate of the man-child,
  The meaning of man;
Known fruit of the unknown;
  Dædalian plan;
Out of sleeping a waking,
  Out of waking a sleep;
Life death overtaking;
  Deep underneath deep?

"Erect as a sunbeam,
  Upspringeth the palm;
The elephant browses,
  Undaunted and calm;
In beautiful motion
  The thrush plies his wings;

Kind leaves of his covert,
Your silence he sings.

" The waves, unashamèd,
In difference sweet,
Play glad with the breezes,
Old playfellows meet;
The journeying atoms,
Primordial wholes,
Firmly draw, firmly drive,
By their animate poles.

" Sea, earth, air, sound, silence,
Plant, quadruped, bird,
By one music enchanted,
One deity stirred, —
Each the other adorning,
Accompany still;
Night veileth the morning,
The vapor the hill.

" The babe by its mother
Lies bathèd in joy;
Glide its hours uncounted, —
The sun is its toy;
Shines the peace of all being,
Without cloud, in its eyes;
And the sum of the world
In soft miniature lies.

" But man crouches and blushes,
    Absconds and conceals ;
He creepeth and peepeth,
    He palters and steals ;
Infirm, melancholy,
    Jealous glancing around,
An oaf, an accomplice,
    He poisons the ground.[1]

" Out spoke the great mother,
    Beholding his fear ; —
At the sound of her accents
    Cold shuddered the sphere : —
' Who has drugged my boy's cup ?
    Who has mixed my boy's bread ?
Who, with sadness and madness,
    Has turned my child's head ? ' " [2]

I heard a poet answer
    Aloud and cheerfully,
" Say on, sweet Sphinx ! thy dirges
    Are pleasant songs to me.
Deep love lieth under
    These pictures of time ;
They fade in the light of
    Their meaning sublime.

" The fiend that man harries
    Is love of the Best ;

Yawns the pit of the Dragon,
  Lit by rays from the Blest.
The Lethe of Nature
  Can't trance him again,
Whose soul sees the perfect,
  Which his eyes seek in vain.

" To vision profounder,
  Man's spirit must dive;
His aye-rolling orb
  At no goal will arrive;
The heavens that now draw him
  With sweetness untold,
Once found, — for new heavens
  He spurneth the old.

" Pride ruined the angels,
  Their shame them restores;
Lurks the joy that is sweetest
  In stings of remorse.
Have I a lover
  Who is noble and free? —
I would he were nobler
  Than to love me.

" Eterne alternation
  Now follows, now flies;
And under pain, pleasure, —
  Under pleasure, pain lies.

Love works at the centre,
 Heart-heaving alway;
Forth speed the strong pulses
 To the borders of day.

" Dull Sphinx, Jove keep thy five wits;
 Thy sight is growing blear;
Rue, myrrh and cummin for the Sphinx,
 Her muddy eyes to clear! "
The old Sphinx bit her thick lip, —
 Said, " Who taught thee me to name?
I am thy spirit, yoke-fellow;
 Of thine eye I am eyebeam.

" Thou art the unanswered question;¹
 Couldst see thy proper eye,
Alway it asketh, asketh;
 And each answer is a lie.
So take thy quest through nature,
 It through thousand natures ply;
Ask on, thou clothed eternity;
 Time is the false reply."

Uprose the merry Sphinx,
 And crouched no more in stone;
She melted into purple cloud,
 She silvered in the moon;
She spired into a yellow flame;
 She flowered in blossoms red;

She flowed into a foaming wave:
She stood Monadnoc's head.

Thorough a thousand voices
Spoke the universal dame;
" Who telleth one of my meanings
Is master of all I am." [1]

ALPHONSO OF CASTILE

I, ALPHONSO, live and learn,
Seeing Nature go astern.
Things deteriorate in kind;
Lemons run to leaves and rind;
Meagre crop of figs and limes;
Shorter days and harder times.
Flowering April cools and dies
In the insufficient skies.
Imps, at high midsummer, blot
Half the sun's disk with a spot;
'T will not now avail to tan
Orange cheek or skin of man.
Roses bleach, the goats are dry,
Lisbon quakes, the people cry.
Yon pale, scrawny fisher fools,
Gaunt as bitterns in the pools,
Are no brothers of my blood; —

They discredit Adamhood.
Eyes of gods! ye must have seen,
O'er your ramparts as ye lean,
The general debility; [1]
Of genius the sterility;
Mighty projects countermanded;
Rash ambition, brokenhanded;
Puny man and scentless rose
Tormenting Pan to double the dose.
Rebuild or ruin: either fill
Of vital force the wasted rill,
Or tumble all again in heap
To weltering Chaos and to sleep. [2]

Say, Seigniors, are the old Niles dry,
Which fed the veins of earth and sky,
That mortals miss the loyal heats,
Which drove them erst to social feats;
Now, to a savage selfness grown,
Think nature barely serves for one;
With science poorly mask their hurt;
And vex the gods with question pert,
Immensely curious whether you
Still are rulers, or Mildew?

Masters, I'm in pain with you;
Masters, I'll be plain with you;
In my palace of Castile,
I, a king, for kings can feel.

There my thoughts the matter roll,
And solve and oft resolve the whole.
And, for I'm styled Alphonse the Wise,
Ye shall not fail for sound advice.
Before ye want a drop of rain,
Hear the sentiment of Spain.

You have tried famine : no more try it;
Ply us now with a full diet;
Teach your pupils now with plenty,
For one sun supply us twenty.
I have thought it thoroughly over, —
State of hermit, state of lover;
We must have society,
We cannot spare variety.
Hear you, then, celestial fellows!
Fits not to be overzealous;
Steads not to work on the clean jump,
Nor wine nor brains perpetual pump.
Men and gods are too extense;
Could you slacken and condense?
Your rank overgrowths reduce
Till your kinds abound with juice?
Earth, crowded, cries, 'Too many men!'
My counsel is, kill nine in ten,
And bestow the shares of all
On the remnant decimal.
Add their nine lives to this cat;
Stuff their nine brains in one hat;

Make his frame and forces square
With the labors he must dare;
Thatch his flesh, and even his years
With the marble which he rears.
There, growing slowly old at ease
No faster than his planted trees,
He may, by warrant of his age,
In schemes of broader scope engage.
So shall ye have a man of the sphere
Fit to grace the solar year.

MITHRIDATES

I CANNOT spare water or wine,
　　Tobacco-leaf, or poppy, or rose;
From the earth-poles to the Line,
　　All between that works or grows,
Every thing is kin of mine.

Give me agates for my meat;
Give me cantharids to eat;
From air and ocean bring me foods,
From all zones and altitudes; —

From all natures, sharp and slimy,
　　Salt and basalt, wild and tame:
Tree and lichen, ape, sea-lion,
　　Bird, and reptile, be my game.

Ivy for my fillet band;
Blinding dog-wood in my hand;
Hemlock for my sherbet cull me,
And the prussic juice to lull me;
Swing me in the upas boughs,
Vampyre-fanned, when I carouse.

Too long shut in strait and few,
Thinly dieted on dew,
I will use the world, and sift it,
To a thousand humors shift it,
As you spin a cherry.
O doleful ghosts, and goblins merry!
O all you virtues, methods, mights,
Means, appliances, delights,
Reputed wrongs and braggart rights,
Smug routine, and things allowed,
Minorities, things under cloud!
Hither! take me, use me, fill me,
Vein and artery, though ye kill me! [1]

TO J. W.

SET not thy foot on graves;
Hear what wine and roses say;
The mountain chase, the summer waves,
The crowded town, thy feet may well delay.

Set not thy foot on graves;
Nor seek to unwind the shroud
Which charitable Time
And Nature have allowed
To wrap the errors of a sage sublime.

Set not thy foot on graves;
Care not to strip the dead
Of his sad ornament,
His myrrh, and wine, and rings,

His sheet of lead,
And trophies burièd:
Go, get them where he earned them when alive;
As resolutely dig or dive.

Life is too short to waste
In critic peep or cynic bark,
Quarrel or reprimand:
'T will soon be dark;
Up! mind thine own aim, and
God speed the mark!

DESTINY

THAT you are fair or wise is vain,
Or strong, or rich, or generous;
You must add the untaught strain
That sheds beauty on the rose.
There's a melody born of melody,
Which melts the world into a sea.
Toil could never compass it;
Art its height could never hit;
It came never out of wit;
But a music music-born
Well may Jove and Juno scorn.
Thy beauty, if it lack the fire
Which drives me mad with sweet desire,
What boots it? What the soldier's mail,
Unless he conquer and prevail?
What all the goods thy pride which lift,
If thou pine for another's gift?
Alas! that one is born in blight,
Victim of perpetual slight:
When thou lookest on his face,
Thy heart saith, ' Brother, go thy ways!
None shall ask thee what thou doest,
Or care a rush for what thou knowest,
Or listen when thou repliest,

Or remember where thou liest,
Or how thy supper is sodden;'
And another is born
To make the sun forgotten.[1]
Surely he carries a talisman
Under his tongue;
Broad his shoulders are and strong;
And his eye is scornful,
Threatening and young.
I hold it of little matter
Whether your jewel be of pure water,
A rose diamond or a white,
But whether it dazzle me with light.
I care not how you are dressed,
In coarsest weeds or in the best;
Nor whether your name is base or brave:
Nor for the fashion of your behavior;
But whether you charm me,
Bid my bread feed and my fire warm me
And dress up Nature in your favor.[2]
One thing is forever good;
That one thing is Success, —
Dear to the Eumenides,
And to all the heavenly brood.
Who bides at home, nor looks abroad,
Carries the eagles, and masters the sword.[3]

GUY

MORTAL mixed of middle clay,
Attempered to the night and day,
Interchangeable with things,
Needs no amulets nor rings.
Guy possessed the talisman
That all things from him began;
And as, of old, Polycrates[1]
Chained the sunshine and the breeze,
So did Guy betimes discover
Fortune was his guard and lover;
In strange junctures, felt, with awe,
His own symmetry with law;
That no mixture could withstand
The virtue of his lucky hand.
He gold or jewel could not lose,
Nor not receive his ample dues.
Fearless Guy had never foes,
He did their weapons decompose.
Aimed at him, the blushing blade
Healed as fast the wounds it made.
If on the foeman fell his gaze,
Him it would straightway blind or craze,
In the street, if he turned round,
His eye the eye 't was seeking found.

It seemed his Genius discreet
Worked on the Maker's own receipt,
And made each tide and element
Stewards of stipend and of rent;
So that the common waters fell
As costly wine into his well.
He had so sped his wise affairs
That he caught Nature in his snares.
Early or late, the falling rain
Arrived in time to swell his grain;
Stream could not so perversely wind
But corn of Guy's was there to grind:
The siroc found it on its way,
To speed his sails, to dry his hay;
And the world's sun seemed to rise
To drudge all day for Guy the wise.
In his rich nurseries, timely skill
Strong crab with nobler blood did fill;
The zephyr in his garden rolled
From plum-trees vegetable gold;
And all the hours of the year
With their own harvest honored were.
There was no frost but welcome came,
Nor freshet, nor midsummer flame.
Belonged to wind and world the toil
And venture, and to Guy the oil.

HAMATREYA

Bulkeley, Hunt, Willard, Hosmer, Meriam, Flint,
Possessed the land which rendered to their toil
Hay, corn, roots, hemp, flax, apples, wool and wood.[1]
Each of these landlords walked amidst his farm,
Saying, ' 'T is mine, my children's and my name's.
How sweet the west wind sounds in my own trees!
How graceful climb those shadows on my hill!
I fancy these pure waters and the flags
Know me, as does my dog: we sympathize;
And, I affirm, my actions smack of the soil.'

Where are these men? Asleep beneath their grounds:
And strangers, fond as they, their furrows plough.
Earth laughs in flowers, to see her boastful boys
Earth-proud, proud of the earth which is not theirs;
Who steer the plough, but cannot steer their feet
Clear of the grave.
They added ridge to valley, brook to pond,
And sighed for all that bounded their domain;
'This suits me for a pasture; that's my park;
We must have clay, lime, gravel, granite-ledge,
And misty lowland, where to go for peat.
The land is well, — lies fairly to the south.
'T is good, when you have crossed the sea and back,

To find the sitfast acres where you left them.'
Ah! the hot owner sees not Death, who adds
Him to his land, a lump of mould the more.
Hear what the Earth says : —

EARTH-SONG

    ' Mine and yours;
      Mine, not yours.
      Earth endures;
      Stars abide —
      Shine down in the old sea;
      Old are the shores;
      But where are old men?
      I who have seen much,
      Such have I never seen.

    ' The lawyer's deed
      Ran sure,
      In tail,
      To them, and to their heirs
      Who shall succeed,
      Without fail,
      Forevermore.

    ' Here is the land,
      Shaggy with wood,
      With its old valley,
      Mound and flood.
      But the heritors? —

Fled like the flood's foam.
The lawyer, and the laws,
And the kingdom,
Clean swept herefrom.

'They called me theirs,
Who so controlled me;
Yet every one
Wished to stay, and is gone,
How am I theirs,
If they cannot hold me,
But I hold them?'

When I heard the Earth-song
I was no longer brave;
My avarice cooled
Like lust in the chill of the grave.

THE RHODORA:

ON BEING ASKED, WHENCE IS THE FLOWER?

In May, when sea-winds pierced our solitudes,
I found the fresh Rhodora in the woods,
Spreading its leafless blooms in a damp nook,
To please the desert and the sluggish brook.
The purple petals, fallen in the pool,

Made the black water with their beauty gay;
Here might the red-bird come his plumes to cool,
And court the flower that cheapens his array.
Rhodora! if the sages ask thee why
This charm is wasted on the earth and sky,
Tell them, dear, that if eyes were made for seeing,
Then Beauty is its own excuse for being: [1]
Why thou wert there, O rival of the rose!
I never thought to ask, I never knew:
But, in my simple ignorance, suppose
The self-same Power that brought me there brought you.

THE HUMBLE-BEE

BURLY, dozing humble-bee,
Where thou art is clime for me.
Let them sail for Porto Rique,
Far-off heats through seas to seek;
I will follow thee alone,
Thou animated torrid-zone!
Zigzag steerer, desert cheerer,
Let me chase thy waving lines;
Keep me nearer, me thy hearer,
Singing over shrubs and vines.

Insect lover of the sun,
Joy of thy dominion!

Sailor of the atmosphere;
Swimmer through the waves of air;
Voyager of light and noon;
Epicurean of June;
Wait, I prithee, till I come
Within earshot of thy hum, —
All without is martyrdom.

When the south wind, in May days,
With a net of shining haze
Silvers the horizon wall,
And with softness touching all,
Tints the human countenance
With a color of romance,
And infusing subtle heats,
Turns the sod to violets,
Thou, in sunny solitudes,
Rover of the underwoods,
The green silence dost displace
With thy mellow, breezy bass.

Hot midsummer's petted crone,
Sweet to me thy drowsy tone
Tells of countless sunny hours,
Long days, and solid banks of flowers;
Of gulfs of sweetness without bound
In Indian wildernesses found;
Of Syrian peace, immortal leisure,
Firmest cheer, and bird-like pleasure.

Aught unsavory or unclean
Hath my insect never seen;
But violets and bilberry bells,
Maple-sap and daffodels,
Grass with green flag half-mast high,
Succory to match the sky,
Columbine with horn of honey,
Scented fern, and agrimony,
Clover, catchfly, adder's-tongue
And brier-roses, dwelt among;
All beside was unknown waste,
All was picture as he passed.

Wiser far than human seer,
Yellow-breeched philosopher!
Seeing only what is fair,
Sipping only what is sweet,
Thou dost mock at fate and care,
Leave the chaff, and take the wheat.[1]
When the fierce northwestern blast
Cools sea and land so far and fast,
Thou already slumberest deep;
Woe and want thou canst outsleep;
Want and woe, which torture us,
Thy sleep makes ridiculous.

BERRYING

' MAY be true what I had heard, —
Earth's a howling wilderness,
Truculent with fraud and force,'
Said I, strolling through the pastures,
And along the river-side.
Caught among the blackberry vines,
Feeding on the Ethiops sweet,
Pleasant fancies overtook me.
I said, ' What influence me preferred,
Elect, to dreams thus beautiful ? '
The vines replied, ' And didst thou deem
No wisdom from our berries went ? ' [1]

THE SNOW–STORM

ANNOUNCED by all the trumpets of the sky,
Arrives the snow, and, driving o'er the fields,
Seems nowhere to alight: the whited air
Hides hills and woods, the river, and the heaven,
And veils the farm-house at the garden's end.
The sled and traveller stopped, the courier's feet
Delayed, all friends shut out, the housemates sit

Around the radiant fireplace, enclosed
In a tumultuous privacy of storm.

Come see the north wind's masonry.
Out of an unseen quarry evermore
Furnished with tile, the fierce artificer
Curves his white bastions with projected roof
Round every windward stake, or tree, or door.
Speeding, the myriad-handed, his wild work
So fanciful, so savage, nought cares he
For number or proportion. Mockingly,
On coop or kennel he hangs Parian wreaths;
A swan-like form invests the hidden thorn;
Fills up the farmer's lane from wall to wall,
Maugre the farmer's sighs; and at the gate
A tapering turret overtops the work.
And when his hours are numbered, and the world
Is all his own, retiring, as he were not,
Leaves, when the sun appears, astonished Art
To mimic in slow structures, stone by stone,
Built in an age, the mad wind's night-work,
The frolic architecture of the snow.

WOODNOTES

I

I

When the pine tosses its cones
To the song of its waterfall tones,
Who speeds to the woodland walks?
To birds and trees who talks?
Cæsar of his leafy Rome,
There the poet is at home.
He goes to the river-side, —
Not hook nor line hath he;
He stands in the meadows wide, —
Nor gun nor scythe to see.[1]
Sure some god his eye enchants:
What he knows nobody wants.
In the wood he travels glad,
Without better fortune had,
Melancholy without bad.
Knowledge this man prizes best
Seems fantastic to the rest:
Pondering shadows, colors, clouds,
Grass-buds and caterpillar-shrouds,
Boughs on which the wild bees settle,
Tints that spot the violet's petal,
Why Nature loves the number five,

And why the star-form she repeats:[g]
Lover of all things alive,
Wonderer at all he meets,
Wonderer chiefly at himself,
Who can tell him what he is?
Or how meet in human elf
Coming and past eternities?

2

And such I knew, a forest seer,
A minstrel of the natural year,
Foreteller of the vernal ides,
Wise harbinger of spheres and tides,
A lover true, who knew by heart
Each joy the mountain dales impart;
It seemed that Nature could not raise
A plant in any secret place,
In quaking bog, on snowy hill,
Beneath the grass that shades the rill,
Under the snow, between the rocks,
In damp fields known to bird and fox.
But he would come in the very hour
It opened in its virgin bower,
As if a sunbeam showed the place,
And tell its long-descended race.
It seemed as if the breezes brought him,
It seemed as if the sparrows taught him;
As if by secret sight he knew
Where, in far fields, the orchis grew.

Many haps fall in the field
Seldom seen by wishful eyes,
But all her shows did Nature yield,
To please and win this pilgrim wise.
He saw the partridge drum in the woods;
He heard the woodcock's evening hymn;
He found the tawny thrushes' broods;
And the shy hawk did wait for him;
What others did at distance hear,
And guessed within the thicket's gloom,
Was shown to this philosopher,
And at his bidding seemed to come.[1]

3

In unploughed Maine he sought the lumberers' gang
Where from a hundred lakes young rivers sprang;
He trode the unplanted forest floor, whereon
The all-seeing sun for ages hath not shone;
Where feeds the moose, and walks the surly bear,
And up the tall mast runs the woodpecker.
He saw beneath dim aisles, in odorous beds,
The slight Linnæa hang its twin-born heads,
And blessed the monument of the man of flowers,
Which breathes his sweet fame through the northern
        bowers.
He heard, when in the grove, at intervals,
With sudden roar the aged pine-tree falls, —
One crash, the death-hymn of the perfect tree,
Declares the close of its green century.

Low lies the plant to whose creation went
Sweet influence from every element;
Whose living towers the years conspired to build,
Whose giddy top the morning loved to gild.
Through these green tents, by eldest Nature dressed,
He roamed, content alike with man and beast.
Where darkness found him he lay glad at night;
There the red morning touched him with its light.
Three moons his great heart him a hermit made,
So long he roved at will the boundless shade.
The timid it concerns to ask their way,
And fear what foe in caves and swamps can stray,
To make no step until the event is known,
And ills to come as evils past bemoan.
Not so the wise; no coward watch he keeps
To spy what danger on his pathway creeps;
Go where he will, the wise man is at home,
His hearth the earth, — his hall the azure dome;
Where his clear spirit leads him, there 's his road
By God's own light illumined and foreshowed.

4

'Twas one of the charmèd days
When the genius of God doth flow;
The wind may alter twenty ways,
A tempest cannot blow;
It may blow north, it still is warm;
Or south, it still is clear;
Or east, it smells like a clover-farm;

Or west, no thunder fear.[1]
The musing peasant, lowly great,
Beside the forest water sate;
The rope-like pine-roots crosswise grown
Composed the network of his throne;
The wide lake, edged with sand and grass,
Was burnished to a floor of glass,
Painted with shadows green and proud
Of the tree and of the cloud.[2]
He was the heart of all the scene;
On him the sun looked more serene;
To hill and cloud his face was known, —
It seemed the likeness of their own;
They knew by secret sympathy
The public child of earth and sky.
' You ask,' he said, ' what guide
Me through trackless thickets led,
Through thick-stemmed woodlands rough and wide.
I found the water's bed.
The watercourses were my guide;
I travelled grateful by their side,
Or through their channel dry;
They led me through the thicket damp,
Through brake and fern, the beavers' camp,
Through beds of granite cut my road,
And their resistless friendship showed.
The falling waters led me,
The foodful waters fed me,
And brought me to the lowest land,

Unerring to the ocean sand.
The moss upon the forest bark
Was pole-star when the night was dark;
The purple berries in the wood
Supplied me necessary food;
For Nature ever faithful is
To such as trust her faithfulness.
When the forest shall mislead me,
When the night and morning lie,
When sea and land refuse to feed me,
'T will be time enough to die;
Then will yet my mother yield
A pillow in her greenest field,
Nor the June flowers scorn to cover
The clay of their departed lover.'

WOODNOTES

II

*As sunbeams stream through liberal space
And nothing jostle or displace,
So waved the pine-tree through my thought
And fanned the dreams it never brought.*

'Whether is better, the gift or the donor?
Come to me,'
Quoth the pine-tree,
'I am the giver of honor.

My garden is the cloven rock,
And my manure the snow;
And drifting sand-heaps feed my stock,
In summer's scorching glow.[1]
He is great who can live by me:
The rough and bearded forester
Is better than the lord;
God fills the scrip and canister,
Sin piles the loaded board.
The lord is the peasant that was,
The peasant the lord that shall be;
The lord is hay, the peasant grass,
One dry, and one the living tree.[2]
Who liveth by the ragged pine
Foundeth a heroic line;
Who liveth in the palace hall
Waneth fast and spendeth all.
He goes to my savage haunts,
With his chariot and his care;
My twilight realm he disenchants,
And finds his prison there.

' What prizes the town and the tower?
  Only what the pine-tree yields;
  Sinew that subdued the fields;
  The wild-eyed boy, who in the woods
  Chants his hymn to hills and floods,
  Whom the city's poisoning spleen
  Made not pale, or fat, or lean;

Whom the rain and the wind purgeth,
Whom the dawn and the day-star urgeth,
In whose cheek the rose-leaf blusheth,
In whose feet the lion rusheth,
Iron arms, and iron mould,
That know not fear, fatigue, or cold.
I give my rafters to his boat,
My billets to his boiler's throat,
And I will swim the ancient sea
To float my child to victory,
And grant to dwellers with the pine
Dominion o'er the palm and vine.
Who leaves the pine-tree, leaves his friend,
Unnerves his strength, invites his end.
Cut a bough from my parent stem,
And dip it in thy porcelain vase;
A little while each russet gem
Will swell and rise with wonted grace;
But when it seeks enlarged supplies,
The orphan of the forest dies.
Whoso walks in solitude
And inhabiteth the wood,
Choosing light, wave, rock and bird,
Before the money-loving herd,
Into that forester shall pass,
From these companions, power and grace.[1]
Clean shall he be, without, within,
From the old adhering sin,
All ill dissolving in the light

Of his triumphant piercing sight:
Not vain, sour, nor frivolous;
Not mad, athirst, nor garrulous;
Grave, chaste, contented, though retired,
And of all other men desired.
On him the light of star and moon
Shall fall with purer radiance down;
All constellations of the sky
Shed their virtue through his eye.
Him Nature giveth for defence
His formidable innocence;
The mounting sap, the shells, the sea,
All spheres, all stones, his helpers be;
He shall meet the speeding year,
Without wailing, without fear;
He shall be happy in his love,
Like to like shall joyful prove;
He shall be happy whilst he wooes,
Muse-born, a daughter of the Muse.
But if with gold she bind her hair,
And deck her breast with diamond,
Take off thine eyes, thy heart forbear,
Though thou lie alone on the ground.

' Heed the old oracles,
  Ponder my spells;
  Song wakes in my pinnacles
  When the wind swells.
  Soundeth the prophetic wind,

The shadows shake on the rock behind,
And the countless leaves of the pine are strings
Tuned to the lay the wood-god sings.
          Hearken! Hearken!
If thou wouldst know the mystic song
Chanted when the sphere was young.
Aloft, abroad, the pæan swells;
O wise man! hear'st thou half it tells?
O wise man! hear'st thou the least part?
'T is the chronicle of art.
To the open ear it sings
Sweet the genesis of things,[1]
Of tendency through endless ages,
Of star-dust, and star-pilgrimages,
Of rounded worlds, of space and time,
Of the old flood's subsiding slime,
Of chemic matter, force and form,
Of poles and powers, cold, wet, and warm:
The rushing metamorphosis
Dissolving all that fixture is,
Melts things that be to things that seem,
And solid nature to a dream.[2]
O, listen to the undersong,
The ever old, the ever young;
And, far within those cadent pauses,
The chorus of the ancient Causes!
Delights the dreadful Destiny
To fling his voice into the tree,
And shock thy weak ear with a note

Breathed from the everlasting throat.
In music he repeats the pang
Whence the fair flock of Nature sprang.
O mortal! thy ears are stones;
These echoes are laden with tones
Which only the pure can hear;
Thou canst not catch what they recite
Of Fate and Will, of Want and Right,
Of man to come, of human life,
Of Death and Fortune, Growth and Strife.'

Once again the pine-tree sung: —
' Speak not thy speech my boughs among:
Put off thy years, wash in the breeze;
My hours are peaceful centuries.
Talk no more with feeble tongue;
No more the fool of space and time,
Come weave with mine a nobler rhyme.
Only thy Americans
Can read thy line, can meet thy glance,
But the runes that I rehearse
Understands the universe;
The least breath my boughs which tossed
Brings again the Pentecost;
To every soul resounding clear
In a voice of solemn cheer, —
" Am I not thine? Are not these thine? "
And they reply, " Forever mine! "
My branches speak Italian,

English, German, Basque, Castilian,
Mountain speech to Highlanders,
Ocean tongues to islanders,
To Fin and Lap and swart Malay,
To each his bosom-secret say.

   ' Come learn with me the fatal song
Which knits the world in music strong,
Come lift thine eyes to lofty rhymes,
Of things with things, of times with times,
Primal chimes of sun and shade,
Of sound and echo, man and maid,
The land reflected in the flood,
Body with shadow still pursued.[1]
For Nature beats in perfect tune,
And rounds with rhyme her every rune,
Whether she work in land or sea,
Or hide underground her alchemy.
Thou canst not wave thy staff in air,
Or dip thy paddle in the lake,
But it carves the bow of beauty there,
And the ripples in rhymes the oar forsake.[2]
The wood is wiser far than thou ;
The wood and wave each other know
Not unrelated, unaffied,
But to each thought and thing allied,
Is perfect Nature's every part,
Rooted in the mighty Heart.
But thou, poor child ! unbound, unrhymed,

Whence camest thou, misplaced, mistimed,
Whence, O thou orphan and defrauded?
Is thy land peeled, thy realm marauded?
Who thee divorced, deceived and left?
Thee of thy faith who hath bereft,
And torn the ensigns from thy brow,
And sunk the immortal eye so low?
Thy cheek too white, thy form too slender,
Thy gait too slow, thy habits tender
For royal man; — they thee confess
An exile from the wilderness, —
The hills where health with health agrees,
And the wise soul expels disease.
Hark! in thy ear I will tell the sign
By which thy hurt thou may'st divine.
When thou shalt climb the mountain cliff,
Or see the wide shore from thy skiff,
To thee the horizon shall express
But emptiness on emptiness;
There lives no man of Nature's worth
In the circle of the earth;
And to thine eye the vast skies fall,
Dire and satirical,
On clucking hens and prating fools,
On thieves, on drudges and on dolls.
And thou shalt say to the Most High,
" Godhead! all this astronomy,
And fate and practice and invention,
Strong art and beautiful pretension,

This radiant pomp of sun and star,
Throes that were, and worlds that are,
Behold! were in vain and in vain; — [1]
It cannot be, — I will look again.
Surely now will the curtain rise,
And earth's fit tenant me surprise; —
But the curtain doth *not* rise,
And Nature has miscarried wholly
Into failure, into folly."

' Alas! thine is the bankruptcy,
Blessed Nature so to see.
Come, lay thee in my soothing shade,
And heal the hurts which sin has made.
I see thee in the crowd alone;
I will be thy companion.
Quit thy friends as the dead in doom,
And build to them a final tomb;
Let the starred shade that nightly falls
Still celebrate their funerals,
And the bell of beetle and of bee
Knell their melodious memory.
Behind thee leave thy merchandise,
Thy churches and thy charities;
And leave thy peacock wit behind;
Enough for thee the primal mind
That flows in streams, that breathes in wind:
Leave all thy pedant lore apart;
God hid the whole world in thy heart.

Love shuns the sage, the child it crowns,
Gives all to them who all renounce.
The rain comes when the wind calls;
The river knows the way to the sea;
Without a pilot it runs and falls,
Blessing all lands with its charity;
The sea tosses and foams to find
Its way up to the cloud and wind;
The shadow sits close to the flying ball;
The date fails not on the palm-tree tall;
And thou, — go burn thy wormy pages, —
Shalt outsee seers, and outwit sages.
Oft didst thou thread the woods in vain
To find what bird had piped the strain: —
Seek not, and the little eremite
Flies gayly forth and sings in sight.

' Hearken once more!
I will tell thee the mundane lore.
Older am I than thy numbers wot,
Change I may, but I pass not.
Hitherto all things fast abide,
And anchored in the tempest ride.
Trenchant time behoves to hurry
All to yean and all to bury:
All the forms are fugitive,
But the substances survive.
Ever fresh the broad creation,
A divine improvisation,

From the heart of God proceeds,
A single will, a million deeds.
Once slept the world an egg of stone,
And pulse, and sound, and light was none;
And God said, " Throb !" and there was motion
And the vast mass became vast ocean.
Onward and on, the eternal Pan,
Who layeth the world's incessant plan,
Halteth never in one shape,
But forever doth escape,
Like wave or flame, into new forms
Of gem, and air, of plants, and worms.
I, that to-day am a pine,
Yesterday was a bundle of grass.
He is free and libertine,
Pouring of his power the wine
To every age, to every race;
Unto every race and age
He emptieth the beverage;
Unto each, and unto all,
Maker and original.
The world is the ring of his spells,
And the play of his miracles.
As he giveth to all to drink,
Thus or thus they are and think.
With one drop sheds form and feature;
With the next a special nature;
The third adds heat's indulgent spark;
The fourth gives light which eats the dark;

Into the fifth himself he flings,
And conscious Law is King of kings.[1]
As the bee through the garden ranges,
From world to world the godhead changes;
As the sheep go feeding in the waste,
From form to form He maketh haste;
This vault which glows immense with light
Is the inn where he lodges for a night.
What recks such Traveller if the bowers
Which bloom and fade like meadow flowers
A bunch of fragrant lilies be,
Or the stars of eternity?
Alike to him the better, the worse, —
The glowing angel, the outcast corse.
Thou metest him by centuries,
And lo! he passes like the breeze;
Thou seek'st in globe and galaxy,
He hides in pure transparency;
Thou askest in fountains and in fires,
He is the essence that inquires.
He is the axis of the star;
He is the sparkle of the spar;
He is the heart of every creature;
He is the meaning of each feature;
And his mind is the sky.
Than all it holds more deep, more high.'

MONADNOC

THOUSAND minstrels woke within me,
  'Our music's in the hills;'—
Gayest pictures rose to win me,
   Leopard-colored rills.
'Up!—If thou knew'st who calls
To twilight parks of beech and pine,
High over the river intervals,
Above the ploughman's highest line,
Over the owner's farthest walls!
Up! where the airy citadel
O'erlooks the surging landscape's swell!
Let not unto the stones the Day
Her lily and rose, her sea and land display.
Read the celestial sign!
Lo! the south answers to the north;
Bookworm, break this sloth urbane;
A greater spirit bids thee forth
Than the gray dreams which thee detain.
Mark how the climbing Oreads
Beckon thee to their arcades;
Youth, for a moment free as they,
Teach thy feet to feel the ground,
Ere yet arrives the wintry day
When Time thy feet has bound.

Take the bounty of thy birth,
Taste the lordship of the earth.'

I heard, and I obeyed, —
Assured that he who made the claim,
Well known, but loving not a name,
Was not to be gainsaid.
Ere yet the summoning voice was still,
I turned to Cheshire's haughty hill.
From the fixed cone the cloud-rack flowed
Like ample banner flung abroad
To all the dwellers in the plains
Round about, a hundred miles,
With salutation to the sea and to the bordering
isles.
In his own loom's garment dressed,
By his proper bounty blessed,
Fast abides this constant giver,
Pouring many a cheerful river;
To far eyes, an aerial isle
Unploughed, which finer spirits pile,
Which morn and crimson evening paint
For bard, for lover and for saint;
An eyemark and the country's core,
Inspirer, prophet evermore;
Pillar which God aloft had set
So that men might it not forget;
It should be their life's ornament,
And mix itself with each event;

Gauge and calendar and dial,
Weatherglass and chemic phial,
Garden of berries, perch of birds,
Pasture of pool-haunting herds,
Graced by each change of sum untold,
Earth-baking heat, stone-cleaving cold.

The Titan heeds his sky-affairs,
Rich rents and wide alliance shares;
Mysteries of color daily laid
By morn and eve in light and shade;
And sweet varieties of chance,
And the mystic seasons' dance;
And thief-like step of liberal hours
Thawing snow-drift into flowers.
O, wondrous craft of plant and stone
By eldest science wrought and shown!

' Happy,' I said, ' whose home is here!
Fair fortunes to the mountaineer!
Boon Nature to his poorest shed
Has royal pleasure-grounds outspread.'
Intent, I searched the region round,
And in low hut the dweller found:
Woe is me for my hope's downfall!
Is yonder squalid peasant all
That this proud nursery could breed
For God's vicegerency and stead?
Time out of mind, this forge of ores;

Quarry of spars in mountain pores;
Old cradle, hunting-ground and bier
Of wolf and otter, bear and deer;
Well-built abode of many a race;
Tower of observance searching space;
Factory of river and of rain;
Link in the Alps' globe-girding chain;
By million changes skilled to tell
What in the Eternal standeth well,
And what obedient Nature can; —
Is this colossal talisman
Kindly to plant and blood and kind,
But speechless to the master's mind?
I thought to find the patriots
In whom the stock of freedom roots;
To myself I oft recount
Tales of many a famous mount, —
Wales, Scotland, Uri, Hungary's dells:
Bards, Roys, Scanderbegs and Tells;
And think how Nature in these towers
Uplifted shall condense her powers,
And lifting man to the blue deep
Where stars their perfect courses keep,
Like wise preceptor, lure his eye
To sound the science of the sky,
And carry learning to its height
Of untried power and sane delight:
The Indian cheer, the frosty skies,
Rear purer wits, inventive eyes, —

Eyes that frame cities where none be,
And hands that stablish what these see:
And by the moral of his place
Hint summits of heroic grace;
Man in these crags a fastness find
To fight pollution of the mind;
In the wide thaw and ooze of wrong,
Adhere like this foundation strong,
The insanity of towns to stem
With simpleness for stratagem.
But if the brave old mould is broke,
And end in churls the mountain folk
In tavern cheer and tavern joke,
Sink, O mountain, in the swamp!
Hide in thy skies, O sovereign lamp!
Perish like leaves, the highland breed
No sire survive, no son succeed!

Soft! let not the offended muse
Toil's hard hap with scorn accuse.
Many hamlets sought I then,
Many farms of mountain men.
Rallying round a parish steeple
Nestle warm the highland people,
Coarse and boisterous, yet mild,
Strong as giant, slow as child.
Sweat and season are their arts,
Their talismans are ploughs and carts;
And well the youngest can command

Honey from the frozen land;
With cloverheads the swamp adorn,
Change the running sand to corn;
For wolf and fox, bring lowing herds,
And for cold mosses, cream and curds:
Weave wood to canisters and mats;
Drain sweet maple juice in vats.
No bird is safe that cuts the air
From their rifle or their snare;
No fish, in river or in lake,
But their long hands it thence will take;
Whilst the country's flinty face,
Like wax, their fashioning skill betrays,
To fill the hollows, sink the hills,
Bridge gulfs, drain swamps, build dams and mills,
And fit the bleak and howling waste
For homes of virtue, sense and taste.[1]
The World-soul knows his own affair,
Forelooking, when he would prepare
For the next ages, men of mould
Well embodied, well ensouled,
He cools the present's fiery glow,
Sets the life-pulse strong but slow:
Bitter winds and fasts austere
His quarantines and grottoes, where
He slowly cures decrepit flesh,
And brings it infantile and fresh.
Toil and tempest are the toys
And games to breathe his stalwart boys:

IX

They bide their time, and well can prove,
If need were, their line from Jove;
Of the same stuff, and so allayed,
As that whereof the sun is made,
And of the fibre, quick and strong,
Whose throbs are love, whose thrills are song.

Now in sordid weeds they sleep,
In dulness now their secret keep;
Yet, will you learn our ancient speech,
These the masters who can teach.
Fourscore or a hundred words
All their vocal muse affords;
But they turn them in a fashion
Past clerks' or statesmen's art or passion.
I can spare the college bell,
And the learned lecture, well;
Spare the clergy and libraries,
Institutes and dictionaries,
For that hardy English root
Thrives here, unvalued, underfoot.
Rude poets of the tavern hearth,
Squandering your unquoted mirth,
Which keeps the ground and never soars,
While Jake retorts and Reuben roars;
Scoff of yeoman strong and stark,
Goes like bullet to its mark;

While the solid curse and jeer
Never balk the waiting ear.[1]

On the summit as I stood,
O'er the floor of plain and flood
Seemed to me, the towering hill
Was not altogether still,
But a quiet sense conveyed:
If I err not, thus it said: —

'Many feet in summer seek,
Oft, my far-appearing peak;
In the dreaded winter time,
None save dappling shadows climb,
Under clouds, my lonely head,
Old as the sun, old almost as the shade;
And comest thou
To see strange forests and new snow,
And tread uplifted land?
And leavest thou thy lowland race,
Here amid clouds to stand?
And wouldst be my companion
Where I gaze, and still shall gaze,
Through tempering nights and flashing days,
When forests fall, and man is gone,
Over tribes and over times,
At the burning Lyre,
Nearing me,

With its stars of northern fire,
In many a thousand years?

'Gentle pilgrim, if thou know
The gamut old of Pan,
And how the hills began,
The frank blessings of the hill
Fall on thee, as fall they will.

'Let him heed who can and will;
Enchantment fixed me here
To stand the hurts of time, until
In mightier chant I disappear.
    If thou trowest
How the chemic eddies play,
Pole to pole, and what they say;
And that these gray crags
Not on crags are hung,
But beads are of a rosary
On prayer and music strung;
And, credulous, through the granite seeming,
Seest the smile of Reason beaming; —
Can thy style-discerning eye
The hidden-working Builder spy,
Who builds, yet makes no chips, no din,
With hammer soft as snowflake's flight; —
Knowest thou this?
O pilgrim, wandering not amiss!

Already my rocks lie light,
And soon my cone will spin.[1]

'For the world was built in order,
And the atoms march in tune;
Rhyme the pipe, and Time the warder,
The sun obeys them and the moon.
Orb and atom forth they prance,
When they hear from far the rune;
None so backward in the troop,
When the music and the dance
Reach his place and circumstance,
But knows the sun-creating sound,
And, though a pyramid, will bound.

'Monadnoc is a mountain strong,
Tall and good my kind among;
But well I know, no mountain can,
Zion or Meru, measure with man.
For it is on zodiacs writ,
Adamant is soft to wit:
And when the greater comes again
With my secret in his brain,
I shall pass, as glides my shadow
Daily over hill and meadow.

'Through all time, in light, in gloom
Well I hear the approaching feet

On the flinty pathway beat
Of him that cometh, and shall come;
Of him who shall as lightly bear
My daily load of woods and streams,
As doth this round sky-cleaving boat
Which never strains its rocky beams;
Whose timbers, as they silent float,
Alps and Caucasus uprear,
And the long Alleghanies here,
And all town-sprinkled lands that be,
Sailing through stars with all their history.

‘ Every morn I lift my head,
See New England underspread,
South from Saint Lawrence to the Sound,
From Katskill east to the sea-bound.
Anchored fast for many an age,
I await the bard and sage,
Who, in large thoughts, like fair pearl-seed,
Shall string Monadnoc like a bead.
Comes that cheerful troubadour,
This mound shall throb his face before,
As when, with inward fires and pain,
It rose a bubble from the plain.
When he cometh, I shall shed,
From this wellspring in my head,
Fountain-drop of spicier worth
Than all vintage of the earth.
There’s fruit upon my barren soil

Costlier far than wine or oil.
There's a berry blue and gold, —
Autumn-ripe, its juices hold
Sparta's stoutness, Bethlehem's heart,
Asia's rancor, Athens' art,
Slowsure Britain's secular might,
And the German's inward sight.
I will give my son to eat
Best of Pan's immortal meat,
Bread to eat, and juice to drain;
So the coinage of his brain
Shall not be forms of stars, but stars,
Nor pictures pale, but Jove and Mars.[1]
He comes, but not of that race bred
Who daily climb my specular head.
Oft as morning wreathes my scarf,
Fled the last plumule of the Dark,
Pants up hither the spruce clerk
From South Cove and City Wharf.
I take him up my rugged sides,
Half-repentant, scant of breath, —
Bead-eyes my granite chaos show,
And my midsummer snow:
Open the daunting map beneath, —
All his county, sea and land,
Dwarfed to measure of his hand;
His day's ride is a furlong space,
His city-tops a glimmering haze.
I plant his eyes on the sky-hoop bounding;

"See there the grim gray rounding
  Of the bullet of the earth
  Whereon ye sail,
  Tumbling steep
  In the uncontinented deep."
He looks on that, and he turns pale.
'T is even so, this treacherous kite,
Farm-furrowed, town-incrusted sphere,
Thoughtless of its anxious freight,
Plunges eyeless on forever;
And he, poor parasite,
Cooped in a ship he cannot steer, —
Who is the captain he knows not,
Port or pilot trows not, —
Risk or ruin he must share.[1]
I scowl on him with my cloud,
With my north wind chill his blood;
I lame him, clattering down the rocks;
And to live he is in fear.
Then, at last, I let him down
Once more into his dapper town,
To chatter, frightened, to his clan
And forget me if he can.'

As in the old poetic fame
The gods are blind and lame,
And the simular despite
Betrays the more abounding might,
So call not waste that barren cone

Above the floral zone,
Where forests starve:
It is pure use; —
What sheaves like those which here we glean
    and bind
Of a celestial Ceres and the Muse?

Ages are thy days,
Thou grand affirmer of the present tense,[1]
And type of permanence!
Firm ensign of the fatal Being,
Amid these coward shapes of joy and grief,
That will not bide the seeing!

Hither we bring
Our insect miseries to thy rocks;
And the whole flight, with folded wing,
Vanish, and end their murmuring, —
Vanish beside these dedicated blocks,
Which who can tell what mason laid?
Spoils of a front none need restore,
Replacing frieze and architrave; —
Where flowers each stone rosette and metope
    brave;
Still is the haughty pile erect
Of the old building Intellect.[2]

Complement of human kind,
Holding us at vantage still,

Our sumptuous indigence,
O barren mound, thy plenties fill!
We fool and prate;
Thou art silent and sedate.
To myriad kinds and times one sense
The constant mountain doth dispense;
Shedding on all its snows and leaves,
One joy it joys, one grief it grieves.
Thou seest, O watchman tall,
Our towns and races grow and fall,
And imagest the stable good
For which we all our lifetime grope,
In shifting form the formless mind,
And though the substance us elude,
We in thee the shadow find.
Thou, in our astronomy
An opaker star,
Seen haply from afar,
Above the horizon's hoop,
A moment, by the railway troop,
As o'er some bolder height they speed, —
By circumspect ambition,
By errant gain,
By feasters and the frivolous, —
Recallest us,
And makest sane.
Mute orator! well skilled to plead,
And send conviction without phrase,
Thou dost succor and remede

The shortness of our days,
And promise, on thy Founder's truth,
Long morrow to this mortal youth.[1]

FABLE

THE mountain and the squirrel
Had a quarrel,
And the former called the latter 'Little Prig;'
Bun replied,
'You are doubtless very big;
But all sorts of things and weather
Must be taken in together,
To make up a year
And a sphere.
And I think it no disgrace
To occupy my place.
If I'm not so large as you,
You are not so small as I,
And not half so spry.
I'll not deny you make
A very pretty squirrel track;
Talents differ; all is well and wisely put;
If I cannot carry forests on my back,
Neither can you crack a nut.'

ODE

INSCRIBED TO W. H. CHANNING

THOUGH loath to grieve
The evil time's sole patriot,
I cannot leave
My honied thought
For the priest's cant,
Or statesman's rant.

If I refuse
My study for their politique,
Which at the best is trick,
The angry Muse
Puts confusion in my brain.

But who is he that prates
Of the culture of mankind,
Of better arts and life?
Go, blindworm, go,
Behold the famous States
Harrying Mexico
With rifle and with knife!

Or who, with accent bolder,
Dare praise the freedom-loving mountaineer?

I found by thee, O rushing Contoocook!
And in thy valleys, Agiochook!
The jackals of the negro-holder.

The God who made New Hampshire
Taunted the lofty land
With little men; —
Small bat and wren
House in the oak: —
If earth-fire cleave
The upheaved land, and bury the folk,
The southern crocodile would grieve.
Virtue palters; Right is hence;
Freedom praised, but hid;
Funeral eloquence
Rattles the coffin-lid.[1]

What boots thy zeal,
O glowing friend,
That would indignant rend
The northland from the south?
Wherefore? to what good end?
Boston Bay and Bunker Hill
Would serve things still; —
Things are of the snake.

The horseman serves the horse,
The neatherd serves the neat,

The merchant serves the purse,
The eater serves his meat;
'T is the day of the chattel,
Web to weave, and corn to grind;
Things are in the saddle,
And ride mankind.

There are two laws discrete,
Not reconciled, —
Law for man, and law for thing;
The last builds town and fleet,
But it runs wild,
And doth the man unking.

'T is fit the forest fall,
The steep be graded,
The mountain tunnelled,
The sand shaded,
The orchard planted,
The glebe tilled,
The prairie granted,
The steamer built.

Let man serve law for man;
Live for friendship, live for love,
For truth's and harmony's behoof;
The state may follow how it can,
As Olympus follows Jove.

Yet do not I implore
The wrinkled shopman to my sounding woods,
Nor bid the unwilling senator
Ask votes of thrushes in the solitudes.
Every one to his chosen work; —
Foolish hands may mix and mar;
Wise and sure the issues are.
Round they roll till dark is light,
Sex to sex, and even to odd; —
The over-god
Who marries Right to Might,
Who peoples, unpeoples, —
He who exterminates
Races by stronger races,
Black by white faces, —
Knows to bring honey
Out of the lion;
Grafts gentlest scion
On pirate and Turk.

The Cossack eats Poland,
Like stolen fruit;
Her last noble is ruined,
Her last poet mute:
Straight, into double band
The victors divide;
Half for freedom strike and stand; —
The astonished Muse finds thousands at her side.

ASTRÆA

EACH the herald is who wrote
His rank, and quartered his own coat.
There is no king nor sovereign state
That can fix a hero's rate;
Each to all is venerable,
Cap-a-pie invulnerable,
Until he write, where all eyes rest,
Slave or master on his breast.
I saw men go up and down,
In the country and the town,
With this tablet on their neck,[1]
' Judgment and a judge we seek.'
Not to monarchs they repair,
Nor to learned jurist's chair;
But they hurry to their peers,
To their kinsfolk and their dears;
Louder than with speech they pray, —
' What am I? companion, say.'
And the friend not hesitates
To assign just place and mates;
Answers not in word or letter,
Yet is understood the better;
Each to each a looking-glass,
Reflects his figure that doth pass.

Every wayfarer he meets
What himself declared repeats,
What himself confessed records,
Sentences him in his words;
The form is his own corporal form,
And his thought the penal worm.

Yet shine forever virgin minds,
Loved by stars and purest winds,
Which, o'er passion throned sedate,
Have not hazarded their state;
Disconcert the searching spy,
Rendering to a curious eye
The durance of a granite ledge.
To those who gaze from the sea's edge
It is there for benefit;
It is there for purging light;
There for purifying storms;
And its depths reflect all forms; [1]
It cannot parley with the mean, —
Pure by impure is not seen.
For there 's no sequestered grot,
Lone mountain tarn, or isle forgot,
But Justice, journeying in the sphere,
Daily stoops to harbor there.

IX

ÉTIENNE DE LA BOÉCE

I SERVE you not, if you I follow,
Shadowlike, o'er hill and hollow;
And bend my fancy to your leading,
All too nimble for my treading.
When the pilgrimage is done,
And we've the landscape overrun,
I am bitter, vacant, thwarted,
And your heart is unsupported.
Vainly valiant, you have missed
The manhood that should yours resist, —
Its complement; but if I could,
In severe or cordial mood,
Lead you rightly to my altar,
Where the wisest Muses falter,
And worship that world-warming spark
Which dazzles me in midnight dark,
Equalizing small and large,
While the soul it doth surcharge,
Till the poor is wealthy grown,
And the hermit never alone, —
The traveller and the road seem one
With the errand to be done, —
That were a man's and lover's part,
That were Freedom's whitest chart.

COMPENSATION

WHY should I keep holiday
    When other men have none?
Why but because, when these are gay,
    I sit and mourn alone?

And why, when mirth unseals all tongues,
    Should mine alone be dumb?
Ah! late I spoke to silent throngs,
    And now their hour is come.

FORBEARANCE

HAST thou named all the birds without a gun?
Loved the wood-rose, and left it on its stalk?
At rich men's tables eaten bread and pulse?
Unarmed, faced danger with a heart of trust?
And loved so well a high behavior,
In man or maid, that thou from speech refrained,
Nobility more nobly to repay?
O, be my friend, and teach me to be thine!

THE PARK

THE prosperous and beautiful
　　To me seem not to wear
The yoke of conscience masterful,
　　Which galls me everywhere.

I cannot shake off the god;
　　On my neck he makes his seat;
I look at my face in the glass, —
　　My eyes his eyeballs meet.

Enchanters! Enchantresses!
　　Your gold makes you seem wise;
The morning mist within your grounds
　　More proudly rolls, more softly lies.

Yet spake yon purple mountain,
　　Yet said yon ancient wood,
That Night or Day, that Love or Crime,
　　Leads all souls to the Good.

FORERUNNERS

Long I followed happy guides,
I could never reach their sides;
Their step is forth, and, ere the day
Breaks up their leaguer, and away.
Keen my sense, my heart was young,
Right good-will my sinews strung,
But no speed of mine avails
To hunt upon their shining trails.
On and away, their hasting feet
Make the morning proud and sweet;
Flowers they strew, — I catch the scent;
Or tone of silver instrument
Leaves on the wind melodious trace;
Yet I could never see their face.
On eastern hills I see their smokes,
Mixed with mist by distant lochs.
I met many travellers
Who the road had surely kept;
They saw not my fine revellers, —
These had crossed them while they slept.
Some had heard their fair report,
In the country or the court.
Fleetest couriers alive
Never yet could once arrive,

As they went or they returned,
At the house where these sojourned.
Sometimes their strong speed they slacken,
Though they are not overtaken;
In sleep their jubilant troop is near, —
I tuneful voices overhear;
It may be in wood or waste, —
At unawares 't is come and past.
Their near camp my spirit knows
By signs gracious as rainbows.
I thenceforward and long after
Listen for their harp-like laughter,
And carry in my heart, for days,
Peace that hallows rudest ways.

SURSUM CORDA

SEEK not the spirit, if it hide
Inexorable to thy zeal:
Trembler, do not whine and chide:
Art thou not also real?
Stoop not then to poor excuse;
Turn on the accuser roundly; say,
'Here am I, here will I abide
Forever to myself soothfast;
Go thou, sweet Heaven, or at thy pleasure stay!'
Already Heaven with thee its lot has cast,
For only it can absolutely deal.

ODE TO BEAUTY

Who gave thee, O Beauty,
The keys of this breast, —
Too credulous lover
Of blest and unblest?
Say, when in lapsed ages
Thee knew I of old?
Or what was the service
For which I was sold?
When first my eyes saw thee,
I found me thy thrall,
By magical drawings,
Sweet tyrant of all!
I drank at thy fountain
False waters of thirst;
Thou intimate stranger,
Thou latest and first!
Thy dangerous glances
Make women of men;
New-born, we are melting
Into nature again.[1]

Lavish, lavish promiser,
Nigh persuading gods to err!
Guest of million painted forms,

Which in turn thy glory warms!
The frailest leaf, the mossy bark,
The acorn's cup, the raindrop's arc,
The swinging spider's silver line,
The ruby of the drop of wine,
The shining pebble of the pond,
Thou inscribest with a bond,
In thy momentary play,
Would bankrupt nature to repay.

Ah, what avails it
To hide or to shun
Whom the Infinite One
Hath granted his throne?
The heaven high over
Is the deep's lover;
The sun and sea,
Informed by thee,
Before me run
And draw me on,
Yet fly me still,
As Fate refuses
To me the heart Fate for me chooses.
Is it that my opulent soul
Was mingled from the generous whole;
Sea-valleys and the deep of skies
Furnished several supplies;
And the sands whereof I'm made
Draw me to them, self-betrayed?

I turn the proud portfolio
Which holds the grand designs
Of Salvator, of Guercino,
And Piranesi's lines.[1]
I hear the lofty pæans
Of the masters of the shell,
Who heard the starry music
And recount the numbers well;
Olympian bards who sung
Divine Ideas below,
Which always find us young
And always keep us so.[2]
Oft, in streets or humblest places,
I detect far-wandered graces,
Which, from Eden wide astray,
In lowly homes have lost their way.

Thee gliding through the sea of form,
Like the lightning through the storm,
Somewhat not to be possessed,
Somewhat not to be caressed,
No feet so fleet could ever find,
No perfect form could ever bind.[3]
Thou eternal fugitive,
Hovering over all that live,
Quick and skilful to inspire
Sweet, extravagant desire,
Starry space and lily-bell
Filling with thy roseate smell,[4]

Wilt not give the lips to taste
Of the nectar which thou hast.

All that's good and great with thee
Works in close conspiracy;
Thou hast bribed the dark and lonely
To report thy features only,
And the cold and purple morning
Itself with thoughts of thee adorning;
The leafy dell, the city mart,
Equal trophies of thine art;
E'en the flowing azure air
Thou hast touched for my despair;
And, if I languish into dreams,
Again I meet the ardent beams.
Queen of things! I dare not die
In Being's deeps past ear and eye;
Lest there I find the same deceiver
And be the sport of Fate forever.
Dread Power, but dear! if God thou be,
Unmake me quite, or give thyself to me! [1]

GIVE ALL TO LOVE

GIVE all to love;
Obey thy heart;
Friends, kindred, days,

Estate, good-fame,
Plans, credit and the Muse, —
Nothing refuse.

'T is a brave master;
Let it have scope:
Follow it utterly,
Hope beyond hope:
High and more high
It dives into noon,
With wing unspent,
Untold intent;
But it is a god,
Knows its own path
And the outlets of the sky.

It was never for the mean;
It requireth courage stout.
Souls above doubt,
Valor unbending,
It will reward, —
They shall return
More than they were,
And ever ascending.

Leave all for love;
Yet, hear me, yet,
One word more thy heart behoved,
One pulse more of firm endeavor, —

Keep thee to-day,
To-morrow, forever,
Free as an Arab
Of thy beloved.[1]

Cling with life to the maid;
But when the surprise,
First vague shadow of surmise
Flits across her bosom young,
Of a joy apart from thee,
Free be she, fancy-free;
Nor thou detain her vesture's hem,
Nor the palest rose she flung
From her summer diadem.

Though thou loved her as thyself,
As a self of purer clay,
Though her parting dims the day,
Stealing grace from all alive;
Heartily know,
When half-gods go,[2]
The gods arrive.

TO ELLEN AT THE SOUTH

THE green grass is bowing,
　　The morning wind is in it;
'T is a tune worth thy knowing,
　　Though it change every minute.

'T is a tune of the Spring;
　　Every year plays it over
To the robin on the wing,
　　And to the pausing lover.

O'er ten thousand, thousand acres,
　　Goes light the nimble zephyr;
The Flowers — tiny sect of Shakers —
　　Worship him ever.

Hark to the winning sound!
　　They summon thee, dearest, —
Saying, 'We have dressed for thee the ground,
　　Nor yet thou appearest.

'O hasten;' 't is our time,
　　Ere yet the red Summer
Scorch our delicate prime,
　　Loved of bee, — the tawny hummer.

'O pride of thy race!
    Sad, in sooth, it were to ours,
If our brief tribe miss thy face,
    We poor New England flowers.

'Fairest, choose the fairest members
    Of our lithe society;
June's glories and September's
    Show our love and piety.

'Thou shalt command us all, —
    April's cowslip, summer's clover,
To the gentian in the fall,
    Blue-eyed pet of blue-eyed lover.

'O come, then, quickly come!
    We are budding, we are blowing;
And the wind that we perfume
    Sings a tune that's worth the knowing.'

TO ELLEN

AND Ellen, when the graybeard years
    Have brought us to life's evening hour,
And all the crowded Past appears
    A tiny scene of sun and shower,

Then, if I read the page aright
   Where Hope, the soothsayer, reads our lot,
Thyself shalt own the page was bright,
   Well that we loved, woe had we not,

When Mirth is dumb and Flattery's fled,
   And mute thy music's dearest tone,
When all but Love itself is dead
   And all but deathless Reason gone.

TO EVA

O FAIR and stately maid, whose eyes
Were kindled in the upper skies
   At the same torch that lighted mine;
For so I must interpret still
Thy sweet dominion o'er my will,
   A sympathy divine.

Ah! let me blameless gaze upon
Features that seem at heart my own;
   Nor fear those watchful sentinels,
Who charm the more their glance forbids,
Chaste-glowing, underneath their lids,
   With fire that draws while it repels.

LINES

WRITTEN BY ELLEN LOUISA TUCKER SHORTLY BEFORE
HER MARRIAGE TO MR. EMERSON

LOVE scatters oil
 On Life's dark sea,
Sweetens its toil —
 Our helmsman he.

Around him hover
 Odorous clouds;
Under this cover
 His arrows he shrouds.

The cloud was around me,
 I knew not why
Such sweetness crowned me,
 While Time shot by.

No pain was within,
 But calm delight,
Like a world without sin,
 Or a day without night.

The shafts of the god
 Were tipped with down,

For they drew no blood,
And they knit no frown.

I knew of them not
Until Cupid laughed loud,
And saying " You 're caught ! "
Flew off in the cloud.

O then I awoke,
And I lived but to sigh,
Till a clear voice spoke, —
And my tears are dry.

THE VIOLET

BY ELLEN LOUISA TUCKER

WHY lingerest thou, pale violet, to see the dying year ;
Are Autumn's blasts fit music for thee, fragile one, to
    hear ;
Will thy clear blue eye, upward bent, still keep its
    chastened glow,
Still tearless lift its slender form above the wintry snow?

Why wilt thou live when none around reflects thy
    pensive ray ?
Thou bloomest here a lonely thing in the clear autumn
    day.

IX

The tall green trees, that shelter thee, their last gay
    dress put on;
There will be nought to shelter thee when their sweet
    leaves are gone.

O Violet, like thee, how blest could I lie down and
    die,
When summer light is fading, and autumn breezes
    sigh;
When Winter reigned I'd close my eye, but wake with
    bursting Spring,
And live with living nature, a pure rejoicing thing.

I had a sister once who seemed just like a violet;
Her morning sun shone bright and calmly purely
    set;
When the violets were in their shrouds, and Summer
    in its pride,
She laid her hopes at rest, and in the year's rich beauty
    died.

THE AMULET

Your picture smiles as first it smiled;
    The ring you gave is still the same;
Your letter tells, O changing child!
    No tidings *since* it came.

Give me an amulet
  That keeps intelligence with you, —
Red when you love, and rosier red,
  And when you love not, pale and blue.

Alas! that neither bonds nor vows
  Can certify possession;
Torments me still the fear that love
  Died in its last expression.

THINE EYES STILL SHINED

THINE eyes still shined for me, though far
  I lonely roved the land or sea:
As I behold yon evening star,
  Which yet beholds not me.[1]

This morn I climbed the misty hill
  And roamed the pastures through;
How danced thy form before my path
  Amidst the deep-eyed dew!

When the redbird spread his sable wing,
  And showed his side of flame;
When the rosebud ripened to the rose,
  In both I read thy name.[2]

EROS

THE sense of the world is short, —
Long and various the report, —
   To love and be beloved;
Men and gods have not outlearned it;
And, how oft soe'er they 've turned it,
   Not to be improved.

HERMIONE

ON a mound an Arab lay,
And sung his sweet regrets
And told his amulets:
The summer bird
His sorrow heard,
And, when he heaved a sigh profound,
The sympathetic swallow swept the ground.

' If it be, as they said, she was not fair,
Beauty 's not beautiful to me,
But sceptred genius, aye inorbed,
Culminating in her sphere.
This Hermione absorbed
The lustre of the land and ocean,

Hills and islands, cloud and tree,
In her form and motion.

'I ask no bauble miniature,
Nor ringlets dead
Shorn from her comely head,
Now that morning not disdains
Mountains and the misty plains
Her colossal portraiture;
They her heralds be,
Steeped in her quality,
And singers of her fame
Who is their Muse and dame.

'Higher, dear swallows! mind not what I say.
Ah! heedless how the weak are strong,
Say, was it just,
In thee to frame, in me to trust,
Thou to the Syrian couldst belong?

'I am of a lineage
That each for each doth fast engage;
In old Bassora's schools, I seemed
Hermit vowed to books and gloom,—
Ill-bestead for gay bridegroom.
I was by thy touch redeemed;
When thy meteor glances came,
We talked at large of worldly fate,
And drew truly every trait.

' Once I dwelt apart,
Now I live with all;
As shepherd's lamp on far hill-side
Seems, by the traveller espied,
A door into the mountain heart,
So didst thou quarry and unlock
Highways for me through the rock.

' Now, deceived, thou wanderest
In strange lands unblest;
And my kindred come to soothe me.
Southwind is my next of blood;
He is come through fragrant wood,
Drugged with spice from climates warm,
And in every twinkling glade,
And twilight nook,
Unveils thy form.
Out of the forest way
Forth paced it yesterday;
And when I sat by the watercourse,
Watching the daylight fade,
It throbbed up from the brook.

' River and rose and crag and bird,
Frost and sun and eldest night,
To me their aid preferred,
To me their comfort plight; —
" Courage ! we are thine allies,
And with this hint be wise, —

The chains of kind
The distant bind;
Deed thou doest she must do,
Above her will, be true;
And, in her strict resort
To winds and waterfalls
And autumn's sunlit festivals,
To music, and to music's thought,
Inextricably bound,
She shall find thee, and be found.
Follow not her flying feet;
Come to us herself to meet." '

INITIAL, DÆMONIC AND CELESTIAL LOVE

I

THE INITIAL LOVE

VENUS, when her son was lost,
Cried him up and down the coast,
In hamlets, palaces and parks,
And told the truant by his marks, —
Golden curls, and quiver and bow.
This befell how long ago!
Time and tide are strangely changed,
Men and manners much deranged:

None will now find Cupid latent
By this foolish antique patent.
He came late along the waste,
Shod like a traveller for haste;
With malice dared me to proclaim him,
That the maids and boys might name him.

Boy no more, he wears all coats,
Frocks and blouses, capes, capotes;
He bears no bow, or quiver, or wand,
Nor chaplet on his head or hand.
Leave his weeds and heed his eyes, —
All the rest he can disguise.
In the pit of his eye 's a spark
Would bring back day if it were dark;
And, if I tell you all my thought,
Though I comprehend it not,
In those unfathomable orbs
Every function he absorbs;
Doth eat, and drink, and fish, and shoot,
And write, and reason, and compute,
And ride, and run, and have, and hold,
And whine, and flatter, and regret,
And kiss, and couple, and beget,
By those roving eyeballs bold.

Undaunted are their courages,
Right Cossacks in their forages;
Fleeter they than any creature, —

They are his steeds, and not his feature;
Inquisitive, and fierce, and fasting,
Restless, predatory, hasting;
And they pounce on other eyes
As lions on their prey;[1]
And round their circles is writ,
Plainer than the day,
Underneath, within, above, —
Love — love — love — love.
He lives in his eyes;
There doth digest, and work, and spin,
And buy, and sell, and lose, and win;
He rolls them with delighted motion,
Joy-tides swell their mimic ocean.
Yet holds he them with tautest rein,
That they may seize and entertain
The glance that to their glance opposes,
Like fiery honey sucked from roses.
He palmistry can understand,
Imbibing virtue by his hand
As if it were a living root;
The pulse of hands will make him mute;
With all his force he gathers balms
Into those wise, thrilling palms.

Cupid is a casuist,
A mystic and a cabalist, —
Can your lurking thought surprise,
And interpret your device.

He is versed in occult science,
In magic and in clairvoyance,
Oft he keeps his fine ear strained,
And Reason on her tiptoe pained
For aëry intelligence,
And for strange coincidence.
But it touches his quick heart
When Fate by omens takes his part,
And chance-dropped hints from Nature's sphere
Deeply soothe his anxious ear.

Heralds high before him run;
He has ushers many a one;
He spreads his welcome where he goes,
And touches all things with his rose.
All things wait for and divine him, —
How shall I dare to malign him,
Or accuse the god of sport?
I must end my true report,
Painting him from head to foot,
In as far as I took note,
Trusting well the matchless power
Of this young-eyed emperor
Will clear his fame from every cloud
With the bards and with the crowd.

He is wilful, mutable,
Shy, untamed, inscrutable,
Swifter-fashioned than the fairies,

Substance mixed of pure contraries;
His vice some elder virtue's token,
And his good is evil-spoken.
Failing sometimes of his own,
He is headstrong and alone;
He affects the wood and wild,
Like a flower-hunting child;
Buries himself in summer waves,
In trees, with beasts, in mines and caves,
Loves nature like a hornèd cow,
Bird, or deer, or caribou.

Shun him, nymphs, on the fleet horses!
He has a total world of wit;
O how wise are his discourses!
But he is the arch-hypocrite,
And, through all science and all art,
Seeks alone his counterpart.
He is a Pundit of the East,
He is an augur and a priest,
And his soul will melt in prayer,
But word and wisdom is a snare;
Corrupted by the present toy
He follows joy, and only joy.
There is no mask but he will wear;
He invented oaths to swear;
He paints, he carves, he chants, he prays,
And holds all stars in his embrace.[1]
He takes a sovran privilege

Not allowed to any liege;
For Cupid goes behind all law,
And right into himself does draw;
For he is sovereignly allied, —
Heaven's oldest blood flows in his side, —
And interchangeably at one
With every king on every throne,
That no god dare say him nay,
Or see the fault, or seen betray:
He has the Muses by the heart,
And the stern Parcæ on his part.

His many signs cannot be told;
He has not one mode, but manifold,
Many fashions and addresses,
Piques, reproaches, hurts, caresses.[1]
He will preach like a friar,
And jump like Harlequin;
He will read like a crier,
And fight like a Paladin.
Boundless is his memory;
Plans immense his term prolong;
He is not of counted age,
Meaning always to be young.
And his wish is intimacy,
Intimater intimacy,
And a stricter privacy;
The impossible shall yet be done,
And, being two, shall still be one.

As the wave breaks to foam on shelves,
Then runs into a wave again,
So lovers melt their sundered selves,
Yet melted would be twain.

II

THE DÆMONIC LOVE

MAN was made of social earth,
Child and brother from his birth,
Tethered by a liquid cord
Of blood through veins of kindred poured.
Next his heart the fireside band
Of mother, father, sister, stand;
Names from awful childhood heard [1]
Throbs of a wild religion stirred;—
Virtue, to love, to hate them, vice;
Till dangerous Beauty came, at last,
Till Beauty came to snap all ties;
The maid, abolishing the past,
With lotus wine obliterates
Dear memory's stone-incarved traits,
And, by herself, supplants alone
Friends year by year more inly known.
When her calm eyes opened bright,
All else grew foreign in their light.
It was ever the self-same tale,

The first experience will not fail;
Only two in the garden walked,
And with snake and seraph talked.[1]

Close, close to men,
Like undulating layer of air,
Right above their heads,
The potent plain of Dæmons spreads.[2]
Stands to each human soul its own,
For watch and ward and furtherance,
In the snares of Nature's dance;
And the lustre and the grace
To fascinate each youthful heart,
Beaming from its counterpart,
Translucent through the mortal covers,
Is the Dæmon's form and face.
To and fro the Genius hies, —
A gleam which plays and hovers
Over the maiden's head,
And dips sometimes as low as to her eyes.[3]
Unknown, albeit lying near,
To men, the path to the Dæmon sphere;
And they that swiftly come and go
Leave no track on the heavenly snow.
Sometimes the airy synod bends,
And the mighty choir descends,
And the brains of men thenceforth,
In crowded and in still resorts,
Teem with unwonted thoughts:

As, when a shower of meteors
Cross the orbit of the earth,
And, lit by fringent air,
Blaze near and far,
Mortals deem the planets bright
Have slipped their sacred bars,
And the lone seaman all the night
Sails, astonished, amid stars.

Beauty of a richer vein,
Graces of a subtler strain,
Unto men these moonmen lend,
And our shrinking sky extend.
So is man's narrow path
By strength and terror skirted;
Also (from the song the wrath
Of the Genii be averted !
The Muse the truth uncolored speaking)
The Dæmons are self-seeking:
Their fierce and limitary will
Draws men to their likeness still.
The erring painter made Love blind, —
Highest Love who shines on all;
Him, radiant, sharpest-sighted god,
None can bewilder;
Whose eyes pierce
The universe,
Path-finder, road-builder,
Mediator, royal giver;

Rightly seeing, rightly seen,
Of joyful and transparent mien.
'T is a sparkle passing
From each to each, from thee to me,
To and fro perpetually ;
Sharing all, daring all,
Levelling, displacing
Each obstruction, it unites
Equals remote, and seeming opposites.
And ever and forever Love
Delights to build a road :
Unheeded Danger near him strides,
Love laughs, and on a lion rides.
But Cupid wears another face,
Born into Dæmons less divine :
His roses bleach apace,
His nectar smacks of wine.
The Dæmon ever builds a wall,
Himself encloses and includes,
Solitude in solitudes :
In like sort his love doth fall.[1]
He doth elect
The beautiful and fortunate,
And the sons of intellect,
And the souls of ample fate,
Who the Future's gates unbar, —
Minions of the Morning Star.
In his prowess he exults,
And the multitude insults.

His impatient looks devour
Oft the humble and the poor;
And, seeing his eye glare,
They drop their few pale flowers,
Gathered with hope to please,
Along the mountain towers, —
Lose courage, and despair.
He will never be gainsaid, —
Pitiless, will not be stayed;
His hot tyranny
Burns up every other tie.
Therefore comes an hour from Jove
Which his ruthless will defies,
And the dogs of Fate unties.
Shiver the palaces of glass;
Shrivel the rainbow-colored walls,
Where in bright Art each god and sibyl dwelt
Secure as in the zodiac's belt;
And the galleries and halls,
Wherein every siren sung,
Like a meteor pass.
For this fortune wanted root
In the core of God's abysm, —
Was a weed of self and schism;
And ever the Dæmonic Love
Is the ancestor of wars
And the parent of remorse.

IX

III

THE CELESTIAL LOVE

BUT God said,
‘ I will have a purer gift ;
There is smoke in the flame ;
New flowerets bring, new prayers uplift,
And love without a name.
Fond children, ye desire
To please each other well ;
Another round, a higher,
Ye shall climb on the heavenly stair,
And selfish preference forbear ;
And in right deserving,
And without a swerving
Each from your proper state,
Weave roses for your mate.

‘ Deep, deep are loving eyes,
Flowed with naphtha fiery sweet ;
And the point is paradise,
Where their glances meet :
Their reach shall yet be more profound,
And a vision without bound :
The axis of those eyes sun-clear
Be the axis of the sphere :

So shall the lights ye pour amain
Go, without check or intervals,
Through from the empyrean walls
Unto the same again.'

Higher far into the pure realm,
Over sun and star,
Over the flickering Dæmon film,
Thou must mount for love;
Into vision where all form
In one only form dissolves;
In a region where the wheel
On which all beings ride
Visibly revolves;
Where the starred, eternal worm
Girds the world with bound and term;
Where unlike things are like;
Where good and ill,
And joy and moan,
Melt into one.

There Past, Present, Future, shoot
Triple blossoms from one root;
Substances at base divided,
In their summits are united;
There the holy essence rolls,
One through separated souls;
And the sunny Æon sleeps
Folding Nature in its deeps,

And every fair and every good,
Known in part, or known impure,
To men below,
In their archetypes endure.
The race of gods,
Or those we erring own,
Are shadows flitting up and down
In the still abodes.
The circles of that sea are laws
Which publish and which hide the cause.

Pray for a beam
Out of that sphere,
Thee to guide and to redeem.
O, what a load
Of care and toil,
By lying use bestowed,
From his shoulders falls who sees
The true astronomy,
The period of peace.
Counsel which the ages kept
Shall the well-born soul accept.
As the overhanging trees
Fill the lake with images, —
As garment draws the garment's hem,
Men their fortunes bring with them.
By right or wrong,
Lands and goods go to the strong.
Property will brutely draw

Still to the proprietor;
Silver to silver creep and wind,
And kind to kind.

Nor less the eternal poles
Of tendency distribute souls.
There need no vows to bind
Whom not each other seek, but find.[1]
They give and take no pledge or oath, —
Nature is the bond of both:
No prayer persuades, no flattery fawns, —
Their noble meanings are their pawns.
Plain and cold is their address,[2]
Power have they for tenderness;
And, so thoroughly is known
Each other's counsel by his own,
They can parley without meeting;
Need is none of forms of greeting;
They can well communicate
In their innermost estate;
When each the other shall avoid,
Shall each by each be most enjoyed.

Not with scarfs or perfumed gloves
Do these celebrate their loves:
Not by jewels, feasts and savors,
Not by ribbons or by favors,
But by the sun-spark on the sea,
And the cloud-shadow on the lea,

The soothing lapse of morn to mirk,
And the cheerful round of work.
Their cords of love so public are,
They intertwine the farthest star:
The throbbing sea, the quaking earth,
Yield sympathy and signs of mirth;
Is none so high, so mean is none,
But feels and seals this union;
Even the fell Furies are appeased,
The good applaud, the lost are eased.

Love's hearts are faithful, but not fond,
Bound for the just, but not beyond;
Not glad, as the low-loving herd,
Of self in other still preferred,
But they have heartily designed
The benefit of broad mankind.
And they serve men austerely,
After their own genius, clearly,[1]
Without a false humility;
For this is Love's nobility, —
Not to scatter bread and gold,
Goods and raiment bought and sold;
But to hold fast his simple sense,
And speak the speech of innocence,
And with hand and body and blood,
To make his bosom-counsel good.
He that feeds men serveth few;
He serves all who dares be true.[2]

THE APOLOGY

THINK me not unkind and rude
  That I walk alone in grove and glen;
I go to the god of the wood
  To fetch his word to men.

Tax not my sloth that I
  Fold my arms beside the brook;
Each cloud that floated in the sky
  Writes a letter in my book.

Chide me not, laborious band,
  For the idle flowers I brought;
Every aster in my hand
  Goes home loaded with a thought.

There was never mystery
  But 't is figured in the flowers;
Was never secret history
  But birds tell it in the bowers.

One harvest from thy field
  Homeward brought the oxen strong;
A second crop thine acres yield,
  Which I gather in a song.

MERLIN

I

THY trivial harp will never please
Or fill my craving ear;
Its chords should ring as blows the breeze,
Free, peremptory, clear.
No jingling serenader's art,
Nor tinkle of piano strings,
Can make the wild blood start
In its mystic springs.
The kingly bard
Must smite the chords rudely and hard,
As with hammer or with mace;
That they may render back
Artful thunder, which conveys
Secrets of the solar track,
Sparks of the supersolar blaze.[1]
Merlin's blows are strokes of fate,
Chiming with the forest tone,
When boughs buffet boughs in the wood;
Chiming with the gasp and moan
Of the ice-imprisoned flood;
With the pulse of manly hearts;
With the voice of orators;
With the din of city arts;

With the cannonade of wars;
With the marches of the brave;
And prayers of might from martyrs' cave.

Great is the art,
Great be the manners, of the bard.
He shall not his brain encumber
With the coil of rhythm and number;
But, leaving rule and pale forethought,
He shall aye climb
For his rhyme.
' Pass in, pass in,' the angels say,
' In to the upper doors,
Nor count compartments of the floors,
But mount to paradise
By the stairway of surprise.' [1]

Blameless master of the games,
King of sport that never shames,
He shall daily joy dispense
Hid in song's sweet influence.
Forms more cheerly live and go,
What time the subtle mind
Sings aloud the tune whereto
Their pulses beat,
And march their feet,
And their members are combined.

By Sybarites beguiled,
He shall no task decline;

Merlin's mighty line
Extremes of nature reconciled, —
Bereaved a tyrant of his will,
And made the lion mild.
Songs can the tempest still,
Scattered on the stormy air,
Mould the year to fair increase,
And bring in poetic peace.

He shall not seek to weave,
In weak, unhappy times,
Efficacious rhymes;
Wait his returning strength.
Bird that from the nadir's floor
To the zenith's top can soar, —
The soaring orbit of the muse exceeds that
    journey's length.
Nor profane affect to hit
Or compass that, by meddling wit,
Which only the propitious mind
Publishes when 't is inclined.
There are open hours
When the God's will sallies free,
And the dull idiot might see
The flowing fortunes of a thousand years; —
Sudden, at unawares,
Self-moved, fly-to the doors,
Nor sword of angels could reveal
What they conceal.

MERLIN

II

THE rhyme of the poet
Modulates the king's affairs;
Balance-loving Nature
Made all things in pairs.
To every foot its antipode;
Each color with its counter glowed;
To every tone beat answering tones,
Higher or graver;
Flavor gladly blends with flavor;
Leaf answers leaf upon the bough;
And match the paired cotyledons.
Hands to hands, and feet to feet,
In one body grooms and brides;
Eldest rite, two married sides
In every mortal meet.[1]
Light's far furnace shines,
Smelting balls and bars,
Forging double stars,
Glittering twins and trines.
The animals are sick with love,
Lovesick with rhyme;
Each with all propitious Time
Into chorus wove.

Like the dancers' ordered band,
Thoughts come also hand in hand;

In equal couples mated,
Or else alternated;
Adding by their mutual gage,
One to other, health and age.[1]
Solitary fancies go
Short-lived wandering to and fro,
Most like to bachelors,
Or an ungiven maid,
Not ancestors,
With no posterity to make the lie afraid,
Or keep truth undecayed.[2]
Perfect-paired as eagle's wings,
Justice is the rhyme of things;
Trade and counting use
The self-same tuneful muse;
And Nemesis,
Who with even matches odd,
Who athwart space redresses
The partial wrong,
Fills the just period,
And finishes the song.

Subtle rhymes, with ruin rife,
Murmur in the house of life,
Sung by the Sisters as they spin;
In perfect time and measure they
Build and unbuild our echoing clay.
As the two twilights of the day
Fold us music-drunken in.[3]

BACCHUS

Bring me wine, but wine which never grew
In the belly of the grape,
Or grew on vine whose tap-roots, reaching through
Under the Andes to the Cape,
Suffer no savor of the earth to scape.

Let its grapes the morn salute
From a nocturnal root,
Which feels the acrid juice
Of Styx and Erebus;
And turns the woe of Night,
By its own craft, to a more rich delight.

We buy ashes for bread;
We buy diluted wine;
Give me of the true,—
Whose ample leaves and tendrils curled
Among the silver hills of heaven
Draw everlasting dew;
Wine of wine,
Blood of the world,
Form of forms, and mould of statures,
That I intoxicated,
And by the draught assimilated,
May float at pleasure through all natures;

The bird-language rightly spell,
And that which roses say so well.

Wine that is shed
Like the torrents of the sun
Up the horizon walls,
Or like the Atlantic streams, which run
When the South Sea calls.

Water and bread,
Food which needs no transmuting,
Rainbow-flowering, wisdom-fruiting,
Wine which is already man,
Food which teach and reason can.

Wine which Music is, —
Music and wine are one, —
That I, drinking this,
Shall hear far Chaos talk with me;
Kings unborn shall walk with me;
And the poor grass shall plot and plan
What it will do when it is man.[1]
Quickened so, will I unlock
Every crypt of every rock.

I thank the joyful juice
For all I know; —
Winds of remembering
Of the ancient being blow,

And seeming-solid walls of use
Open and flow.

Pour, Bacchus! the remembering wine;
Retrieve the loss of me and mine!
Vine for vine be antidote,
And the grape requite the lote!
Haste to cure the old despair,—
Reason in Nature's lotus drenched,
The memory of ages quenched;
Give them again to shine;
Let wine repair what this undid;
And where the infection slid,
A dazzling memory revive;
Refresh the faded tints,
Recut the aged prints,
And write my old adventures with the pen
Which on the first day drew,
Upon the tablets blue,
The dancing Pleiads and eternal men.

MEROPS

WHAT care I, so they stand the same,—
  Things of the heavenly mind,—
How long the power to give them name
  Tarries yet behind?

Thus far to-day your favors reach,
  O fair, appeasing presences!
Ye taught my lips a single speech,
  And a thousand silences.

Space grants beyond his fated road
  No inch to the god of day;
And copious language still bestowed
  One word, no more, to say.

THE HOUSE

THERE is no architect
  Can build as the Muse can;
She is skilful to select
  Materials for her plan;

Slow and warily to choose
  Rafters of immortal pine,
Or cedar incorruptible,
  Worthy her design,

She threads dark Alpine forests
  Or valleys by the sea,
In many lands, with painful steps,
  Ere she can find a tree.

She ransacks mines and ledges
   And quarries every rock,
To hew the famous adamant
   For each eternal block —

She lays her beams in music,
   In music every one,
To the cadence of the whirling world
   Which dances round the sun —

That so they shall not be displaced
   By lapses or by wars,
But for the love of happy souls
   Outlive the newest stars.

SAADI

Trees in groves,
Kine in droves,
In ocean sport the scaly herds,
Wedge-like cleave the air the birds,
To northern lakes fly wind-borne ducks,
Browse the mountain sheep in flocks,
Men consort in camp and town,
But the poet dwells alone.

God, who gave to him the lyre,
Of all mortals the desire,

IX

For all breathing men's behoof,
Straitly charged him, ' Sit aloof;'
Annexed a warning, poets say,
To the bright premium, —
Ever, when twain together play,
Shall the harp be dumb.

Many may come,
But one shall sing;
Two touch the string,
The harp is dumb.
Though there come a million,
Wise Saadi dwells alone.

Yet Saadi loved the race of men, —
No churl, immured in cave or den;
In bower and hall
He wants them all,
Nor can dispense
With Persia for his audience;
They must give ear,
Grow red with joy and white with fear;
But he has no companion;
Come ten, or come a million,
Good Saadi dwells alone.

Be thou ware where Saadi dwells;
Wisdom of the gods is he, —
Entertain it reverently.

Gladly round that golden lamp
Sylvan deities encamp,
And simple maids and noble youth
Are welcome to the man of truth.
Most welcome they who need him most,
They feed the spring which they exhaust;
For greater need
Draws better deed:
But, critic, spare thy vanity,
Nor show thy pompous parts,
To vex with odious subtlety
The cheerer of men's hearts.

Sad-eyed Fakirs swiftly say
Endless dirges to decay,
Never in the blaze of light
Lose the shudder of midnight;
Pale at overflowing noon
Hear wolves barking at the moon;
In the bower of dalliance sweet
Hear the far Avenger's feet:
And shake before those awful Powers,
Who in their pride forgive not ours.
Thus the sad-eyed Fakirs preach:
‘ Bard, when thee would Allah teach,
And lift thee to his holy mount,
He sends thee from his bitter fount
Wormwood, — saying, " Go thy ways;
Drink not the Malaga of praise,¹

But do the deed thy fellows hate,
And compromise thy peaceful state;
Smite the white breasts which thee fed,
Stuff sharp thorns beneath the head
Of them thou shouldst have comforted;
For out of woe and out of crime
Draws the heart a lore sublime." '
And yet it seemeth not to me
That the high gods love tragedy;
For Saadi sat in the sun,
And thanks was his contrition;
For haircloth and for bloody whips,
Had active hands and smiling lips;
And yet his runes he rightly read,
And to his folk his message sped.
Sunshine in his heart transferred
Lighted each transparent word,
And well could honoring Persia learn
What Saadi wished to say;
For Saadi's nightly stars did burn
Brighter than Jami's day.

Whispered the Muse in Saadi's cot:
' O gentle Saadi, listen not,
Tempted by thy praise of wit,
Or by thirst and appetite
For the talents not thine own,
To sons of contradiction.
Never, son of eastern morning,

Follow falsehood, follow scorning.
Denounce who will, who will deny,
And pile the hills to scale the sky;
Let theist, atheist, pantheist,
Define and wrangle how they list,
Fierce conserver, fierce destroyer, —
But thou, joy-giver and enjoyer,
Unknowing war, unknowing crime,
Gentle Saadi, mind thy rhyme;
Heed not what the brawlers say,
Heed thou only Saadi's lay.[1]

' Let the great world bustle on
With war and trade, with camp and town;
A thousand men shall dig and eat;
At forge and furnace thousands sweat;
And thousands sail the purple sea,
And give or take the stroke of war,
Or crowd the market and bazaar;
Oft shall war end, and peace return,
And cities rise where cities burn,
Ere one man my hill shall climb,
Who can turn the golden rhyme.
Let them manage how they may,
Heed thou only Saadi's lay.
Seek the living among the dead, —
Man in man is imprisonèd;
Barefooted Dervish is not poor,
If fate unlock his bosom's door,

So that what his eye hath seen
His tongue can paint as bright, as keen;
And what his tender heart hath felt
With equal fire thy heart shalt melt.
For, whom the Muses smile upon,
And touch with soft persuasion,
His words like a storm-wind can bring
Terror and beauty on their wing;
In his every syllable
Lurketh Nature veritable;
And though he speak in midnight dark, —
In heaven no star, on earth no spark, —
Yet before the listener's eye
Swims the world in ecstasy,
The forest waves, the morning breaks,
The pastures sleep, ripple the lakes,
Leaves twinkle, flowers like persons be,
And life pulsates in rock or tree.
Saadi, so far thy words shall reach:
Suns rise and set in Saadi's speech!'

And thus to Saadi said the Muse:
'Eat thou the bread which men refuse;
Flee from the goods which from thee flee;
Seek nothing, — Fortune seeketh thee.
Nor mount, nor dive; all good things keep
The midway of the eternal deep.
Wish not to fill the isles with eyes
To fetch thee birds of paradise:

On thine orchard's edge belong
All the brags of plume and song;
Wise Ali's sunbright sayings pass
For proverbs in the market-place:
Through mountains bored by regal art,
Toil whistles as he drives his cart.
Nor scour the seas, nor sift mankind,
A poet or a friend to find:
Behold, he watches at the door!
Behold his shadow on the floor! [1]
Open innumerable doors
The heaven where unveiled Allah pours
The flood of truth, the flood of good,
The Seraph's and the Cherub's food.
Those doors are men: the Pariah hind
Admits thee to the perfect Mind.
Seek not beyond thy cottage wall
Redeemers that can yield thee all:
While thou sittest at thy door
On the desert's yellow floor,
Listening to the gray-haired crones,
Foolish gossips, ancient drones,
Saadi, see! they rise in stature
To the height of mighty Nature,
And the secret stands revealed
Fraudulent Time in vain concealed, —
That blessed gods in servile masks
Plied for thee thy household tasks.' [2]

HOLIDAYS

From fall to spring, the russet acorn,
    Fruit beloved of maid and boy,
Lent itself beneath the forest,
    To be the children's toy.

Pluck it now! In vain, — thou canst not;
    Its root has pierced yon shady mound;
Toy no longer — it has duties;
    It is anchored in the ground.

Year by year the rose-lipped maiden,
    Playfellow of young and old,
Was frolic sunshine, dear to all men,
    More dear to one than mines of gold.

Whither went the lovely hoyden?
    Disappeared in blessed wife;
Servant to a wooden cradle,
    Living in a baby's life.

Still thou playest; — short vacation
    Fate grants each to stand aside;
Now must thou be man and artist, —
    'T is the turning of the tide.

XENOPHANES

By fate, not option, frugal Nature gave
One scent to hyson and to wall-flower,
One sound to pine-groves and to waterfalls,
One aspect to the desert and the lake.
It was her stern necessity: all things
Are of one pattern made; bird, beast and flower,
Song, picture, form, space, thought and character
Deceive us, seeming to be many things,
And are but one. Beheld far off, they part
As God and devil; bring them to the mind,
They dull its edge with their monotony.
To know one element, explore another,
And in the second reappears the first.
The specious panorama of a year
But multiplies the image of a day, —
A belt of mirrors round a taper's flame;
And universal Nature, through her vast
And crowded whole, an infinite paroquet,
Repeats one note.[1]

THE DAY'S RATION

WHEN I was born,
From all the seas of strength Fate filled a chalice,
Saying, ' This be thy portion, child; this chalice,
Less than a lily's, thou shalt daily draw
From my great arteries, — nor less, nor more.'
All substances the cunning chemist Time
Melts down into that liquor of my life, —
Friends, foes, joys, fortunes, beauty and disgust.
And whether I am angry or content,
Indebted or insulted, loved or hurt,
All he distils into sidereal wine
And brims my little cup; heedless, alas!
Of all he sheds how little it will hold,
How much runs over on the desert sands.
If a new Muse draw me with splendid ray,
And I uplift myself into its heaven,
The needs of the first sight absorb my blood,
And all the following hours of the day
Drag a ridiculous age.
To-day, when friends approach, and every hour
Brings book, or starbright scroll of genius,
The little cup will hold not a bead more,
And all the costly liquor runs to waste;
Nor gives the jealous lord one diamond drop

So to be husbanded for poorer days.
Why need I volumes, if one word suffice?
Why need I galleries, when a pupil's draught
After the master's sketch fills and o'erfills
My apprehension? Why seek Italy,
Who cannot circumnavigate the sea
Of thoughts and things at home, but still adjourn
The nearest matters for a thousand days?

BLIGHT

GIVE me truths;
For I am weary of the surfaces,
And die of inanition. If I knew
Only the herbs and simples of the wood,
Rue, cinquefoil, gill, vervain and agrimony,
Blue-vetch and trillium, hawkweed, sassafras,
Milkweeds and murky brakes, quaint pipes and sun-
    dew,
And rare and virtuous roots, which in these woods
Draw untold juices from the common earth,
Untold, unknown, and I could surely spell
Their fragrance, and their chemistry apply
By sweet affinities to human flesh,
Driving the foe and stablishing the friend, —
O, that were much, and I could be a part
Of the round day, related to the sun

And planted world, and full executor
Of their imperfect functions.[1]
But these young scholars, who invade our hills,
Bold as the engineer who fells the wood,
And travelling often in the cut he makes,
Love not the flower they pluck, and know it not,
And all their botany is Latin names.
The old men studied magic in the flowers,
And human fortunes in astronomy,
And an omnipotence in chemistry,
Preferring things to names, for these were men,
Were unitarians of the united world,
And, wheresoever their clear eye-beams fell,
They caught the footsteps of the SAME.[2] Our eyes
Are armed, but we are strangers to the stars,
And strangers to the mystic beast and bird,
And strangers to the plant and to the mine.
The injured elements say, 'Not in us;'
And night and day, ocean and continent,
Fire, plant and mineral say, 'Not in us;'
And haughtily return us stare for stare.[3]
For we invade them impiously for gain;
We devastate them unreligiously,
And coldly ask their pottage, not their love.
Therefore they shove us from them, yield to us
Only what to our griping toil is due;
But the sweet affluence of love and song,
The rich results of the divine consents
Of man and earth, of world beloved and lover,

The nectar and ambrosia, are withheld;
And in the midst of spoils and slaves, we thieves
And pirates of the universe, shut out
Daily to a more thin and outward rind,
Turn pale and starve. Therefore, to our sick eyes,
The stunted trees look sick, the summer short,
Clouds shade the sun, which will not tan our hay,
And nothing thrives to reach its natural term;
And life, shorn of its venerable length,
Even at its greatest space is a defeat,
And dies in anger that it was a dupe;
And, in its highest noon and wantonness,
Is early frugal, like a beggar's child;
Even in the hot pursuit of the best aims
And prizes of ambition, checks its hand,
Like Alpine cataracts frozen as they leaped,
Chilled with a miserly comparison
Of the toy's purchase with the length of life.

MUSKETAQUID

BECAUSE I was content with these poor fields,
Low, open meads, slender and sluggish streams,
And found a home in haunts which others scorned,
The partial wood-gods overpaid my love,
And granted me the freedom of their state,
And in their secret senate have prevailed

With the dear, dangerous lords that rule our life,[1]
Made moon and planets parties to their bond,
And through my rock-like, solitary wont
Shot million rays of thought and tenderness.
For me, in showers, in sweeping showers, the Spring
Visits the valley; — break away the clouds, —
I bathe in the morn's soft and silvered air,
And loiter willing by yon loitering stream.
Sparrows far off, and nearer, April's bird,
Blue-coated, — flying before from tree to tree,
Courageous sing a delicate overture
To lead the tardy concert of the year.
Onward and nearer rides the sun of May;
And wide around, the marriage of the plants
Is sweetly solemnized. Then flows amain
The surge of summer's beauty; dell and crag,
Hollow and lake, hillside and pine arcade,
Are touched with genius. Yonder ragged cliff
Has thousand faces in a thousand hours.

Beneath low hills, in the broad interval
Through which at will our Indian rivulet
Winds mindful still of sannup and of squaw,
Whose pipe and arrow oft the plough unburies,
Here in pine houses built of new-fallen trees,
Supplanters of the tribe, the farmers dwell.
Traveller, to thee, perchance, a tedious road,
Or, it may be, a picture; to these men,
The landscape is an armory of powers,

Which, one by one, they know to draw and use.
They harness beast, bird, insect, to their work;
They prove the virtues of each bed of rock,
And, like the chemist 'mid his loaded jars,
Draw from each stratum its adapted use
To drug their crops or weapon their arts withal.
They turn the frost upon their chemic heap,
They set the wind to winnow pulse and grain,
They thank the spring-flood for its fertile slime,
And, on cheap summit-levels of the snow,
Slide with the sledge to inaccessible woods
O'er meadows bottomless. So, year by year,
They fight the elements with elements
(That one would say, meadow and forest walked,
Transmuted in these men to rule their like),
And by the order in the field disclose
The order regnant in the yeoman's brain.

What these strong masters wrote at large in miles,
I followed in small copy in my acre;
For there's no rood has not a star above it;[1]
The cordial quality of pear or plum
Ascends as gladly in a single tree
As in broad orchards resonant with bees;
And every atom poises for itself,
And for the whole. The gentle deities
Showed me the lore of colors and of sounds,
The innumerable tenements of beauty,
The miracle of generative force,

Far-reaching concords of astronomy [1]
Felt in the plants and in the punctual birds;
Better, the linked purpose of the whole,
And, chiefest prize, found I true liberty
In the glad home plain-dealing Nature gave.
The polite found me impolite; the great
Would mortify me, but in vain; for still
I am a willow of the wilderness,
Loving the wind that bent me. All my hurts
My garden spade can heal. A woodland walk,
A quest of river-grapes, a mocking thrush,
A wild-rose, or rock-loving columbine,
Salve my worst wounds.
For thus the wood-gods murmured in my ear:
[3] Dost love our manners? Canst thou silent lie?
Canst thou, thy pride forgot, like Nature pass
Into the winter night's extinguished mood?
Canst thou shine now, then darkle,
And being latent, feel thyself no less?
As, when the all-worshipped moon attracts the eye,
The river, hill, stems, foliage are obscure,
Yet envies none, none are unenviable.'

DIRGE

CONCORD, 1838

I REACHED the middle of the mount
  Up which the incarnate soul must climb,
And paused for them, and looked around,
  With me who walked through space and time,

Five rosy boys with morning light
  Had leaped from one fair mother's arms,
Fronted the sun with hope as bright,
  And greeted God with childhood's psalms.

Knows he who tills this lonely field
  To reap its scanty corn,
What mystic fruit his acres yield
  At midnight and at morn?

In the long sunny afternoon
  The plain was full of ghosts;
I wandered up, I wandered down,
  Beset by pensive hosts.

IX

The winding Concord gleamed below,
　　Pouring as wide a flood
As when my brothers, long ago,
　　Came with me to the wood.

But they are gone, — the holy ones
　　Who trod with me this lovely vale;
The strong, star-bright companions
　　Are silent, low and pale.

My good, my noble, in their prime,
　　Who made this world the feast it was,
Who learned with me the lore of time,
　　Who loved this dwelling-place!

They took this valley for their toy,
　　They played with it in every mood;
A cell for prayer, a hall for joy, —
　　They treated Nature as they would.

They colored the horizon round;
　　Stars flamed and faded as they bade,
All echoes hearkened for their sound, —
　　They made the woodlands glad or mad.

I touch this flower of silken leaf,
　　Which once our childhood knew;
Its soft leaves wound me with a grief
　　Whose balsam never grew.[1]

Hearken to yon pine-warbler
 Singing aloft in the tree!
Hearest thou, O traveller,
 What he singeth to me?

Not unless God made sharp thine ear
 With sorrow such as mine,
Out of that delicate lay could'st thou
 Its heavy tale divine.

'Go, lonely man,' it saith;
 'They loved thee from their birth;
Their hands were pure, and pure their faith,—
 There are no such hearts on earth.

'Ye drew one mother's milk,
 One chamber held ye all;
A very tender history
 Did in your childhood fall.

'You cannot unlock your heart,
 The key is gone with them;
The silent organ loudest chants
 The master's requiem.'

THRENODY

THE South-wind brings
Life, sunshine and desire,
And on every mount and meadow
Breathes aromatic fire;
But over the dead he has no power,
The lost, the lost, he cannot restore;
And, looking over the hills, I mourn
The darling who shall not return.

I see my empty house,
I see my trees repair their boughs;
And he, the wondrous child,
Whose silver warble wild
Outvalued every pulsing sound
Within the air's cerulean round,—
The hyacinthine boy, for whom
Morn well might break and April bloom,
The gracious boy, who did adorn
The world whereinto he was born,
And by his countenance repay
The favor of the loving Day,—
Has disappeared from the Day's eye;
Far and wide she cannot find him;
My hopes pursue, they cannot bind him.

Returned this day, the South-wind searches,
And finds young pines and budding birches;
But finds not the budding man;
Nature, who lost, cannot remake him;
Fate let him fall, Fate can't retake him;
Nature, Fate, men, him seek in vain.

And whither now, my truant wise and sweet,
O, whither tend thy feet?
I had the right, few days ago,
Thy steps to watch, thy place to know:
How have I forfeited the right?
Hast thou forgot me in a new delight?
I hearken for thy household cheer,
O eloquent child!
Whose voice, an equal messenger,
Conveyed thy meaning mild.
What though the pains and joys
Whereof it spoke were toys
Fitting his age and ken,
Yet fairest dames and bearded men,
Who heard the sweet request,
So gentle, wise and grave,
Bended with joy to his behest
And let the world's affairs go by,
A while to share his cordial game,
Or mend his wicker wagon-frame,
Still plotting how their hungry ear
That winsome voice again might hear;

For his lips could well pronounce
Words that were persuasions.[1]

Gentlest guardians marked serene
His early hope, his liberal mien;
Took counsel from his guiding eyes
To make this wisdom earthly wise.
Ah, vainly do these eyes recall
The school-march, each day's festival,
When every morn my bosom glowed
To watch the convoy on the road;
The babe in willow wagon closed,
With rolling eyes and face composed;
With children forward and behind,
Like Cupids studiously inclined;
And he the chieftain paced beside,
The centre of the troop allied,
With sunny face of sweet repose,
To guard the babe from fancied foes.
The little captain innocent
Took the eye with him as he went;
Each village senior paused to scan
And speak the lovely caravan.
From the window I look out
To mark thy beautiful parade,
Stately marching in cap and coat
To some tune by fairies played; —
A music heard by thee alone
To works as noble led thee on.

Now Love and Pride, alas! in vain,
Up and down their glances strain.
The painted sled stands where it stood;
The kennel by the corded wood;
His gathered sticks to stanch the wall
Of the snow-tower, when snow should fall;
The ominous hole he dug in the sand,
And childhood's castles built or planned;
His daily haunts I well discern, —
The poultry-yard, the shed, the barn, —
And every inch of garden ground
Paced by the blessed feet around,
From the roadside to the brook
Whereinto he loved to look.
Step the meek fowls where erst they ranged;
The wintry garden lies unchanged;
The brook into the stream runs on;
But the deep-eyed boy is gone.[1]

On that shaded day,
Dark with more clouds than tempests are,
When thou didst yield thy innocent breath
In birdlike heavings unto death,
Night came, and Nature had not thee;
I said, 'We are mates in misery.'
The morrow dawned with needless glow;
Each snowbird chirped, each fowl must crow;
Each tramper started; but the feet
Of the most beautiful and sweet

Of human youth had left the hill
And garden, — they were bound and still.
There's not a sparrow or a wren,
There's not a blade of autumn grain,
Which the four seasons do not tend
And tides of life and increase lend;
And every chick of every bird,
And weed and rock-moss is preferred.
O ostrich-like forgetfulness!
O loss of larger in the less!
Was there no star that could be sent,
No watcher in the firmament,
No angel from the countless host
That loiters round the crystal coast,
Could stoop to heal that only child,
Nature's sweet marvel undefiled,
And keep the blossom of the earth,
Which all her harvests were not worth?
Not mine, — I never called thee mine,
But Nature's heir, — if I repine,
And seeing rashly torn and moved
Not what I made, but what I loved,
Grow early old with grief that thou
Must to the wastes of Nature go, —
'T is because a general hope
Was quenched, and all must doubt and grope.
For flattering planets seemed to say
This child should ills of ages stay,
By wondrous tongue, and guided pen,

Bring the flown Muses back to men.
Perchance not he but Nature ailed,
The world and not the infant failed.
It was not ripe yet to sustain
A genius of so fine a strain,
Who gazed upon the sun and moon
As if he came unto his own,
And, pregnant with his grander thought,
Brought the old order into doubt.
His beauty once their beauty tried;
They could not feed him, and he died,
And wandered backward as in scorn,
To wait an æon to be born.
Ill day which made this beauty waste,
Plight broken, this high face defaced!
Some went and came about the dead;
And some in books of solace read;
Some to their friends the tidings say;
Some went to write, some went to pray;
One tarried here, there hurried one;
But their heart abode with none.
Covetous death bereaved us all,
To aggrandize one funeral.
The eager fate which carried thee
Took the largest part of me:
For this losing is true dying;
This is lordly man's down-lying,
This his slow but sure reclining,
Star by star his world resigning.

O child of paradise,
Boy who made dear his father's home,
In whose deep eyes
Men read the welfare of the times to come,
I am too much bereft.
The world dishonored thou hast left.
O truth's and nature's costly lie!
O trusted broken prophecy!
O richest fortune sourly crossed!
Born for the future, to the future lost!

The deep Heart answered, 'Weepest thou?
Worthier cause for passion wild
If I had not taken the child.
And deemest thou as those who pore,
With aged eyes, short way before, —
Think'st Beauty vanished from the coast
Of matter, and thy darling lost?
Taught he not thee — the man of eld,
Whose eyes within his eyes beheld
Heaven's numerous hierarchy span
The mystic gulf from God to man?
To be alone wilt thou begin
When worlds of lovers hem thee in?
To-morrow, when the masks shall fall
That dizen Nature's carnival,
The pure shall see by their own will,
Which overflowing Love shall fill,

'T is not within the force of fate
The fate-conjoined to separate.
But thou, my votary, weepest thou?
I gave thee sight — where is it now?
I taught thy heart beyond the reach
Of ritual, bible, or of speech;
Wrote in thy mind's transparent table,
As far as the incommunicable;
Taught thee each private sign to raise
Lit by the supersolar blaze.
Past utterance, and past belief,
And past the blasphemy of grief,
The mysteries of Nature's heart;
And though no Muse can these impart,
Throb thine with Nature's throbbing breast,
And all is clear from east to west.

I came to thee as to a friend;
Dearest, to thee I did not send
Tutors, but a joyful eye,
Innocence that matched the sky,
Lovely locks, a form of wonder,
Laughter rich as woodland thunder,
That thou might'st entertain apart
The richest flowering of all art:
And, as the great all-loving Day
Through smallest chambers takes its way,
That thou might'st break thy daily bread

With prophet, savior and head;
That thou might'st cherish for thine own
The riches of sweet Mary's Son,
Boy-Rabbi, Israel's paragon.
And thoughtest thou such guest
Would in thy hall take up his rest?
Would rushing life forget her laws,
Fate's glowing revolution pause?
High omens ask diviner guess;
Not to be conned to tediousness
And know my higher gifts unbind
The zone that girds the incarnate mind.
When the scanty shores are full
With Thought's perilous, whirling pool;
When frail Nature can no more,
Then the Spirit strikes the hour:
My servant Death, with solving rite,
Pours finite into infinite.
Wilt thou freeze love's tidal flow,
Whose streams through Nature circling go?
Nail the wild star to its track
On the half-climbed zodiac?
Light is light which radiates,
Blood is blood which circulates,
Life is life which generates,
And many-seeming life is one, —
Wilt thou transfix and make it none?
Its onward force too starkly pent
In figure, bone and lineament?

Wilt thou, uncalled, interrogate,
Talker! the unreplying Fate?
Nor see the genius of the whole
Ascendant in the private soul,
Beckon it when to go and come,
Self-announced its hour of doom?
Fair the soul's recess and shrine,
Magic-built to last a season;
Masterpiece of love benign,
Fairer that expansive reason
Whose omen 't is, and sign.
Wilt thou not ope thy heart to know
What rainbows teach, and sunsets show?
Verdict which accumulates
From lengthening scroll of human fates,
Voice of earth to earth returned,
Prayers of saints that inly burned, —
Saying, *What is excellent,*
As God lives, is permanent;
Hearts are dust, hearts' loves remain;
Heart's love will meet thee again.
Revere the Maker; fetch thine eye
Up to his style, and manners of the sky.
Not of adamant and gold
Built he heaven stark and cold;
No, but a nest of bending reeds,
Flowering grass and scented weeds;
Or like a traveller's fleeing tent,
Or bow above the tempest bent;

Built of tears and sacred flames,
And virtue reaching to its aims;
Built of furtherance and pursuing,
Not of spent deeds, but of doing.
Silent rushes the swift Lord
Through ruined systems still restored,
Broadsowing, bleak and void to bless,
Plants with worlds the wilderness; [1]
Waters with tears of ancient sorrow
Apples of Eden ripe to-morrow.
House and tenant go to ground,
Lost in God, in Godhead found.'

CONCORD HYMN

SUNG AT THE COMPLETION OF THE BATTLE
MONUMENT, JULY 4, 1837 [2]

By the rude bridge that arched the flood,
  Their flag to April's breeze unfurled,
Here once the embattled farmers stood
. And fired the shot heard round the world.

The foe long since in silence slept;
  Alike the conqueror silent sleeps;
And Time the ruined bridge has swept
  Down the dark stream which seaward creeps.

On this green bank, by this soft stream,
   We set to-day a votive stone;
That memory may their deed redeem,
   When, like our sires, our sons are gone.

Spirit, that made those heroes dare
   To die, and leave their children free,
Bid Time and Nature gently spare
   The shaft we raise to them and thee.

II

MAY–DAY AND OTHER PIECES

MAY-DAY

Daughter of Heaven and Earth, coy Spring,
With sudden passion languishing,
Teaching barren moors to smile,
Painting pictures mile on mile,
Holds a cup with cowslip-wreaths,
Whence a smokeless incense breathes.[1]
The air is full of whistlings bland;
What was that I heard
Out of the hazy land?
Harp of the wind, or song of bird,[2]
Or vagrant booming of the air,
Voice of a meteor lost in day?
Such tidings of the starry sphere
Can this elastic air convey.
Or haply 't was the cannonade
Of the pent and darkened lake,
Cooled by the pendent mountain's shade,
Whose deeps, till beams of noonday break,
Afflicted moan, and latest hold
Even into May the iceberg cold.
Was it a squirrel's pettish bark,
Or clarionet of jay? or hark

Where yon wedged line the Nestor leads,
Steering north with raucous cry
Through tracts and provinces of sky,
Every night alighting down
In new landscapes of romance,
Where darkling feed the clamorous clans
By lonely lakes to men unknown.
Come the tumult whence it will,
Voice of sport, or rush of wings,
It is a sound, it is a token
That the marble sleep is broken,
And a change has passed on things.

When late I walked, in earlier days,
All was stiff and stark;
Knee-deep snows choked all the ways,
In the sky no spark;
Firm-braced I sought my ancient woods,
Struggling through the drifted roads;
The whited desert knew me not,
Snow-ridges masked each darling spot;
The summer dells, by genius haunted,
One arctic moon had disenchanted.
All the sweet secrets therein hid
By Fancy, ghastly spells undid.
Eldest mason, Frost, had piled
Swift cathedrals in the wild;
The piny hosts were sheeted ghosts
In the star-lit minster aisled.

I found no joy: the icy wind
Might rule the forest to his mind.
Who would freeze on frozen lakes?
Back to books and sheltered home,
And wood-fire flickering on the walls,
To hear, when, 'mid our talk and games,
Without the baffled North-wind calls.
But soft! a sultry morning breaks; [1]
The ground-pines wash their rusty green,
The maple-tops their crimson tint,
On the soft path each track is seen,
The girl's foot leaves its neater print.
The pebble loosened from the frost
Asks of the urchin to be tost.
In flint and marble beats a heart,
The kind Earth takes her children's part, [2]
The green lane is the school-boy's friend,
Low leaves his quarrel apprehend,
The fresh ground loves his top and ball,
The air rings jocund to his call,
The brimming brook invites a leap,
He dives the hollow, climbs the steep. [3]
The youth sees omens where he goes,
And speaks all languages the rose,
The wood-fly mocks with tiny voice
The far halloo of human voice;
The perfumed berry on the spray
Smacks of faint memories far away.
A subtle chain of countless rings

The next into the farthest brings,
And, striving to be man, the worm
Mounts through all the spires of form.[1]

The cagèd linnet in the Spring
Hearkens for the choral glee,
When his fellows on the wing
Migrate from the Southern Sea ;
When trellised grapes their flowers unmask,
And the new-born tendrils twine,
The old wine darkling in the cask
Feels the bloom on the living vine,
And bursts the hoops at hint of Spring : [2]
And so, perchance, in Adam's race,
Of Eden's bower some dream-like trace
Survived the Flight and swam the Flood,
And wakes the wish in youngest blood
To tread the forfeit Paradise,
And feed once more the exile's eyes ;
And ever when the happy child
In May beholds the blooming wild,
And hears in heaven the bluebird sing,
' Onward,' he cries, ' your baskets bring, —
In the next field is air more mild,
And o'er yon hazy crest is Eden's balmier spring.'

Not for a regiment's parade,
Nor evil laws or rulers made,
Blue Walden rolls its cannonade,

But for a lofty sign
Which the Zodiac threw,
That the bondage-days are told,
And waters free as winds shall flow.[1]
Lo! how all the tribes combine
To rout the flying foe.
See, every patriot oak-leaf throws
His elfin length upon the snows,
Not idle, since the leaf all day
Draws to the spot the solar ray,
Ere sunset quarrying inches down,
And halfway to the mosses brown;
While the grass beneath the rime
Has hints of the propitious time,
And upward pries and perforates
Through the cold slab a thousand gates,
Till green lances peering through
Bend happy in the welkin blue.

As we thaw frozen flesh with snow,
So Spring will not her time forerun,
Mix polar night with tropic glow,
Nor cloy us with unshaded sun,
Nor wanton skip with bacchic dance,
But she has the temperance
Of the gods, whereof she is one, —
Masks her treasury of heat
Under east winds crossed with sleet.
Plants and birds and humble creatures

Well accept her rule austere;
Titan-born, to hardy natures
Cold is genial and dear.
As Southern wrath to Northern right
Is but straw to anthracite;
As in the day of sacrifice,
When heroes piled the pyre,
The dismal Massachusetts ice
Burned more than others' fire,
So Spring guards with surface cold
The garnered heat of ages old.
Hers to sow the seed of bread,
That man and all the kinds be fed;
And, when the sunlight fills the hours,
Dissolves the crust, displays the flowers.

Beneath the calm, within the light,
A hid unruly appetite
Of swifter life, a surer hope,
Strains every sense to larger scope,
Impatient to anticipate
The halting steps of aged Fate.
Slow grows the palm, too slow the pearl:
When Nature falters, fain would zeal
Grasp the felloes of her wheel,
And grasping give the orbs another whirl.
Turn swiftlier round, O tardy ball!
And sun this frozen side.
Bring hither back the robin's call,
Bring back the tulip's pride.

Why chidest thou the tardy Spring?
The hardy bunting does not chide;
The blackbirds make the maples ring
With social cheer and jubilee;
The redwing flutes his *o-ka-lee*,
The robins know the melting snow;
The sparrow meek, prophetic-eyed,
Her nest beside the snow-drift weaves,
Secure the osier yet will hide
Her callow brood in mantling leaves, —
And thou, by science all undone,
Why only must thy reason fail
To see the southing of the sun? [1]

The world rolls round, — mistrust it not, —
Befalls again what once befell;
All things return, both sphere and mote,
And I shall hear my bluebird's note,
And dream the dream of Auburn dell. [2]

April cold with dropping rain
Willows and lilacs brings again,
The whistle of returning birds,
And trumpet-lowing of the herds.
The scarlet maple-keys betray
What potent blood hath modest May,
What fiery force the earth renews,
The wealth of forms, the flush of hues;
What joy in rosy waves outpoured
Flows from the heart of Love, the Lord.

Hither rolls the storm of heat;
I feel its finer billows beat
Like a sea which me infolds; [1]
Heat with viewless fingers moulds,
Swells, and mellows, and matures,
Paints, and flavors, and allures,
Bird and brier inly warms,
Still enriches and transforms,
Gives the reed and lily length,
Adds to oak and oxen strength, [2]
Transforming what it doth infold,
Life out of death, new out of old,
Painting fawns' and leopards' fells,
Seethes the gulf-encrimsoning shells,
Fires gardens with a joyful blaze
Of tulips, in the morning's rays.
The dead log touched bursts into leaf,
The wheat-blade whispers of the sheaf.
What god is this imperial Heat,
Earth's prime secret, sculpture's seat?
Doth it bear hidden in its heart
Water-line patterns of all art?
Is it Dædalus? is it Love?
Or walks in mask almighty Jove,
And drops from Power's redundant horn
All seeds of beauty to be born?

Where shall we keep the holiday,
And duly greet the entering May?

Too strait and low our cottage doors,
And all unmeet our carpet floors;
Nor spacious court, nor monarch's hall,
Suffice to hold the festival.
Up and away! where haughty woods
Front the liberated floods:
We will climb the broad-backed hills,
Hear the uproar of their joy;
We will mark the leaps and gleams
Of the new-delivered streams,
And the murmuring rivers of sap
Mount in the pipes of the trees,
Giddy with day, to the topmost spire,
Which for a spike of tender green
Bartered its powdery cap;
And the colors of joy in the bird,
And the love in its carol heard,
Frog and lizard in holiday coats,
And turtle brave in his golden spots;
While cheerful cries of crag and plain
Reply to the thunder of river and main.[1]

As poured the flood of the ancient sea
Spilling over mountain chains,
Bending forests as bends the sedge,
Faster flowing o'er the plains, —
A world-wide wave with a foaming edge
That rims the running silver sheet, —
So pours the deluge of the heat

Broad northward o'er the land,
Painting artless paradises,
Drugging herbs with Syrian spices,[1]
Fanning secret fires which glow
In columbine and clover-blow,
Climbing the northern zones,
Where a thousand pallid towns
Lie like cockles by the main,
Or tented armies on a plain.
The million-handed sculptor moulds
Quaintest bud and blossom folds,
The million-handed painter pours
Opal hues and purple dye;
Azaleas flush the island floors,
And the tints of heaven reply.

Wreaths for the May! for happy Spring
To-day shall all her dowry bring,
The love of kind, the joy, the grace,
Hymen of element and race,
Knowing well to celebrate
With song and hue and star and state,
With tender light and youthful cheer,
The spousals of the new-born year.

Spring is strong and virtuous,
Broad-sowing, cheerful, plenteous,
Quickening underneath the mould
Grains beyond the price of gold.

So deep and large her bounties are,
That one broad, long midsummer day
Shall to the planet overpay
The ravage of a year of war.

Drug the cup, thou butler sweet,
And send the nectar round;
The feet that slid so long on sleet
Are glad to feel the ground.
Fill and saturate each kind
With good according to its mind,
Fill each kind and saturate
With good agreeing with its fate,
And soft perfection of its plan—
Willow and violet, maiden and man.

The bitter-sweet, the haunting air
Creepeth, bloweth everywhere;
It preys on all, all prey on it,
Blooms in beauty, thinks in wit,
Stings the strong with enterprise,
Makes travellers long for Indian skies,
And where it comes this courier fleet
Fans in all hearts expectance sweet,
As if to-morrow should redeem
The vanished rose of evening's dream.
By houses lies a fresher green,
On men and maids a ruddier mien,
As if Time brought a new relay

Of shining virgins every May,
And Summer came to ripen maids
To a beauty that not fades.

I saw the bud-crowned Spring go forth,
Stepping daily onward north
To greet staid ancient cavaliers
Filing single in stately train.
And who, and who are the travellers?
They were Night and Day, and Day and Night,
Pilgrims wight with step forthright.
I saw the Days deformed and low,
Short and bent by cold and snow;
The merry Spring threw wreaths on them,
Flower-wreaths gay with bud and bell;
Many a flower and many a gem,
They were refreshed by the smell,
They shook the snow from hats and shoon,
They put their April raiment on;
And those eternal forms,
Unhurt by a thousand storms,
Shot up to the height of the sky again,
And danced as merrily as young men.
I saw them mask their awful glance
Sidewise meek in gossamer lids;
And to speak my thought if none forbids
It was as if the eternal gods,
Tired of their starry periods,
Hid their majesty in cloth

Woven of tulips and painted moth.
On carpets green the maskers march
Below May's well-appointed arch,
Each star, each god, each grace amain,
Every joy and virtue speed,
Marching duly in her train,
And fainting Nature at her need
Is made whole again.[1]

'T was the vintage-day of field and wood,
When magic wine for bards is brewed;
Every tree and stem and chink
Gushed with syrup to the brink.
The air stole into the streets of towns,
Refreshed the wise, reformed the clowns,
And betrayed the fund of joy
To the high-school and medalled boy:
On from hall to chamber ran,
From youth to maid, from boy to man,
To babes, and to old eyes as well.
'Once more,' the old man cried, 'ye clouds,
Airy turrets purple-piled,
Which once my infancy beguiled,
Beguile me with the wonted spell.
I know ye skilful to convoy
The total freight of hope and joy
Into rude and homely nooks,
Shed mocking lustres on shelf of books,
On farmer's byre, on pasture rude,

And stony pathway to the wood.
I care not if the pomps you show
Be what they soothfast appear,
Or if yon realms in sunset glow
Be bubbles of the atmosphere.
And if it be to you allowed
To fool me with a shining cloud,
So only new griefs are consoled
By new delights, as old by old,
Frankly I will be your guest,
Count your change and cheer the best.
The world hath overmuch of pain, —
If Nature give me joy again,
Of such deceit I 'll not complain.'

Ah! well I mind the calendar,
Faithful through a thousand years,
Of the painted race of flowers,
Exact to days, exact to hours,
Counted on the spacious dial
Yon broidered zodiac girds.
I know the trusty almanac
Of the punctual coming-back,
On their due days, of the birds.
I marked them yestermorn,
A flock of finches darting
Beneath the crystal arch,
Piping, as they flew, a march, —
Belike the one they used in parting

Last year from yon oak or larch;
Dusky sparrows in a crowd,
Diving, darting northward free,
Suddenly betook them all,
Every one to his hole in the wall,
Or to his niche in the apple-tree.
I greet with joy the choral trains
Fresh from palms and Cuba's canes.
Best gems of Nature's cabinet,
With dews of tropic morning wet,
Beloved of children, bards and Spring,
O birds, your perfect virtues bring,
Your song, your forms, your rhythmic flight,
Your manners for the heart's delight,
Nestle in hedge, or barn, or roof,
Here weave your chamber weather-proof,
Forgive our harms, and condescend
To man, as to a lubber friend,
And, generous, teach his awkward race
Courage and probity and grace! [1]

Poets praise that hidden wine
Hid in milk we drew
At the barrier of Time,
When our life was new.
We had eaten fairy fruit,
We were quick from head to foot,
All the forms we looked on shone
As with diamond dews thereon.

IX

What cared we for costly joys,
The Museum's far-fetched toys?
Gleam of sunshine on the wall
Poured a deeper cheer than all
The revels of the Carnival.
We a pine-grove did prefer
To a marble theatre,
Could with gods on mallows dine,
Nor cared for spices or for wine.
Wreaths of mist and rainbow spanned,
Arch on arch, the grimmest land;
Whistle of a woodland bird
Made the pulses dance,
Note of horn in valleys heard
Filled the region with romance.

None can tell how sweet,
How virtuous, the morning air;
Every accent vibrates well;
Not alone the wood-bird's call,
Or shouting boys that chase their ball,
Pass the height of minstrel skill,
But the ploughman's thoughtless cry,
Lowing oxen, sheep that bleat,
And the joiner's hammer-beat,
Softened are above their will,
Take tones from groves they wandered through
Or flutes which passing angels blew.
All grating discords melt,

No dissonant note is dealt,
And though thy voice be shrill
Like rasping file on steel,
Such is the temper of the air,
Echo waits with art and care,
And will the faults of song repair.

So by remote Superior Lake,
And by resounding Mackinac,
When northern storms the forest shake,
And billows on the long beach break,
The artful Air will separate
Note by note all sounds that grate,
Smothering in her ample breast
All but godlike words,
Reporting to the happy ear
Only purified accords.
Strangely wrought from barking waves,
Soft music daunts the Indian braves,—
Convent-chanting which the child
Hears pealing from the panther's cave
And the impenetrable wild.[1]

Soft on the South-wind sleeps the haze:
So on thy broad mystic van
Lie the opal-colored days,
And waft the miracle to man.
Soothsayer of the eldest gods,
Repairer of what harms betide,

Revealer of the inmost powers
Prometheus proffered, Jove denied;
Disclosing treasures more than true,
Or in what far to-morrow due;
Speaking by the tongues of flowers,
By the ten-tongued laurel speaking,
Singing by the oriole songs,
Heart of bird the man's heart seeking;
Whispering hints of treasure hid
Under Morn's unlifted lid,
Islands looming just beyond
The dim horizon's utmost bound; —
Who can, like thee, our rags upbraid,
Or taunt us with our hope decayed?
Or who like thee persuade,
Making the splendor of the air,
The morn and sparkling dew, a snare?
Or who resent
Thy genius, wiles and blandishment?

There is no orator prevails
To beckon or persuade
Like thee the youth or maid : [1]
Thy birds, thy songs, thy brooks, thy gales,
Thy blooms, thy kinds,
Thy echoes in the wilderness,
Soothe pain, and age, and love's distress,
Fire fainting will, and build heroic minds.

For thou, O Spring! canst renovate
All that high God did first create.
Be still his arm and architect,
Rebuild the ruin, mend defect;
Chemist to vamp old worlds with new,
Coat sea and sky with heavenlier blue,
New tint the plumage of the birds,
And slough decay from grazing herds,
Sweep ruins from the scarped mountain,
Cleanse the torrent at the fountain,
Purge alpine air by towns defiled,
Bring to fair mother fairer child,
Not less renew the heart and brain,
Scatter the sloth, wash out the stain,
Make the aged eye sun-clear,
To parting soul bring grandeur near.
Under gentle types, my Spring
Masks the might of Nature's king,
An energy that searches thorough
From Chaos to the dawning morrow;
Into all our human plight,
The soul's pilgrimage and flight;
In city or in solitude,
Step by step, lifts bad to good,
Without halting, without rest,
Lifting Better up to Best;
Planting seeds of knowledge pure,
Through earth to ripen, through heaven endure.

THE ADIRONDACS

A JOURNAL

DEDICATED TO MY FELLOW TRAVELLERS IN AUGUST, 1858

> Wise and polite, — and if I drew
> Their several portraits, you would own
> Chaucer had no such worthy crew,
> Nor Boccace in Decameron.

WE crossed Champlain to Keeseville with our friends,
Thence, in strong country carts, rode up the forks
Of the Ausable stream, intent to reach
The Adirondac lakes. At Martin's Beach
We chose our boats ; each man a boat and guide, —
Ten men, ten guides, our company all told.

Next morn, we swept with oars the Saranac,
With skies of benediction, to Round Lake,
Where all the sacred mountains drew around us,
Taháwus, Seaward, MacIntyre, Baldhead,
And other Titans without muse or name.
Pleased with these grand companions, we glide on,
Instead of flowers, crowned with a wreath of hills.
We made our distance wider, boat from boat,
As each would hear the oracle alone.
By the bright morn the gay flotilla slid

Through files of flags that gleamed like bayonets,
Through gold-moth-haunted beds of pickerel-flower,
Through scented banks of lilies white and gold,
Where the deer feeds at night, the teal by day,
On through the Upper Saranac, and up
Père Raquette stream, to a small tortuous pass
Winding through grassy shallows in and out,
Two creeping miles of rushes, pads and sponge,
To Follansbee Water and the Lake of Loons.

Northward the length of Follansbee we rowed,
Under low mountains, whose unbroken ridge
Ponderous with beechen forest sloped the shore.
A pause and council: then, where near the head
Due east a bay makes inward to the land
Between two rocky arms, we climb the bank,
And in the twilight of the forest noon
Wield the first axe these echoes ever heard.
We cut young trees to make our poles and thwarts,
Barked the white spruce to weatherfend the roof,
Then struck a light and kindled the camp-fire.

The wood was sovran with centennial trees, —
Oak, cedar, maple, poplar, beech and fir,
Linden and spruce. In strict society
Three conifers, white, pitch and Norway pine,
Five-leaved, three-leaved and two-leaved, grew thereby.
Our patron pine was fifteen feet in girth,
The maple eight, beneath its shapely tower.

' Welcome ! ' the wood-god murmured through the
    leaves, —
' Welcome, though late, unknowing, yet known to
    me.'
Evening drew on ; stars peeped through maple-boughs,
Which o'erhung, like a cloud, our camping fire.
Decayed millennial trunks, like moonlight flecks,
Lit with phosphoric crumbs the forest floor.

Ten scholars, wonted to lie warm and soft
In well-hung chambers daintily bestowed,
Lie here on hemlock-boughs, like Sacs and Sioux,
And greet unanimous the joyful change.
So fast will Nature acclimate her sons,
Though late returning to her pristine ways.
Off soundings, seamen do not suffer cold ;
And, in the forest, delicate clerks, unbrowned,
Sleep on the fragrant brush, as on down-beds.
Up with the dawn, they fancied the light air
That circled freshly in their forest dress
Made them to boys again. Happier that they
Slipped off their pack of duties, leagues behind,
At the first mounting of the giant stairs.
No placard on these rocks warned to the polls,
No door-bell heralded a visitor,
No courier waits, no letter came or went,
Nothing was ploughed, or reaped, or bought, or sold ;
The frost might glitter, it would blight no crop,
The falling rain will spoil no holiday.

We were made freemen of the forest laws,
All dressed, like Nature, fit for her own ends,
Essaying nothing she cannot perform.

                     In Adirondac lakes,
At morn or noon, the guide rows bareheaded:
Shoes, flannel shirt, and kersey trousers make
His brief toilette: at night, or in the rain,
He dons a surcoat which he doffs at morn:
A paddle in the right hand, or an oar,
And in the left, a gun, his needful arms.
By turns we praised the stature of our guides,
Their rival strength and suppleness, their skill
To row, to swim, to shoot, to build a camp,
To climb a lofty stem, clean without boughs
Full fifty feet, and bring the eaglet down:
Temper to face wolf, bear, or catamount,
And wit to trap or take him in his lair.
Sound, ruddy men, frolic and innocent,
In winter, lumberers; in summer, guides;
Their sinewy arms pull at the oar untired
Three times ten thousand strokes, from morn to eve.

Look to yourselves, ye polished gentlemen!
No city airs or arts pass current here.
Your rank is all reversed; let men of cloth
Bow to the stalwart churls in overalls:
They are the doctors of the wilderness,
And we the low-prized laymen.

In sooth, red flannel is a saucy test
Which few can put on with impunity.
What make you, master, fumbling at the oar?
Will you catch crabs? Truth tries pretension here.
The sallow knows the basket-maker's thumb;
The oar, the guide's. Dare you accept the tasks
He shall impose, to find a spring, trap foxes,
Tell the sun's time, determine the true north,
Or stumbling on through vast self-similar woods
To thread by night the nearest way to camp?

Ask you, how went the hours?
All day we swept the lake, searched every cove,
North from Camp Maple, south to Osprey Bay,
Watching when the loud dogs should drive in deer,
Or whipping its rough surface for a trout;
Or, bathers, diving from the rock at noon;
Challenging Echo by our guns and cries;
Or listening to the laughter of the loon;
Or, in the evening twilight's latest red,
Beholding the procession of the pines; [1]
Or, later yet, beneath a lighted jack,
In the boat's bows, a silent night-hunter
Stealing with paddle to the feeding-grounds
Of the red deer, to aim at a square mist. [2]
Hark to that muffled roar! a tree in the woods
Is fallen: but hush! it has not scared the buck
Who stands astonished at the meteor light,
Then turns to bound away, — is it too late?

Our heroes tried their rifles at a mark,
Six rods, sixteen, twenty, or forty-five;
Sometimes their wits at sally and retort,
With laughter sudden as the crack of rifle;
Or parties scaled the near acclivities
Competing seekers of a rumored lake,
Whose unauthenticated waves we named
Lake Probability, — our carbuncle,
Long sought, not found.

                   Two Doctors in the camp
Dissected the slain deer, weighed the trout's brain,
Captured the lizard, salamander, shrew,
Crab, mice, snail, dragon-fly, minnow and moth;
Insatiate skill in water or in air
Waved the scoop-net, and nothing came amiss;
The while, one leaden pot of alcohol
Gave an impartial tomb to all the kinds.
Not less the ambitious botanist sought plants,
Orchis and gentian, fern and long whip-scirpus,
Rosy polygonum, lake-margin's pride,
Hypnum and hydnum, mushroom, sponge and
        moss,
Or harebell nodding in the gorge of falls.
Above, the eagle flew, the osprey screamed,
The raven croaked, owls hooted, the woodpecker
Loud hammered, and the heron rose in the swamp.
As water poured through hollows of the hills
To feed this wealth of lakes and rivulets,

So Nature shed all beauty lavishly
From her redundant horn.

                  Lords of this realm,
Bounded by dawn and sunset, and the day
Rounded by hours where each outdid the last
In miracles of pomp, we must be proud,
As if associates of the sylvan gods.
We seemed the dwellers of the zodiac,
So pure the Alpine element we breathed,
So light, so lofty pictures came and went.
We trode on air, contemned the distant town,
Its timorous ways, big trifles, and we planned
That we should build, hard-by, a spacious lodge
And how we should come hither with our sons,
Hereafter, — willing they, and more adroit.[1]

Hard fare, hard bed and comic misery, —
The midge, the blue-fly and the mosquito
Painted our necks, hands, ankles, with red bands:
But, on the second day, we heed them not,
Nay, we saluted them Auxiliaries,
Whom earlier we had chid with spiteful names.
For who defends our leafy tabernacle
From bold intrusion of the travelling crowd, —
Who but the midge, mosquito and the fly,
Which past endurance sting the tender cit,
But which we learn to scatter with a smudge,
Or baffle by a veil, or slight by scorn?

Our foaming ale we drank from hunters' pans,
Ale, and a sup of wine. Our steward gave
Venison and trout, potatoes, beans, wheat-bread;
All ate like abbots, and, if any missed
Their wonted convenance, cheerly hid the loss
With hunters' appetite and peals of mirth.
And Stillman, our guides' guide, and Commodore,
Crusoe, Crusader, Pius Æneas, said aloud,
" Chronic dyspepsia never came from eating
Food indigestible " : — then murmured some,
Others applauded him who spoke the truth.[1]

Nor doubt but visitings of graver thought
Checked in these souls the turbulent heyday
'Mid all the hints and glories of the home.
For who can tell what sudden privacies
Were sought and found, amid the hue and cry
Of scholars furloughed from their tasks and let
Into this Oreads' fended Paradise,
As chapels in the city's thoroughfares,
Whither gaunt Labor slips to wipe his brow
And meditate a moment on Heaven's rest.
Judge with what sweet surprises Nature spoke
To each apart, lifting her lovely shows
To spiritual lessons pointed home,
And as through dreams in watches of the night,
So through all creatures in their form and ways
Some mystic hint accosts the vigilant,
Not clearly voiced, but waking a new sense

Inviting to new knowledge, one with old.
Hark to that petulant chirp! what ails the warbler?
Mark his capricious ways to draw the eye.
Now soar again. What wilt thou, restless bird,
Seeking in that chaste blue a bluer light,
Thirsting in that pure for a purer sky?

And presently the sky is changed; O world!
What pictures and what harmonies are thine!
The clouds are rich and dark, the air serene,
So like the soul of me, what if 't were me?
A melancholy better than all mirth.
Comes the sweet sadness at the retrospect,
Or at the foresight of obscurer years?
Like yon slow-sailing cloudy promontory
Whereon the purple iris dwells in beauty
Superior to all its gaudy skirts.
And, that no day of life may lack romance,
The spiritual stars rise nightly, shedding down
A private beam into each several heart.
Daily the bending skies solicit man,
The seasons chariot him from this exile,
The rainbow hours bedeck his glowing chair,
The storm-winds urge the heavy weeks along,
Suns haste to set, that so remoter lights
Beckon the wanderer to his vaster home.

With a vermilion pencil mark the day
When of our little fleet three cruising skiffs

Entering Big Tupper, bound for the foaming Falls
Of loud Bog River, suddenly confront
Two of our mates returning with swift oars.
One held a printed journal waving high
Caught from a late-arriving traveller,
Big with great news, and shouted the report
For which the world had waited, now firm fact,
Of the wire-cable laid beneath the sea,
And landed on our coast, and pulsating
With ductile fire. Loud, exulting cries
From boat to boat, and to the echoes round,
Greet the glad miracle. Thought's new-found
          path
Shall supplement henceforth all trodden ways,
Match God's equator with a zone of art,
And lift man's public action to a height
Worthy the enormous cloud of witnesses,
When linkèd hemispheres attest his deed.
We have few moments in the longest life
Of such delight and wonder as there grew, —
Nor yet unsuited to that solitude :
A burst of joy, as if we told the fact
To ears intelligent ; as if gray rock
And cedar grove and cliff and lake should know
This feat of wit, this triumph of mankind ;
As if we men were talking in a vein
Of sympathy so large, that ours was theirs,
And a prime end of the most subtle element
Were fairly reached at last. Wake, echoing caves !

Bend nearer, faint day-moon ! Yon thundertops,
Let them hear well ! 't is theirs as much as ours.[1]

A spasm throbbing through the pedestals
Of Alp and Andes, isle and continent,
Urging astonished Chaos with a thrill
To be a brain, or serve the brain of man.[2]
The lightning has run masterless too long;
He must to school and learn his verb and noun
And teach his nimbleness to earn his wage,
Spelling with guided tongue man's messages
Shot through the weltering pit of the salt sea.
And yet I marked, even in the manly joy
Of our great-hearted Doctor in his boat
(Perchance I erred), a shade of discontent;
Or was it for mankind a generous shame,
As of a luck not quite legitimate,
Since fortune snatched from wit the lion's part?
Was it a college pique of town and gown,
As one within whose memory it burned
That not academicians, but some lout,
Found ten years since the Californian gold?
And now, again, a hungry company
Of traders, led by corporate sons of trade,
Perversely borrowing from the shop the tools
Of science, not from the philosophers,
Had won the brightest laurel of all time.
'T was always thus, and will be; hand and head
Are ever rivals : but, though this be swift,

The other slow, — this the Prometheus,
And that the Jove, — yet, howsoever hid,
It was from Jove the other stole his fire,
And, without Jove, the good had never been.
It is not Iroquois or cannibals,
But ever the free race with front sublime,
And these instructed by their wisest too,
Who do the feat, and lift humanity.
Let not him mourn who best entitled was,
Nay, mourn not one: let him exult,
Yea, plant the tree that bears best apples, plant,
And water it with wine, nor watch askance
Whether thy sons or strangers eat the fruit:
Enough that mankind eat and are refreshed.

We flee away from cities, but we bring
The best of cities with us, these learned classifiers,
Men knowing what they seek, armed eyes of experts.
We praise the guide, we praise the forest life:
But will we sacrifice our dear-bought lore
Of books and arts and trained experiment,
Or count the Sioux a match for Agassiz?
O no, not we! Witness the shout that shook
Wild Tupper Lake; witness the mute all-hail
The joyful traveller gives, when on the verge
Of craggy Indian wilderness he hears
From a log cabin stream Beethoven's notes
On the piano, played with master's hand.
'Well done!' he cries; 'the bear is kept at bay,

IX

The lynx, the rattlesnake, the flood, the fire;
All the fierce enemies, ague, hunger, cold,
This thin spruce roof, this clayed log-wall,
This wild plantation will suffice to chase.
Now speed the gay celerities of art,
What in the desert was impossible
Within four walls is possible again, —
Culture and libraries, mysteries of skill,
Traditioned fame of masters, eager strife
Of keen competing youths, joined or alone
To outdo each other and extort applause.
Mind wakes a new-born giant from her sleep.
Twirl the old wheels! Time takes fresh start again,
On for a thousand years of genius more.'

The holidays were fruitful, but must end;
One August evening had a cooler breath;
Into each mind intruding duties crept;
Under the cinders burned the fires of home;
Nay, letters found us in our paradise:
So in the gladness of the new event
We struck our camp and left the happy hills.
The fortunate star that rose on us sank not;
The prodigal sunshine rested on the land,
The rivers gambolled onward to the sea,
And Nature, the inscrutable and mute,
Permitted on her infinite repose
Almost a smile to steal to cheer her sons,
As if one riddle of the Sphinx were guessed.

BRAHMA

IF the red slayer think he slays,
  Or if the slain think he is slain,
They know not well the subtle ways
  I keep, and pass, and turn again.

Far or forgot to me is near;
  Shadow and sunlight are the same;
The vanished gods to me appear;
  And one to me are shame and fame.

They reckon ill who leave me out;
  When me they fly, I am the wings;
I am the doubter and the doubt,
  And I the hymn the Brahmin sings.

The strong gods pine for my abode,
  And pine in vain the sacred Seven;
But thou, meek lover of the good!
  Find me, and turn thy back on heaven.

NEMESIS

Already blushes on thy cheek
The bosom thought which thou must speak;
The bird, how far it haply roam
By cloud or isle, is flying home;
The maiden fears, and fearing runs
Into the charmed snare she shuns;
And every man, in love or pride,
Of his fate is never wide.

Will a woman's fan the ocean smooth?
Or prayers the stony Parcæ soothe,
Or coax the thunder from its mark?
Or tapers light the chaos dark?
In spite of Virtue and the Muse,
Nemesis will have her dues,
And all our struggles and our toils
Tighter wind the giant coils.

FATE

Deep in the man sits fast his fate
To mould his fortunes, mean or great:
Unknown to Cromwell as to me
Was Cromwell's measure or degree;
Unknown to him as to his horse,
If he than his groom be better or worse.
He works, plots, fights, in rude affairs,
With squires, lords, kings, his craft compares,
Till late he learned, through doubt and fear,
Broad England harbored not his peer:
Obeying time, the last to own
The Genius from its cloudy throne.
For the prevision is allied
Unto the thing so signified;
Or say, the foresight that awaits
Is the same Genius that creates.

FREEDOM

Once I wished I might rehearse
Freedom's pæan in my verse,
That the slave who caught the strain
Should throb until he snapped his chain.
But the Spirit said, 'Not so;
Speak it not, or speak it low;
Name not lightly to be said,
Gift too precious to be prayed,
Passion not to be expressed
But by heaving of the breast:
Yet, — wouldst thou the mountain find
Where this deity is shrined,
Who gives to seas and sunset skies
Their unspent beauty of surprise,
And, when it lists him, waken can
Brute or savage into man;
Or, if in thy heart he shine,
Blends the starry fates with thine,
Draws angels nigh to dwell with thee,
And makes thy thoughts archangels be;
Freedom's secret wilt thou know? —
Counsel not with flesh and blood;
Loiter not for cloak or food;
Right thou feelest, rush to do.'

ODE

SUNG IN THE TOWN HALL, CONCORD, JULY 4, 1857

O TENDERLY the haughty day
    Fills his blue urn with fire;
One morn is in the mighty heaven,
    And one in our desire.

The cannon booms from town to town,
    Our pulses beat not less,
The joy-bells chime their tidings down,
    Which children's voices bless.

For He that flung the broad blue fold
    O'er-mantling land and sea,
One third part of the sky unrolled
    For the banner of the free.

The men are ripe of Saxon kind
    To build an equal state, —
To take the statute from the mind
    And make of duty fate.

United States! the ages plead, —
    Present and Past in under-song, —
Go put your creed into your deed,
    Nor speak with double tongue.

For sea and land don't understand,
   Nor skies without a frown
See rights for which the one hand fights
   By the other cloven down.

Be just at home; then write your scroll
   Of honor o'er the sea,
And bid the broad Atlantic roll,
   A ferry of the free.

And henceforth there shall be no chain,
   Save underneath the sea
The wires shall murmur through the main
   Sweet songs of liberty.

The conscious stars accord above,
   The waters wild below,
And under, through the cable wove,
   Her fiery errands go.

For He that worketh high and wise,
   Nor pauses in his plan,
Will take the sun out of the skies
   Ere freedom out of man.

BOSTON HYMN

READ IN MUSIC HALL, JANUARY 1, 1863

THE word of the Lord by night
To the watching Pilgrims came,
As they sat by the seaside,
And filled their hearts with flame.

God said, I am tired of kings,
I suffer them no more;
Up to my ear the morning brings
The outrage of the poor.

Think ye I made this ball
A field of havoc and war,
Where tyrants great and tyrants small
Might harry the weak and poor?

My angel, — his name is Freedom, —
Choose him to be your king;
He shall cut pathways east and west
And fend you with his wing.

Lo! I uncover the land
Which I hid of old time in the West,
As the sculptor uncovers the statue
When he has wrought his best;

I show Columbia, of the rocks
Which dip their foot in the seas
And soar to the air-borne flocks
Of clouds and the boreal fleece.

I will divide my goods;
Call in the wretch and slave:
None shall rule but the humble,
And none but Toil shall have.

I will have never a noble,
No lineage counted great;
Fishers and choppers and ploughmen
Shall constitute a state.

Go, cut down trees in the forest
And trim the straightest boughs;
Cut down trees in the forest
And build me a wooden house.

Call the people together,
The young men and the sires,
The digger in the harvest-field,
Hireling and him that hires;

And here in a pine state-house
They shall choose men to rule
In every needful faculty,
In church and state and school.

Lo, now! if these poor men
Can govern the land and sea
And make just laws below the sun,
As planets faithful be.

And ye shall succor men;
'T is nobleness to serve;
Help them who cannot help again:
Beware from right to swerve.

I break your bonds and masterships,
And I unchain the slave:
Free be his heart and hand henceforth
As wind and wandering wave.

I cause from every creature
His proper good to flow:
As much as he is and doeth,
So much he shall bestow.

But, laying hands on another
To coin his labor and sweat,
He goes in pawn to his victim
For eternal years in debt.

To-day unbind the captive,
So only are ye unbound;
Lift up a people from the dust,
Trump of their rescue, sound!

Pay ransom to the owner
And fill the bag to the brim.[1]
Who is the owner? The slave is owner,
And ever was. Pay him.

O North! give him beauty for rags,
And honor, O South! for his shame;
Nevada! coin thy golden crags
With Freedom's image and name.

Up! and the dusky race
That sat in darkness long, —
Be swift their feet as antelopes,
And as behemoth strong.

Come, East and West and North,
By races, as snow-flakes,
And carry my purpose forth,
Which neither halts nor shakes.

My will fulfilled shall be,
For, in daylight or in dark,
My thunderbolt has eyes to see
His way home to the mark.

VOLUNTARIES

I

Low and mournful be the strain,
Haughty thought be far from me;
Tones of penitence and pain,
Moanings of the tropic sea;
Low and tender in the cell
Where a captive sits in chains,
Crooning ditties treasured well
From his Afric's torrid plains.
Sole estate his sire bequeathed,—
Hapless sire to hapless son,—
Was the wailing song he breathed,
And his chain when life was done.

What his fault, or what his crime?
Or what ill planet crossed his prime?
Heart too soft and will too weak
To front the fate that crouches near,—
Dove beneath the vulture's beak;—
Will song dissuade the thirsty spear?
Dragged from his mother's arms and breast,
Displaced, disfurnished here,
His wistful toil to do his best
Chilled by a ribald jeer.

Great men in the Senate sate,
Sage and hero, side by side,
Building for their sons the State,
Which they shall rule with pride.
They forbore to break the chain
Which bound the dusky tribe,
Checked by the owners' fierce disdain,
Lured by 'Union' as the bribe.
Destiny sat by, and said,
'Pang for pang your seed shall pay,
Hide in false peace your coward head,
I bring round the harvest day.'

II

FREEDOM all winged expands,
Nor perches in a narrow place;
Her broad van seeks unplanted lands;
She loves a poor and virtuous race.
Clinging to a colder zone
Whose dark sky sheds the snowflake down,
The snowflake is her banner's star,
Her stripes the boreal streamers are.
Long she loved the Northman well;
Now the iron age is done,
She will not refuse to dwell
With the offspring of the Sun;
Foundling of the desert far,
Where palms plume, siroccos blaze,

He roves unhurt the burning ways
In climates of the summer star.
He has avenues to God
Hid from men of Northern brain,
Far beholding, without cloud,
What these with slowest steps attain.
If once the generous chief arrive
To lead him willing to be led,
For freedom he will strike and strive,
And drain his heart till he be dead.[1]

III

IN an age of fops and toys,
Wanting wisdom, void of right,
Who shall nerve heroic boys
To hazard all in Freedom's fight, —
Break sharply off their jolly games,
Forsake their comrades gay
And quit proud homes and youthful dames
For famine, toil and fray?
Yet on the nimble air benign
Speed nimbler messages,
That waft the breath of grace divine
To hearts in sloth and ease.
So nigh is grandeur to our dust,
So near is God to man,
When Duty whispers low, *Thou must*,
The youth replies, *I can*.

IV

O, WELL for the fortunate soul
Which Music's wings infold,
Stealing away the memory
Of sorrows new and old !
Yet happier he whose inward sight,
Stayed on his subtile thought,
Shuts his sense on toys of time,
To vacant bosoms brought.
But best befriended of the God
He who, in evil times,
Warned by an inward voice,
Heeds not the darkness and the dread,
Biding by his rule and choice,
Feeling only the fiery thread
Leading over heroic ground,
Walled with mortal terror round,
To the aim which him allures,
And the sweet heaven his deed secures.
Peril around, all else appalling,
Cannon in front and leaden rain
Him duty through the clarion calling
To the van called not in vain.[1]

Stainless soldier on the walls,
Knowing this, — and knows no more, —
Whoever fights, whoever falls,
Justice conquers evermore,

Justice after as before, ——
And he who battles on her side,
God, though he were ten times slain,
Crowns him victor glorified,
Victor over death and pain.

V

BLOOMS the laurel which belongs
To the valiant chief who fights;
I see the wreath, I hear the songs
Lauding the Eternal Rights,
Victors over daily wrongs:
Awful victors, they misguide
Whom they will destroy,
And their coming triumph hide
In our downfall, or our joy:
They reach no term, they never sleep,
In equal strength through space abide;
Though, feigning dwarfs, they crouch and creep,
The strong they slay, the swift outstride:
Fate's grass grows rank in valley clods,
And rankly on the castled steep, ——
Speak it firmly, these are gods,
All are ghosts beside.[1]

IX

LOVE AND THOUGHT

Two well-assorted travellers use
The highway, Eros and the Muse.
From the twins is nothing hidden,
To the pair is nought forbidden;
Hand in hand the comrades go
Every nook of Nature through:
Each for other they were born,
Each can other best adorn;
They know one only mortal grief
Past all balsam or relief;
When, by false companions crossed,
The pilgrims have each other lost.

UNA

Roving, roving, as it seems,
Una lights my clouded dreams;
Still for journeys she is dressed;
We wander far by east and west.

In the homestead, homely thought,
At my work I ramble not;
If from home chance draw me wide,
Half-seen Una sits beside.

In my house and garden-plot,
Though beloved, I miss her not;
But one I seek in foreign places,
One face explore in foreign faces.

At home a deeper thought may light
The inward sky with chrysolite,
And I greet from far the ray,
Aurora of a dearer day.

But if upon the seas I sail,
Or trundle on the glowing rail,
I am but a thought of hers,
Loveliest of travellers.

So the gentle poet's name
To foreign parts is blown by fame;
Seek him in his native town,
He is hidden and unknown.

BOSTON

SICUT PATRIBUS, SIT DEUS NOBIS

THE rocky nook with hilltops three
  Looked eastward from the farms,
And twice each day the flowing sea
  Took Boston in its arms;
The men of yore were stout and poor,
And sailed for bread to every shore.

And where they went on trade intent
  They did what freemen can,
Their dauntless ways did all men praise,
  The merchant was a man.
The world was made for honest trade, —
To plant and eat be none afraid.

The waves that rocked them on the deep
  To them their secret told;
Said the winds that sung the lads to sleep,
  ' Like us be free and bold ! '
The honest waves refused to slaves
The empire of the ocean caves.

Old Europe groans with palaces,
  Has lords enough and more; —

We plant and build by foaming seas
  A city of the poor; —
For day by day could Boston Bay
Their honest labor overpay.

We grant no dukedoms to the few,
  We hold like rights, and shall; —
Equal on Sunday in the pew,
  On Monday in the mall,
For what avail the plough or sail,
Or land or life, if freedom fail?

The noble craftsman we promote,
  Disown the knave and fool;
Each honest man shall have his vote,
  Each child shall have his school.
A union then of honest men,
Or union never more again.

The wild rose and the barberry thorn
  Hung out their summer pride,
Where now on heated pavements worn
  The feet of millions stride.

Fair rose the planted hills behind
  The good town on the bay,
And where the western hills declined
  The prairie stretched away.

What care though rival cities soar
   Along the stormy coast,
Penn's town, New York and Baltimore,
   If Boston knew the most!

They laughed to know the world so wide;
   The mountains said, ' Good-day!
We greet you well, you Saxon men,
   Up with your towns and stay!'
The world was made for honest trade,—
To plant and eat be none afraid.

' For you,' they said, ' no barriers be,
   For you no sluggard rest;
Each street leads downward to the sea,
   Or landward to the west.'

O happy town beside the sea,
   Whose roads lead everywhere to all;
Than thine no deeper moat can be,
   No stouter fence, no steeper wall!

Bad news from George on the English throne;
   ' You are thriving well,' said he;
' Now by these presents be it known
   You shall pay us a tax on tea;
'T is very small,— no load at all,—
Honor enough that we send the call.'

'Not so,' said Boston, 'good my lord,
  We pay your governors here
Abundant for their bed and board,
  Six thousand pounds a year.
(Your Highness knows our homely word)
  Millions for self-government,
  But for tribute never a cent.'

The cargo came! and who could blame
  If *Indians* seized the tea,
And, chest by chest, let down the same,
  Into the laughing sea?
For what avail the plough or sail,
Or land or life, if freedom fail?

The townsmen braved the English king,
  Found friendship in the French,
And honor joined the patriot ring
  Low on their wooden bench.

O bounteous seas that never fail!
  O day remembered yet!
O happy port that spied the sail
  Which wafted Lafayette!
Pole-star of light in Europe's night,
That never faltered from the right.

Kings shook with fear, old empires crave
  The secret force to find
Which fired the little State to save
  The rights of all mankind.

But right is might through all the world;
  Province to province faithful clung,
Through good and ill the war-bolt hurled,
  Till Freedom cheered and joy-bells rung.

The sea returning day by day
  Restores the world-wide mart;
So let each dweller on the Bay
  Fold Boston in his heart,
Till these echoes be choked with snows,
Or over the town blue ocean flows.

Let the blood of her hundred thousands
  Throb in each manly vein;
And the wits of all her wisest,
  Make sunshine in her brain.
For you can teach the lightning speech,
And round the globe your voices reach.

And each shall care for other,
  And each to each shall bend,
To the poor a noble brother,
  To the good an equal friend.

A blessing through the ages thus
　　Shield all thy roofs and towers !
GOD WITH THE FATHERS, SO WITH US,
　　Thou darling town of ours ! [1]

LETTERS

EVERY day brings a ship,
Every ship brings a word ;
Well for those who have no fear,
Looking seaward, well assured
That the word the vessel brings
Is the word they wish to hear. [2]

RUBIES

THEY brought me rubies from the mine,
　　And held them to the sun ;
I said, they are drops of frozen wine
　　From Eden's vats that run.

I looked again, — I thought them hearts
　　Of friends to friends unknown ;
Tides that should warm each neighboring life
　　Are locked in sparkling stone.

But fire to thaw that ruddy snow,
　　To break enchanted ice,
And give love's scarlet tides to flow, —
　　When shall that sun arise ? '

MERLIN'S SONG

I

Of Merlin wise I learned a song, —
Sing it low or sing it loud,
It is mightier than the strong,
And punishes the proud.
I sing it to the surging crowd, —
Good men it will calm and cheer,
Bad men it will chain and cage —
In the heart of the music peals a strain
Which only angels hear;
Whether it waken joy or rage
Hushed myriads hark in vain,
Yet they who hear it shed their age,
And take their youth again.

II

Hear what British Merlin sung,
Of keenest eye and truest tongue.
Say not, the chiefs who first arrive
Usurp the seats for which all strive;

The forefathers this land who found
Failed to plant the vantage-ground;
Ever from one who comes to-morrow
Men wait their good and truth to borrow.
But wilt thou measure all thy road,
See thou lift the lightest load.
Who has little, to him who has less, can spare,
And thou, Cyndyllan's son! beware
Ponderous gold and stuffs to bear,
To falter ere thou thy task fulfil,—
Only the light-armed climb the hill.
The richest of all lords is Use,
And ruddy Health the loftiest Muse.
Live in the sunshine, swim the sea,
Drink the wild air's salubrity:
When the star Canope shines in May,
Shepherds are thankful and nations gay.
The music that can deepest reach,
And cure all ill, is cordial speech:
Mask thy wisdom with delight,
Toy with the bow, yet hit the white.
Of all wit's uses, the main one
Is to live well with who has none.

THE TEST

(Musa loquitur.)

I HUNG my verses in the wind,
Time and tide their faults may find.
All were winnowed through and through,
Five lines lasted sound and true;
Five were smelted in a pot
Than the South more fierce and hot;
These the siroc could not melt,
Fire their fiercer flaming felt,
And the meaning was more white
Than July's meridian light.
Sunshine cannot bleach the snow,
Nor time unmake what poets know.
Have you eyes to find the five
Which five hundred did survive? [1]

SOLUTION

I am the Muse who sung alway
By Jove, at dawn of the first day.
Star-crowned, sole-sitting, long I wrought
To fire the stagnant earth with thought:

On spawning slime my song prevails,
Wolves shed their fangs, and dragons scales;
Flushed in the sky the sweet May-morn,
Earth smiled with flowers, and man was born.[1]
Then Asia yeaned her shepherd race,
And Nile substructs her granite base, —
Tented Tartary, columned Nile, —
And, under vines, on rocky isle,
Or on wind-blown sea-marge bleak,
Forward stepped the perfect Greek:
That wit and joy might find a tongue,
And earth grow civil, HOMER sung.

Flown to Italy from Greece,
I brooded long and held my peace,
For I am wont to sing uncalled,
And in days of evil plight
Unlock doors of new delight;
And sometimes mankind I appalled
With a bitter horoscope,
With spasms of terror for balm of hope.
Then by better thought I lead
Bards to speak what nations need;
So I folded me in fears,
And DANTE searched the triple spheres,
Moulding Nature at his will,
So shaped, so colored, swift or still,
And, sculptor-like, his large design
Etched on Alp and Apennine.[2]

Seethed in mists of Penmanmaur,
Taught by Plinlimmon's Druid power,
England's genius filled all measure
Of heart and soul, of strength and pleasure,
Gave to the mind its emperor,
And life was larger than before:
Nor sequent centuries could hit
Orbit and sum of SHAKSPEARE's wit.
The men who lived with him became
Poets, for the air was fame.

Far in the North, where polar night
Holds in check the frolic light,
In trance upborne past mortal goal
The Swede EMANUEL leads the soul.
Through snows above, mines underground,
The inks of Erebus he found;
Rehearsed to men the damnèd wails
On which the seraph music sails.
In spirit-worlds he trod alone,
But walked the earth unmarked, unknown.
The near bystander caught no sound, —
Yet they who listened far aloof
Heard rendings of the skyey roof,
And felt, beneath, the quaking ground;
And his air-sown, unheeded words,
In the next age, are flaming swords.

In newer days of war and trade,
Romance forgot, and faith decayed,
When Science armed and guided war,
And clerks the Janus-gates unbar,
When France, where poet never grew,
Halved and dealt the globe anew,
GOETHE, raised o'er joy and strife,
Drew the firm lines of Fate and Life
And brought Olympian wisdom down
To court and mart, to gown and town.
Stooping, his finger wrote in clay
The open secret of to-day.

So bloom the unfading petals five,
And verses that all verse outlive.

HYMN

SUNG AT THE SECOND CHURCH, AT THE ORDINATION
OF REV. CHANDLER ROBBINS

WE love the venerable house
  Our fathers built to God; —
In heaven are kept their grateful vows,
  Their dust endears the sod.

Here holy thoughts a light have shed
    From many a radiant face,
And prayers of humble virtue made
    The perfume of the place.

And anxious hearts have pondered here
    The mystery of life,
And prayed the eternal Light to clear
    Their doubts, and aid their strife.

From humble tenements around
    Came up the pensive train,
And in the church a blessing found
    That filled their homes again;

For faith and peace and mighty love
    That from the Godhead flow,
Showed them the life of Heaven above
    Springs from the life below.

They live with God; their homes are dust;
    Yet here their children pray,
And in this fleeting lifetime trust
    To find the narrow way.

On him who by the altar stands,
    On him thy blessing fall,
Speak through his lips thy pure commands,
    Thou heart that lovest all.

NATURE

I

WINTERS know
Easily to shed the snow,
And the untaught Spring is wise
In cowslips and anemonies.
Nature, hating art and pains,
Baulks and baffles plotting brains;
Casualty and Surprise
Are the apples of her eyes;
But she dearly loves the poor,
And, by marvel of her own,
Strikes the loud pretender down.
For Nature listens in the rose
And hearkens in the berry's bell
To help her friends, to plague her foes,
And like wise God she judges well.
Yet doth much her love excel
To the souls that never fell,
To swains that live in happiness
And do well because they please,
Who walk in ways that are unfamed,
And feats achieve before they're named.

IX

NATURE

II

SHE is gamesome and good,
But of mutable mood, —
No dreary repeater now and again,
She will be all things to all men.
She who is old, but nowise feeble,
Pours her power into the people,
Merry and manifold without bar,
Makes and moulds them what they are,
And what they call their city way
Is not their way, but hers,
And what they say they made to-day,
They learned of the oaks and firs.
She spawneth men as mallows fresh,
Hero and maiden, flesh of her flesh;
She drugs her water and her wheat
With the flavors she finds meet,
And gives them what to drink and eat;
And having thus their bread and growth,
They do her bidding, nothing loath.
What's most theirs is not their own,
But borrowed in atoms from iron and stone,
And in their vaunted works of Art
The master-stroke is still her part.[1]

THE ROMANY GIRL

THE sun goes down, and with him takes
The coarseness of my poor attire;
The fair moon mounts, and aye the flame
Of Gypsy beauty blazes higher.

Pale Northern girls! you scorn our race;
You captives of your air-tight halls,
Wear out indoors your sickly days,
But leave us the horizon walls.[1]

And if I take you, dames, to task,
And say it frankly without guile,
Then you are Gypsies in a mask,
And I the lady all the while.

If on the heath, below the moon,
I court and play with paler blood,
Me false to mine dare whisper none, —
One sallow horseman knows me good.

Go, keep your cheek's rose from the rain,
For teeth and hair with shopmen deal;
My swarthy tint is in the grain,
The rocks and forest know it real.

The wild air bloweth in our lungs,
The keen stars twinkle in our eyes,
The birds gave us our wily tongues,
The panther in our dances flies.

You doubt we read the stars on high,
Nathless we read your fortunes true;
The stars may hide in the upper sky,
But without glass we fathom you.

DAYS

Daughters of Time, the hypocritic Days,
Muffled and dumb like barefoot dervishes,
And marching single in an endless file,
Bring diadems and fagots in their hands.
To each they offer gifts after his will,
Bread, kingdoms, stars, and sky that holds them
    all.
I, in my pleached garden, watched the pomp,
Forgot my morning wishes, hastily
Took a few herbs and apples, and the Day
Turned and departed silent. I, too late,
Under her solemn fillet saw the scorn.

MY GARDEN

If I could put my woods in song
And tell what 's there enjoyed,
All men would to my gardens throng,
And leave the cities void.[1]

In my plot no tulips blow, —
Snow-loving pines and oaks instead;
And rank the savage maples grow
From Spring's faint flush to Autumn red.

My garden is a forest ledge
Which older forests bound;
The banks slope down to the blue lake-edge,
Then plunge to depths profound.

Here once the Deluge ploughed,
Laid the terraces, one by one;
Ebbing later whence it flowed,
They bleach and dry in the sun.

The sowers made haste to depart, —
The wind and the birds which sowed it;
Not for fame, nor by rules of art,
Planted these, and tempests flowed it.

Waters that wash my garden-side
Play not in Nature's lawful web,
They heed not moon or solar tide, —
Five years elapse from flood to ebb.[1]

Hither hasted, in old time, Jove,
And every god, — none did refuse;
And be sure at last came Love,
And after Love, the Muse.

Keen ears can catch a syllable,
As if one spake to another,
In the hemlocks tall, untamable,
And what the whispering grasses smother.

Æolian harps in the pine
Ring with the song of the Fates;
Infant Bacchus in the vine, —
Far distant yet his chorus waits.

Canst thou copy in verse one chime
Of the wood-bell's peal and cry,
Write in a book the morning's prime,
Or match with words that tender sky?

Wonderful verse of the gods,
Of one import, of varied tone;
They chant the bliss of their abodes
To man imprisoned in his own.[2]

Ever the words of the gods resound;
But the porches of man's ear
Seldom in this low life's round
Are unsealed, that he may hear.

Wandering voices in the air
And murmurs in the wold
Speak what I cannot declare,
Yet cannot all withhold.

When the shadow fell on the lake,
The whirlwind in ripples wrote
Air-bells of fortune that shine and break,
And omens above thought.

But the meanings cleave to the lake,
Cannot be carried in book or urn;
Go thy ways now, come later back,
On waves and hedges still they burn.

These the fates of men forecast,
Of better men than live to-day;
If who can read them comes at last
He will spell in the sculpture, 'Stay.'

THE CHARTIST'S COMPLAINT

Day! hast thou two faces,
Making one place two places?
One, by humble farmer seen,
Chill and wet, unlighted, mean,
Useful only, triste and damp,
Serving for a laborer's lamp?
Have the same mists another side,
To be the appanage of pride,
Gracing the rich man's wood and lake,
His park where amber mornings break,
And treacherously bright to show
His planted isle where roses glow?
O Day! and is your mightiness
A sycophant to smug success?
Will the sweet sky and ocean broad
Be fine accomplices to fraud?
O Sun! I curse thy cruel ray:
Back, back to chaos, harlot Day!

THE TITMOUSE

You shall not be overbold
When you deal with arctic cold,
As late I found my lukewarm blood
Chilled wading in the snow-choked wood.
How should I fight? my foeman fine
Has million arms to one of mine:
East, west, for aid I looked in vain,
East, west, north, south, are his domain.
Miles off, three dangerous miles, is home;
Must borrow his winds who there would
      come.
Up and away for life! be fleet! —
The frost-king ties my fumbling feet,
Sings in my ears, my hands are stones,
Curdles the blood to the marble bones,
Tugs at the heart-strings, numbs the sense,
And hems in life with narrowing fence.
Well, in this broad bed lie and sleep, —
The punctual stars will vigil keep, —
Embalmed by purifying cold;
The winds shall sing their dead-march old,
The snow is no ignoble shroud,
The moon thy mourner, and the cloud.

Softly, — but this way fate was pointing,
'T was coming fast to such anointing,
When piped a tiny voice hard by,
Gay and polite, a cheerful cry,
Chic-chic-a-dee-dee! saucy note
Out of sound heart and merry throat,
As if it said, ' Good day, good sir!
Fine afternoon, old passenger!
Happy to meet you in these places,
Where January brings few faces.'

This poet, though he live apart,
Moved by his hospitable heart,
Sped, when I passed his sylvan fort,
To do the honors of his court,
As fits a feathered lord of land;
Flew near, with soft wing grazed my hand,
Hopped on the bough, then, darting low,
Prints his small impress on the snow,
Shows feats of his gymnastic play,
Head downward, clinging to the spray.

Here was this atom in full breath,
Hurling defiance at vast death;
This scrap of valor just for play
Fronts the north-wind in waistcoat gray,
As if to shame my weak behavior;
I greeted loud my little savior,

'You pet! what dost here? and what for?
In these woods, thy small Labrador,
At this pinch, wee San Salvador!
What fire burns in that little chest
So frolic, stout and self-possest?
Henceforth I wear no stripe but thine;
Ashes and jet all hues outshine.
Why are not diamonds black and gray,
To ape thy dare-devil array?
And I affirm, the spacious North
Exists to draw thy virtue forth.
I think no virtue goes with size;
The reason of all cowardice
Is, that men are overgrown,
And, to be valiant, must come down
To the titmouse dimension.'

'T is good will makes intelligence,
And I began to catch the sense
Of my bird's song: 'Live out of doors
In the great woods, on prairie floors.
I dine in the sun; when he sinks in the sea,
I too have a hole in a hollow tree;
And I like less when Summer beats
With stifling beams on these retreats,
Than noontide twilights which snow makes
With tempest of the blinding flakes.
For well the soul, if stout within,
Can arm impregnably the skin;

And polar frost my frame defied,
Made of the air that blows outside.'

With glad remembrance of my debt,
I homeward turn; farewell, my pet!
When here again thy pilgrim comes,
He shall bring store of seeds and crumbs.
Doubt not, so long as earth has bread,
Thou first and foremost shalt be fed;
The Providence that is most large
Takes hearts like thine in special charge,
Helps who for their own need are strong,
And the sky doats on cheerful song.
Henceforth I prize thy wiry chant
O'er all that mass and minster vaunt;
For men mis-hear thy call in Spring,
As 't would accost some frivolous wing,
Crying out of the hazel copse, *Phe-be!*
And, in winter, *Chic-a-dee-dee!*
I think old Cæsar must have heard
In northern Gaul my dauntless bird,
And, echoed in some frosty wold,
Borrowed thy battle-numbers bold.
And I will write our annals new,
And thank thee for a better clew,
I, who dreamed not when I came here
To find the antidote of fear,
Now hear thee say in Roman key,
Pæan! Veni, vidi, vici.

THE HARP

ONE musician is sure,
His wisdom will not fail,
He has not tasted wine impure,
Nor bent to passion frail.
Age cannot cloud his memory,
Nor grief untune his voice,
Ranging down the ruled scale
From tone of joy to inward wail,
Tempering the pitch of all
In his windy cave.
He all the fables knows,
And in their causes tells, —
Knows Nature's rarest moods,
Ever on her secret broods.
The Muse of men is coy,
Oft courted will not come;
In palaces and market squares
Entreated, she is dumb;
But my minstrel knows and tells
The counsel of the gods,
Knows of Holy Book the spells,
Knows the law of Night and Day,
And the heart of girl and boy,
The tragic and the gay,

And what is writ on Table Round
Of Arthur and his peers;
What sea and land discoursing say
In sidereal years.
He renders all his lore
In numbers wild as dreams,
Modulating all extremes, —
What the spangled meadow saith
To the children who have faith;
Only to children children sing,
Only to youth will spring be spring.

Who is the Bard thus magnified?
When did he sing? and where abide?

Chief of song where poets feast
Is the wind-harp which thou seest
In the casement at my side.

Æolian harp,
How strangely wise thy strain!
Gay for youth, gay for youth,
(Sweet is art, but sweeter truth,)
In the hall at summer eve
Fate and Beauty skilled to weave.
From the eager opening strings
Rung loud and bold the song.
Who but loved the wind-harp's note?
How should not the poet doat

On its mystic tongue,
With its primeval memory,
Reporting what old minstrels told
Of Merlin locked the harp within, —
Merlin paying the pain of sin,
Pent in a dungeon made of air, —
And some attain his voice to hear,
Words of pain and cries of fear,
But pillowed all on melody,
As fits the griefs of bards to be.[1]
And what if that all-echoing shell,
Which thus the buried Past can tell,
Should rive the Future, and reveal
What his dread folds would fain conceal?
It shares the secret of the earth,
And of the kinds that owe her birth.
Speaks not of self that mystic tone,
But of the Overgods alone:
It trembles to the cosmic breath, —
As it heareth, so it saith;
Obeying meek the primal Cause,
It is the tongue of mundane laws.
And this, at least, I dare affirm,
Since genius too has bound and term,
There is no bard in all the choir,
Not Homer's self, the poet sire,
Wise Milton's odes of pensive pleasure,
Or Shakspeare, whom no mind can measure,
Nor Collins' verse of tender pain,

Nor Byron's clarion of disdain,
Scott, the delight of generous boys,
Or Wordsworth, Pan's recording voice, —
Not one of all can put in verse,
Or to this presence could rehearse
The sights and voices ravishing
The boy knew on the hills in spring,
When pacing through the oaks he heard
Sharp queries of the sentry-bird,
The heavy grouse's sudden whir,
The rattle of the kingfisher;
Saw bonfires of the harlot flies
In the lowland, when day dies;
Or marked, benighted and forlorn,
The first far signal-fire of morn.
These syllables that Nature spoke,
And the thoughts that in him woke,
Can adequately utter none
Save to his ear the wind-harp lone.[1]
Therein I hear the Parcæ reel
The threads of man at their humming wheel,
The threads of life and power and pain,
So sweet and mournful falls the strain.
And best can teach its Delphian chord
How Nature to the soul is moored,
If once again that silent string,
As erst it wont, would thrill and ring.

Not long ago at eventide,
It seemed, so listening, at my side
A window rose, and, to say sooth,
I looked forth on the fields of youth:
I saw fair boys bestriding steeds,
I knew their forms in fancy weeds,
Long, long concealed by sundering fates,
Mates of my youth, — yet not my mates,
Stronger and bolder far than I,
With grace, with genius, well attired,
And then as now from far admired,
Followed with love
They knew not of,
With passion cold and shy.
O joy, for what recoveries rare!
Renewed, I breathe Elysian air,
See youth's glad mates in earliest bloom, —
Break not my dream, obtrusive tomb!
Or teach thou, Spring! the grand recoil
Of life resurgent from the soil
Wherein was dropped the mortal spoil.

SEASHORE

I HEARD or seemed to hear the chiding Sea
Say, Pilgrim, why so late and slow to come?
Am I not always here, thy summer home?
Is not my voice thy music, morn and eve?
My breath thy healthful climate in the heats,
My touch thy antidote, my bay thy bath?
Was ever building like my terraces?
Was ever couch magnificent as mine?
Lie on the warm rock-ledges, and there learn
A little hut suffices like a town.
I make your sculptured architecture vain,
Vain beside mine. I drive my wedges home,
And carve the coastwise mountain into caves.
Lo! here is Rome and Nineveh and Thebes,
Karnak and Pyramid and Giant's Stairs
Half piled or prostrate; and my newest slab
Older than all thy race.

     Behold the Sea,
The opaline, the plentiful and strong,
Yet beautiful as is the rose in June,
Fresh as the trickling rainbow of July;
Sea full of food, the nourisher of kinds,
Purger of earth, and medicine of men;
Creating a sweet climate by my breath,

Washing out harms and griefs from memory,
And, in my mathematic ebb and flow,
Giving a hint of that which changes not.
Rich are the sea-gods : — who gives gifts but they ?
They grope the sea for pearls, but more than pearls :
They pluck Force thence, and give it to the wise.
For every wave is wealth to Dædalus,
Wealth to the cunning artist who can work
This matchless strength. Where shall he find, O
       waves !
A load your Atlas shoulders cannot lift ?

I with my hammer pounding evermore
The rocky coast, smite Andes into dust,
Strewing my bed, and, in another age,
Rebuild a continent of better men.
Then I unbar the doors : my paths lead out
The exodus of nations : I disperse
Men to all shores that front the hoary main.

I too have arts and sorceries ;
Illusion dwells forever with the wave.
I know what spells are laid. Leave me to deal
With credulous and imaginative man ;
For, though he scoop my water in his palm,
A few rods off he deems it gems and clouds.
Planting strange fruits and sunshine on the shore,
I make some coast alluring, some lone isle,
To distant men, who must go there, or die.

SONG OF NATURE

MINE are the night and morning,
The pits of air, the gulf of space,
The sportive sun, the gibbous moon,
The innumerable days.

I hide in the solar glory,
I am dumb in the pealing song,
I rest on the pitch of the torrent,
In slumber I am strong.

No numbers have counted my tallies,
No tribes my house can fill,
I sit by the shining Fount of Life
And pour the deluge still;

And ever by delicate powers
Gathering along the centuries
From race on race the rarest flowers,
My wreath shall nothing miss.

And many a thousand summers
My gardens ripened well,
And light from meliorating stars
With firmer glory fell.[1]

I wrote the past in characters
Of rock and fire the scroll,
The building in the coral sea,
The planting of the coal.

And thefts from satellites and rings
And broken stars I drew,
And out of spent and aged things
I formed the world anew;

What time the gods kept carnival,
Tricked out in star and flower,
And in cramp elf and saurian forms
They swathed their too much power.

Time and Thought were my surveyors,
They laid their courses well,
They boiled the sea, and piled the layers
Of granite, marl and shell.

But he, the man-child glorious, —
Where tarries he the while?
The rainbow shines his harbinger,
The sunset gleams his smile.

My boreal lights leap upward,
Forthright my planets roll,
And still the man-child is not born,
The summit of the whole.

Must time and tide forever run?
Will never my winds go sleep in the west?
Will never my wheels which whirl the sun
And satellites have rest?

Too much of donning and doffing,
Too slow the rainbow fades,
I weary of my robe of snow,
My leaves and my cascades;

I tire of globes and races,
Too long the game is played;
What without him is summer's pomp,
Or winter's frozen shade?

I travail in pain for him,
My creatures travail and wait;
His couriers come by squadrons,
He comes not to the gate.

Twice I have moulded an image,
And thrice outstretched my hand,
Made one of day and one of night
And one of the salt sea-sand.[1]

One in a Judæan manger,
And one by Avon stream,
One over against the mouths of Nile,
And one in the Academe.

I moulded kings and saviors,
And bards o'er kings to rule ; —
But fell the starry influence short,
The cup was never full.

Yet whirl the glowing wheels once more,
And mix the bowl again ;
Seethe, Fate ! the ancient elements,
Heat, cold, wet, dry, and peace, and pain.

Let war and trade and creeds and song
Blend, ripen race on race,
The sunburnt world a man shall breed
Of all the zones and countless days.

No ray is dimmed, no atom worn,
My oldest force is good as new,
And the fresh rose on yonder thorn
Gives back the bending heavens in dew.[1]

TWO RIVERS

Thy summer voice, Musketaquit,
Repeats the music of the rain;
But sweeter rivers pulsing flit
Through thee, as thou through Concord Plain.

Thou in thy narrow banks art pent:
The stream I love unbounded goes
Through flood and sea and firmament;
Through light, through life, it forward flows.

I see the inundation sweet,
I hear the spending of the stream
Through years, through men, through Nature fleet,
Through love and thought, through power and dream.[1]

Musketaquit, a goblin strong,
Of shard and flint makes jewels gay;
They lose their grief who hear his song,
And where he winds is the day of day.

So forth and brighter fares my stream, —
Who drink it shall not thirst again;[2]
No darkness stains its equal gleam,
And ages drop in it like rain.

WALDEINSAMKEIT

I DO not count the hours I spend
In wandering by the sea;
The forest is my loyal friend,
Like God it useth me.

In plains that room for shadows make
Of skirting hills to lie,
Bound in by streams which give and take
Their colors from the sky;

Or on the mountain-crest sublime,
Or down the oaken glade,
O what have I to do with time?
For this the day was made.[1]

Cities of mortals woe-begone
Fantastic care derides,
But in the serious landscape lone
Stern benefit abides.

Sheen will tarnish, honey cloy,
And merry is only a mask of sad,
But, sober on a fund of joy,
The woods at heart are glad.[2]

There the great Planter plants
Of fruitful worlds the grain,
And with a million spells enchants
The souls that walk in pain.

Still on the seeds of all he made
The rose of beauty burns;
Through times that wear and forms that fade,
Immortal youth returns.

The black ducks mounting from the lake,
The pigeon in the pines,
The bittern's boom, a desert make
Which no false art refines.

Down in yon watery nook,
Where bearded mists divide,
The gray old gods whom Chaos knew,
The sires of Nature, hide.

Aloft, in secret veins of air,
Blows the sweet breath of song,
O, few to scale those uplands dare,
Though they to all belong!

See thou bring not to field or stone
The fancies found in books;
Leave authors' eyes, and fetch your own,
To brave the landscape's looks.

Oblivion here thy wisdom is,
Thy thrift, the sleep of cares;
For a proud idleness like this
Crowns all thy mean affairs.

TERMINUS

It is time to be old,
To take in sail : —
The god of bounds,
Who sets to seas a shore,
Came to me in his fatal rounds,
And said : ' No more !
No farther shoot
Thy broad ambitious branches, and thy root.
Fancy departs : no more invent;
Contract thy firmament
To compass of a tent.
There 's not enough for this and that,
Make thy option which of two;
Economize the failing river,
Not the less revere the Giver,
Leave the many and hold the few.
Timely wise accept the terms,
Soften the fall with wary foot;
A little while
Still plan and smile,

And, — fault of novel germs, —
Mature the unfallen fruit.
Curse, if thou wilt, thy sires,
Bad husbands of their fires,
Who, when they gave thee breath,
Failed to bequeath
The needful sinew stark as once,
The Baresark marrow to thy bones,
But left a legacy of ebbing veins,
Inconstant heat and nerveless reins, —
Amid the Muses, left thee deaf and dumb,
Amid the gladiators, halt and numb.' [1]

As the bird trims her to the gale,
I trim myself to the storm of time,
I man the rudder, reef the sail,
Obey the voice at eve obeyed at prime:
Lowly faithful, banish fear,
Right onward drive unharmed;
The port, well worth the cruise, is near,
And every wave is charmed.' [2]

THE NUN'S ASPIRATION

THE yesterday doth never smile,
The day goes drudging through the while,
Yet, in the name of Godhead, I
The morrow front, and can defy;
Though I am weak, yet God, when prayed,
Cannot withhold his conquering aid.
Ah me! it was my childhood's thought,
If He should make my web a blot
On life's fair picture of delight,
My heart's content would find it right.
But O, these waves and leaves, —
When happy stoic Nature grieves,
No human speech so beautiful
As their murmurs mine to lull.
On this altar God hath built
I lay my vanity and guilt;
Nor me can Hope or Passion urge
Hearing as now the lofty dirge
Which blasts of Northern mountains hymn,
Nature's funeral high and dim, —
Sable pageantry of clouds,
Mourning summer laid in shrouds.
Many a day shall dawn and die,
Many an angel wander by,

And passing, light my sunken turf
Moist perhaps by ocean surf,
Forgotten amid splendid tombs,
Yet wreathed and hid by summer blooms.
On earth I dream; — I die to be:
Time, shake not thy bald head at me.
I challenge thee to hurry past
Or for my turn to fly too fast.
Think me not numbed or halt with age,
Or cares that earth to earth engage,
Caught with love's cord of twisted beams,
Or mired by climate's gross extremes.
I tire of shams, I rush to be:
I pass with yonder comet free, —
Pass with the comet into space
Which mocks thy æons to embrace;
Æons which tardily unfold
Realm beyond realm, — extent untold;
No early morn, no evening late, —
Realms self-upheld, disdaining Fate,
Whose shining sons, too great for fame,
Never heard thy weary name;
Nor lives the tragic bard to say
How drear the part I held in one,
How lame the other limped away.[1]

APRIL

THE April winds are magical
And thrill our tuneful frames;
The garden walks are passional
To bachelors and dames.
The hedge is gemmed with diamonds,
The air with Cupids full,
The cobweb clues of Rosamond
Guide lovers to the pool.
Each dimple in the water,
Each leaf that shades the rock
Can cozen, pique and flatter,
Can parley and provoke.
Goodfellow, Puck and goblins,
Know more than any book.
Down with your doleful problems,
And court the sunny brook.
The south-winds are quick-witted,
The schools are sad and slow,
The masters quite omitted
The lore we care to know.

MAIDEN SPEECH OF THE ÆOLIAN HARP

Soft and softlier hold me, friends!
Thanks if your genial care
Unbind and give me to the air.
Keep your lips or finger-tips
For flute or spinet's dancing chips;
I await a tenderer touch,
I ask more or not so much:
Give me to the atmosphere, —
Where is the wind, my brother, — where?
Lift the sash, lay me within,
Lend me your ears, and I begin.
For gentle harp to gentle hearts
The secret of the world imparts;
And not to-day and not to-morrow
Can drain its wealth of hope and sorrow;
But day by day, to loving ear
Unlocks new sense and loftier cheer.
I 've come to live with you, sweet friends,
This home my minstrel-journeyings ends.
Many and subtle are my lays,
The latest better than the first,
For I can mend the happiest days
And charm the anguish of the worst.[1]

CUPIDO

The solid, solid universe
Is pervious to Love;
With bandaged eyes he never errs,
Around, below, above.
His blinding light
He flingeth white
On God's and Satan's brood,
And reconciles
By mystic wiles
The evil and the good.

THE PAST

The debt is paid,
The verdict said,
The Furies laid,
The plague is stayed.
All fortunes made;
Turn the key and bolt the door,
Sweet is death forevermore.
Nor haughty hope, nor swart chagrin,
Nor murdering hate, can enter in.

IX

All is now secure and fast;
Not the gods can shake the Past;
Flies-to the adamantine door
Bolted down forevermore.
None can reënter there, —
No thief so politic,
No Satan with a royal trick
Steal in by window, chink, or hole,
To bind or unbind, add what lacked,
Insert a leaf, or forge a name,
New-face or finish what is packed,
Alter or mend eternal Fact.[1]

THE LAST FAREWELL

LINES WRITTEN BY THE AUTHOR'S BROTHER,
EDWARD BLISS EMERSON, WHILST SAILING OUT
OF BOSTON HARBOR, BOUND FOR THE ISLAND OF
PORTO RICO, IN 1832[2]

FAREWELL, ye lofty spires
That cheered the holy light!
Farewell, domestic fires
That broke the gloom of night!
Too soon those spires are lost,
Too fast we leave the bay,
Too soon by ocean tost
From hearth and home away,
        Far away, far away.

Farewell the busy town,
The wealthy and the wise,
Kind smile and honest frown
From bright, familiar eyes.
All these are fading now;
Our brig hastes on her way,
Her unremembering prow
Is leaping o'er the sea,
   Far away, far away.

Farewell, my mother fond,
Too kind, too good to me;
Nor pearl nor diamond
Would pay my debt to thee.
But even thy kiss denies
Upon my cheek to stay;
The winged vessel flies,
And billows round her play,
   Far away, far away.

Farewell, my brothers true,
My betters, yet my peers;
How desert without you
My few and evil years!
But though aye one in heart,
Together sad or gay,
Rude ocean doth us part;
We separate to-day,
   Far away, far away.

Farewell, thou fairest one,
Unplighted yet to me,
Uncertain of thine own
I gave my heart to thee.
That untold early love
I leave untold to-day,
My lips in whisper move
Farewell to . . . . . !
   Far away, far away.

Farewell I breathe again
To dim New England's shore;
My heart shall beat not when
I pant for thee no more.
In yon green palmy isle,
Beneath the tropic ray,
I murmur never while
For thee and thine I pray;
   Far away, far away.

IN MEMORIAM

E. B. E.

I mourn upon this battle-field,
But not for those who perished here.
Behold the river-bank
Whither the angry farmers came,
In sloven dress and broken rank,
Nor thought of fame.
Their deed of blood
All mankind praise;
Even the serene Reason says,
It was well done.
The wise and simple have one glance
To greet yon stern head-stone,
Which more of pride than pity gave
To mark the Briton's friendless grave.
Yet it is a stately tomb;
The grand return
Of eve and morn,
The year's fresh bloom,
The silver cloud,
Might grace the dust that is most proud.[1]

Yet not of these I muse
In this ancestral place,
But of a kindred face
That never joy or hope shall here diffuse.

Ah, brother of the brief but blazing star!
What hast thou to do with these
Haunting this bank's historic trees?
Thou born for noblest life,
For action's field, for victor's car,
Thou living champion of the right?
To these their penalty belonged:
I grudge not these their bed of death,
But thine to thee, who never wronged
The poorest that drew breath.

All inborn power that could
Consist with homage to the good
Flamed from his martial eye;
He who seemed a soldier born,
He should have the helmet worn,
All friends to fend, all foes defy,
Fronting foes of God and man,
Frowning down the evil-doer,
Battling for the weak and poor.
His from youth the leader's look
Gave the law which others took,
And never poor beseeching glance
Shamed that sculptured countenance.

There is no record left on earth,
Save in tablets of the heart,
Of the rich inherent worth,
Of the grace that on him shone,
Of eloquent lips, of joyful wit:
He could not frame a word unfit,
An act unworthy to be done;
Honor prompted every glance,
Honor came and sat beside him,
In lowly cot or painful road,
And evermore the cruel god
Cried "Onward!" and the palm-crown showed,
Born for success he seemed,
With grace to win, with heart to hold,
With shining gifts that took all eyes,
With budding power in college-halls,
As pledged in coming days to forge
Weapons to guard the State, or scourge
Tyrants despite their guards or walls.
On his young promise Beauty smiled,
Drew his free homage unbeguiled,
And prosperous Age held out his hand,
And richly his large future planned,
And troops of friends enjoyed the tide, —
All, all was given, and only health denied.

I see him with superior smile
Hunted by Sorrow's grisly train
In lands remote, in toil and pain,

With angel patience labor on,
With the high port he wore erewhile,
When, foremost of the youthful band,
The prizes in all lists he won :
Nor bate one jot of heart or hope,[1]
And, least of all, the loyal tie
Which holds to home 'neath every sky,
The joy and pride the pilgrim feels
In hearts which round the hearth at home
Keep pulse for pulse with those who roam.

What generous beliefs console
The brave whom Fate denies the goal !
If others reach it, is content ;
To Heaven's high will his will is bent.
Firm on his heart relied,
What lot soe'er betide,
Work of his hand
He nor repents nor grieves,
Pleads for itself the fact,
As unrepenting Nature leaves
Her every act.

Fell the bolt on the branching oak ;
The rainbow of his hope was broke ;
No craven cry, no secret tear, —
He told no pang, he knew no fear ;

Its peace sublime his aspect kept,
His purpose woke, his features slept;
And yet between the spasms of pain
His genius beamed with joy again.

O'er thy rich dust the endless smile
Of Nature in thy Spanish isle
Hints never loss or cruel break
And sacrifice for love's dear sake,
Nor mourn the unalterable Days
That Genius goes and Folly stays.
What matters how, or from what ground,
The freed soul its Creator found?
Alike thy memory embalms
That orange-grove, that isle of palms,
And these loved banks, whose oak-boughs bold
Root in the blood of heroes old.

III

ELEMENTS AND MOTTOES

EXPERIENCE

THE lords of life, the lords of life, —
I saw them pass
In their own guise,
Like and unlike,
Portly and grim, —
Use and Surprise,
Surface and Dream,
Succession swift and spectral Wrong,
Temperament without a tongue,
And the inventor of the game
Omnipresent without name ; —
Some to see, some to be guessed,
They marched from east to west :
Little man, least of all,
Among the legs of his guardians tall,
Walked about with puzzled look.
Him by the hand dear Nature took,
Dearest Nature, strong and kind,
Whispered, ' Darling, never mind !
To-morrow they will wear another face,
The founder thou ; these are thy race ! '

COMPENSATION

The wings of Time are black and white,
Pied with morning and with night.
Mountain tall and ocean deep
Trembling balance duly keep.
In changing moon and tidal wave
Glows the feud of Want and Have.
Gauge of more and less through space,
Electric star or pencil plays,
The lonely Earth amid the balls
That hurry through the eternal halls,
A makeweight flying to the void,
Supplemental asteroid,
Or compensatory spark,
Shoots across the neutral Dark.

Man 's the elm, and Wealth the vine;
Stanch and strong the tendrils twine:
Though the frail ringlets thee deceive,
None from its stock that vine can reave.
Fear not, then, thou child infirm,
There 's no god dare wrong a worm;
Laurel crowns cleave to deserts,
And power to him who power exerts.
Hast not thy share? On winged feet,
Lo! it rushes thee to meet;

And all that Nature made thy own,
Floating in air or pent in stone,
Will rive the hills and swim the sea,
And, like thy shadow, follow thee.[1]

POLITICS

GOLD and iron are good
To buy iron and gold;
All earth's fleece and food
For their like are sold.
Boded Merlin wise,
Proved Napoleon great,
Nor kind nor coinage buys
Aught above its rate.
Fear, Craft and Avarice
Cannot rear a State.
Out of dust to build
What is more than dust, —
Walls Amphion piled
Phœbus stablish must.
When the Muses nine
With the Virtues meet,
Find to their design
An Atlantic seat,
By green orchard boughs
Fended from the heat,

Where the statesman ploughs
Furrow for the wheat, —
When the Church is social worth,
When the state-house is the hearth,
Then the perfect State is come,
The republican at home.

HEROISM

RUBY wine is drunk by knaves,
Sugar spends to fatten slaves,
Rose and vine-leaf deck buffoons;
Thunder-clouds are Jove's festoons,
Drooping oft in wreaths of dread,
Lightning-knotted round his head;
The hero is not fed on sweets,
Daily his own heart he eats;
Chambers of the great are jails,
And head-winds right for royal sails.°

CHARACTER

THE sun set, but set not his hope:
Stars rose ; his faith was earlier up :
Fixed on the enormous galaxy,
Deeper and older seemed his eye ;
And matched his sufferance sublime
The taciturnity of time.[1]
He spoke, and words more soft than rain
Brought the Age of Gold again :
His action won such reverence sweet
As hid all measure of the feat.

CULTURE

CAN rules or tutors educate
The semigod whom we await ?
He must be musical,
Tremulous, impressional,
Alive to gentle influence
Of landscape and of sky,
And tender to the spirit-touch
Of man's or maiden's eye :
But, to his native centre fast,
Shall into Future fuse the Past,
And the world's flowing fates in his own mould recast.[2]

FRIENDSHIP

A RUDDY drop of manly blood
The surging sea outweighs,
The world uncertain comes and goes;
The lover rooted stays.
I fancied he was fled, —
And, after many a year,
Glowed unexhausted kindliness,
Like daily sunrise there.
My careful heart was free again,
O friend, my bosom said,
Through thee alone the sky is arched,
Through thee the rose is red;
All things through thee take nobler form,
And look beyond the earth,
The mill-round of our fate appears
A sun-path in thy worth.
Me too thy nobleness has taught
To master my despair;
The fountains of my hidden life
Are through thy friendship fair.[1]

SPIRITUAL LAWS

THE living Heaven thy prayers respect,
House at once and architect,
Quarrying man's rejected hours,
Builds therewith eternal towers;
Sole and self-commanded works,
Fears not undermining days,
Grows by decays,
And, by the famous might that lurks
In reaction and recoil,
Makes flame to freeze and ice to boil;
Forging, through swart arms of Offence,
The silver seat of Innocence.[1]

BEAUTY

WAS never form and never face
So sweet to SEYD as only grace
Which did not slumber like a stone,
But hovered gleaming and was gone.
Beauty chased he everywhere,
In flame, in storm, in clouds of air.
He smote the lake to feed his eye

With the beryl beam of the broken wave;
He flung in pebbles well to hear
The moment's music which they gave.
Oft pealed for him a lofty tone
From nodding pole and belting zone.
He heard a voice none else could hear
From centred and from errant sphere.
The quaking earth did quake in rhyme,
Seas ebbed and flowed in epic chime.
In dens of passion, and pits of woe,
He saw strong Eros struggling through,
To sun the dark and solve the curse,
And beam to the bounds of the universe.
While thus to love he gave his days
In loyal worship, scorning praise,
How spread their lures for him in vain
Thieving Ambition and paltering Gain!
He thought it happier to be dead,
To die for Beauty, than live for bread.[1]

MANNERS

GRACE, Beauty and Caprice
Build this golden portal;
Graceful women, chosen men,
Dazzle every mortal.
Their sweet and lofty countenance

His enchanted food;
He need not go to them, their forms
Beset his solitude.
He looketh seldom in their face,
His eyes explore the ground, —
The green grass is a looking-glass
Whereon their traits are found.[1]
Little and less he says to them,
So dances his heart in his breast;
Their tranquil mien bereaveth him
Of wit, of words, of rest.
Too weak to win, too fond to shun
The tyrants of his doom,
The much deceived Endymion
Slips behind a tomb.[2]

ART

Give to barrows, trays and pans
Grace and glimmer of romance;
Bring the moonlight into noon
Hid in gleaming piles of stone;
On the city's paved street
Plant gardens lined with lilacs sweet;
Let spouting fountains cool the air,
Singing in the sun-baked square;
Let statue, picture, park and hall,

Ballad, flag and festival,
The past restore, the day adorn,
And make to-morrow a new morn.
So shall the drudge in dusty frock
Spy behind the city clock
Retinues of airy kings,
Skirts of angels, starry wings,
His fathers shining in bright fables,
His children fed at heavenly tables.
'T is the privilege of Art
Thus to play its cheerful part,
Man on earth to acclimate
And bend the exile to his fate,
And, moulded of one element
With the days and firmament,
Teach him on these as stairs to climb,
And live on even terms with Time;
Whilst upper life the slender rill
Of human sense doth overfill.

UNITY[1]

SPACE is ample, east and west,
But two cannot go abreast,
Cannot travel in it two:
Yonder masterful cuckoo
Crowds every egg out of the nest,
Quick or dead, except its own;
A spell is laid on sod and stone,
Night and Day were tampered with,
Every quality and pith
Surcharged and sultry with a power
That works its will on age and hour.

WORSHIP

THIS is he, who, felled by foes,
Sprung harmless up, refreshed by blows:
He to captivity was sold,
But him no prison-bars would hold:
Though they sealed him in a rock,
Mountain chains he can unlock:
Thrown to lions for their meat,
The crouching lion kissed his feet;

Bound to the stake, no flames appalled,
But arched o'er him an honoring vault.
This is he men miscall Fate,
Threading dark ways, arriving late,
But ever coming in time to crown
The truth, and hurl wrong-doers down.[1]
He is the oldest, and best known,
More near than aught thou call'st thy own,
Yet, greeted in another's eyes,
Disconcerts with glad surprise.[2]
This is Jove, who, deaf to prayers,
Floods with blessings unawares.
Draw, if thou canst, the mystic line
Severing rightly his from thine,
Which is human, which divine.

PRUDENCE

THEME no poet gladly sung,
Fair to old and foul to young;
Scorn not thou the love of parts,
And the articles of arts.
Grandeur of the perfect sphere
Thanks the atoms that cohere.

NATURE

I

A SUBTLE chain of countless rings
The next unto the farthest brings ;
The eye reads omens where it goes,
And speaks all languages the rose;
And, striving to be man, the worm
Mounts through all the spires of form.

II

The rounded world is fair to see,
Nine times folded in mystery :
Though baffled seers cannot impart
The secret of its laboring heart,
Throb thine with Nature's throbbing breast,
And all is clear from east to west.
Spirit that lurks each form within
Beckons to spirit of its kin ;
Self-kindled every atom glows
And hints the future which it owes.

THE INFORMING SPIRIT

I

THERE is no great and no small
To the Soul that maketh all :
And where it cometh, all things are ;
And it cometh everywhere.

II

I am owner of the sphere,
Of the seven stars and the solar year,
Of Cæsar's hand, and Plato's brain,
Of Lord Christ's heart, and Shakspeare's strain.

CIRCLES

NATURE centres into balls,
And her proud ephemerals,
Fast to surface and outside,
Scan the profile of the sphere ;
Knew they what that signified,
A new genesis were here.

INTELLECT

Go, speed the stars of Thought
On to their shining goals ; —
The sower scatters broad his seed ;
The wheat thou strew'st be souls.

GIFTS

GIFTS of one who loved me, —
'T was high time they came ;
When he ceased to love me,
Time they stopped for shame.

PROMISE

IN countless upward-striving waves
The moon-drawn tide-wave strives ;
In thousand far-transplanted grafts
The parent fruit survives ;
So, in the new-born millions,
The perfect Adam lives.

Not less are summer mornings dear
To every child they wake,
And each with novel life his sphere
Fills for his proper sake.

CARITAS

In the suburb, in the town,
On the railway, in the square,
Came a beam of goodness down
Doubling daylight everywhere:
Peace now each for malice takes,
Beauty for his sinful weeds,
For the angel Hope aye makes
Him an angel whom she leads.

POWER

His tongue was framed to music,
And his hand was armed with skill;
His face was the mould of beauty,
And his heart the throne of will.

WEALTH

Who shall tell what did befall,
Far away in time, when once,
Over the lifeless ball,
Hung idle stars and suns?
What god the element obeyed?
Wings of what wind the lichen bore,
Wafting the puny seeds of power,
Which, lodged in rock, the rock abrade?
And well the primal pioneer
Knew the strong task to it assigned,
Patient through Heaven's enormous year
To build in matter home for mind.
From air the creeping centuries drew
The matted thicket low and wide,
This must the leaves of ages strew
The granite slab to clothe and hide,
Ere wheat can wave its golden pride.
What smiths, and in what furnace, rolled
(In dizzy æons dim and mute
The reeling brain can ill compute)
Copper and iron, lead and gold?
What oldest star the fame can save
Of races perishing to pave
The planet with a floor of lime?

Dust is their pyramid and mole:
Who saw what ferns and palms were pressed
Under the tumbling mountain's breast,
In the safe herbal of the coal ?
But when the quarried means were piled,
All is waste and worthless, till
Arrives the wise selecting will,
And, out of slime and chaos, Wit
Draws the threads of fair and fit.
Then temples rose, and towns, and marts,
The shop of toil, the hall of arts ;
Then flew the sail across the seas
To feed the North from tropic trees ;
The storm-wind wove, the torrent span,
Where they were bid, the rivers ran;
New slaves fulfilled the poet's dream,
Galvanic wire, strong-shouldered steam.
Then docks were built, and crops were stored,
And ingots added to the hoard.
But though light-headed man forget,
Remembering Matter pays her debt :
Still, through her motes and masses, draw
Electric thrills and ties of law,
Which bind the strengths of Nature wild
To the conscience of a child.

ILLUSIONS

Flow, flow the waves hated,
Accursed, adored,
The waves of mutation;
No anchorage is.
Sleep is not, death is not;
Who seem to die live.
House you were born in,
Friends of your spring-time,
Old man and young maid,
Day's toil and its guerdon,
They are all vanishing,
Fleeing to fables,
Cannot be moored.
See the stars through them,
Through treacherous marbles.
Know the stars yonder,
The stars everlasting,
Are fugitive also,
And emulate, vaulted,
The lambent heat lightning
And fire-fly's flight.

When thou dost return
On the wave's circulation,

Behold the shimmer,
The wild dissipation,
And, out of endeavor
To change and to flow,
The gas become solid,
And phantoms and nothings
Return to be things,
And endless imbroglio
Is law and the world, —
Then first shalt thou know,
That in the wild turmoil,
Horsed on the Proteus,
Thou ridest to power,
And to endurance.

IV

QUATRAINS AND TRANSLA-
TIONS

QUATRAINS

A. H.

HIGH was her heart, and yet was well inclined,
Her manners made of bounty well refined ;
Far capitals and marble courts, her eye still seemed to
see,
Minstrels and kings and high-born dames, and of the
best that be.

HUSH !

EVERY thought is public,
Every nook is wide ;
Thy gossips spread each whisper,
And the gods from side to side.

ORATOR

HE who has no hands
Perforce must use his tongue ;
Foxes are so cunning
Because they are not strong.

ARTIST

QUIT the hut, frequent the palace,
Reck not what the people say ;
For still, where'er the trees grow biggest,
Huntsmen find the easiest way.[1]

POET

Ever the Poet *from* the land
Steers his bark and trims his sail;
Right out to sea his courses stand,
New worlds to find in pinnace frail.

POET

To clothe the fiery thought
In simple words succeeds,
For still the craft of genius is
To mask a king in weeds.[1]

BOTANIST

Go thou to thy learned task,
I stay with the flowers of Spring:
Do thou of the Ages ask
What me the Hours will bring.

GARDENER

True Brahmin, in the morning meadows wet,
Expound the Vedas of the violet,
Or, hid in vines, peeping through many a loop,
See the plum redden, and the beurré stoop.[2]

FORESTER

He took the color of his vest
From rabbit's coat or grouse's breast;
For, as the wood-kinds lurk and hide,
So walks the woodman, unespied.[3]

NORTHMAN

THE gale that wrecked you on the sand,
It helped my rowers to row;
The storm is my best galley hand
And drives me where I go.[1]

FROM ALCUIN

THE sea is the road of the bold,
Frontier of the wheat-sown plains,
The pit wherein the streams are rolled
And fountain of the rains.

EXCELSIOR

OVER his head were the maple buds,
And over the tree was the moon,
And over the moon were the starry studs
That drop from the angels' shoon.[2]

S. H.

WITH beams December planets dart
His cold eye truth and conduct scanned,
July was in his sunny heart,
October in his liberal hand.[3]

BORROWING

FROM THE FRENCH

SOME of your hurts you have cured,
And the sharpest you still have survived,
But what torments of grief you endured
From evils which never arrived!

NATURE

BOON Nature yields each day a brag which we now
first behold,
And trains us on to slight the new, as if it were
the old:
But blest is he, who, playing deep, yet haply asks
not why,
Too busied with the crowded hour to fear to live or
die.[1]

FATE

HER planted eye to-day controls,
Is in the morrow most at home,
And sternly calls to being souls
That curse her when they come.

HOROSCOPE

ERE he was born, the stars of fate
Plotted to make him rich and great:
When from the womb the babe was loosed,
The gate of gifts behind him closed.[2]

POWER

Cast the bantling on the rocks,
Suckle him with the she-wolf's teat,
Wintered with the hawk and fox,
Power and speed be hands and feet.[1]

CLIMACTERIC

I am not wiser for my age,
Nor skilful by my grief;
Life loiters at the book's first page, —
Ah! could we turn the leaf.

HERI, CRAS, HODIE

Shines the last age, the next with hope is seen,
To-day slinks poorly off unmarked between:
Future or Past no richer secret folds,
O friendless Present! than thy bosom holds.

MEMORY

Night-dreams trace on Memory's wall
Shadows of the thoughts of day,
And thy fortunes, as they fall,
The bias of the will betray.[2]

LOVE

Love on his errand bound to go
Can swim the flood and wade through snow,
Where way is none, 't will creep and wind
And eat through Alps its home to find.[3]

SACRIFICE

Though love repine, and reason chafe,
There came a voice without reply, —
'T is man's perdition to be safe,
When for the truth he ought to die.' [1]

PERICLES

Well and wisely said the Greek,
Be thou faithful, but not fond;
To the altar's foot thy fellow seek, —
The Furies wait beyond. [2]

CASELLA

Test of the poet is knowledge of love,
For Eros is older than Saturn or Jove;
Never was poet, of late or of yore,
Who was not tremulous with love-lore. [3]

SHAKSPEARE

I see all human wits
Are measured but a few;
Unmeasured still my Shakspeare sits,
Lone as the blessed Jew.

HAFIZ

Her passions the shy violet
From Hafiz never hides;
Love-longings of the raptured bird
The bird to him confides.

NATURE IN LEASTS

As sings the pine-tree in the wind,
So sings in the wind a sprig of the pine;
Her strength and soul has laughing France
Shed in each drop of wine.

ΑΔΑΚΡΥΝ ΝΕΜΟΝΤΑΙ ΑΙΩΝΑ

' A NEW commandment,' said the smiling Muse,
' I give my darling son, Thou shalt not preach'; —
Luther, Fox, Behmen, Swedenborg, grew pale,
And, on the instant, rosier clouds upbore
Hafiz and Shakspeare with their shining choirs.[1]

TRANSLATIONS

SONNET OF MICHEL ANGELO BUONAROTTI

NEVER did sculptor's dream unfold
A form which marble doth not hold
In its white block; yet it therein shall find
Only the hand secure and bold
Which still obeys the mind.
So hide in thee, thou heavenly dame,
The ill I shun, the good I claim;
I alas! not well alive,
Miss the aim whereto I strive.
Not love, nor beauty's pride,
Nor Fortune, nor thy coldness, can I chide,
If, whilst within thy heart abide
Both death and pity, my unequal skill
Fails of the life, but draws the death and ill.

THE EXILE

FROM THE PERSIAN OF KERMANI

IN Farsistan the violet spreads
Its leaves to the rival sky;
I ask how far is the Tigris flood,
And the vine that grows thereby?

Except the amber morning wind,
Not one salutes me here;
There is no lover in all Bagdat
To offer the exile cheer.

I know that thou, O morning wind!
O'er Kernan's meadow blowest,
And thou, heart-warming nightingale!
My father's orchard knowest.

The merchant hath stuffs of price,
And gems from the sea-washed strand,
And princes offer me grace
To stay in the Syrian land;

But what is gold *for*, but for gifts?
And dark, without love, is the day;
And all that I see in Bagdat
Is the Tigris to float me away.

FROM HAFIZ

I SAID to heaven that glowed above,
O hide yon sun-filled zone,
Hide all the stars you boast;
For, in the world of love
And estimation true,
The heaped-up harvest of the moon
Is worth one barley-corn at most,
The Pleiads' sheaf but two.

If my darling should depart,
And search the skies for prouder friends,
God forbid my angry heart
In other love should seek amends.

When the blue horizon's hoop
Me a little pinches here,
Instant to my grave I stoop,
And go find thee in the sphere.

EPITAPH

Bethink, poor heart, what bitter kind of jest
Mad Destiny this tender stripling played;
For a warm breast of maiden to his breast,
She laid a slab of marble on his head.

They say, through patience, chalk
Becomes a ruby stone;
Ah, yes! but by the true heart's blood
The chalk is crimson grown.

FRIENDSHIP

Thou foolish Hafiz! Say, do churls
Know the worth of Oman's pearls?
Give the gem which dims the moon
To the noblest, or to none.[1]

DEAREST, where thy shadow falls,
Beauty sits and Music calls;
Where thy form and favor come,
All good creatures have their home.

ON prince or bride no diamond stone
Half so gracious ever shone,
As the light of enterprise
Beaming from a young man's eyes.

FROM OMAR KHAYYAM

EACH spot where tulips prank their state
Has drunk the life-blood of the great;
The violets yon field which stain
Are moles of beauties Time hath slain.

UNBAR the door, since thou the Opener art,
Show me the forward way, since thou art guide,
I put no faith in pilot or in chart,
Since they are transient, and thou dost abide.

FROM ALI BEN ABU TALEB

HE who has a thousand friends has not a friend to
spare,
And he who has one enemy will meet him everywhere.

ON two days it steads not to run from thy grave,
The appointed, and the unappointed day;
On the first, neither balm nor physician can save,
Nor thee, on the second, the Universe slay.

FROM IBN JEMIN

Two things thou shalt not long for, if thou love a
mind serene; —
A woman to thy wife, though she were a crowned
queen;
And the second, borrowed money, — though the smil-
ing lender say
That he will not demand the debt until the Judgment
Day.

THE FLUTE

FROM HILALI

HARK what, now loud, now low, the pining flute com-
plains,
Without tongue, yellow-cheeked, full of winds that
wail and sigh;
Saying, Sweetheart! the old mystery remains, —
If I am I; thou, thou; or thou art I?

TO THE SHAH

FROM HAFIZ

THY foes to hunt, thy enviers to strike down,
Poises Arcturus aloft morning and evening his spear.

TO THE SHAH

FROM ENWERI

NOT in their houses stand the stars,
But o'er the pinnacles of thine!

TO THE SHAH

FROM ENWERI

FROM thy worth and weight the stars gravitate,
And the equipoise of heaven is thy house's equipoise.

SONG OF SEYD NIMETOLLAH OF KUHISTAN

[Among the religious customs of the dervishes is an astronomical dance, in which the dervish imitates the movements of the heavenly bodies, by spinning on his own axis, whilst at the same time he revolves round the Sheikh in the centre, representing the sun; and, as he spins, he sings the Song of Seyd Nimetollah of Kuhistan.]

SPIN the ball! I reel, I burn,
Nor head from foot can I discern,
Nor my heart from love of mine,
Nor the wine-cup from the wine.
All my doing, all my leaving,
Reaches not to my perceiving;
Lost in whirling spheres I rove,
And know only that I love.

I am seeker of the stone,
Living gem of Solomon;
From the shore of souls arrived,
In the sea of sense I dived;
But what is land, or what is wave,
To me who only jewels crave?
Love is the air-fed fire intense,
And my heart the frankincense;
As the rich aloes flames, I glow,
Yet the censer cannot know.
I'm all-knowing, yet unknowing;
Stand not, pause not, in my going.

Ask not me, as Muftis can,
To recite the Alcoran;
Well I love the meaning sweet, —
I tread the book beneath my feet.

Lo! the God's love blazes higher,
Till all difference expire.
What are Moslems? what are Giaours?
All are Love's, and all are ours.
I embrace the true believers,
But I reck not of deceivers.
Firm to Heaven my bosom clings,
Heedless of inferior things;
Down on earth there, underfoot,
What men chatter know I not.

IX

V

APPENDIX

THE POET

I

RIGHT upward on the road of fame
With sounding steps the poet came;
Born and nourished in miracles,
His feet were shod with golden bells,
Or where he stepped the soil did peal
As if the dust were glass and steel.
The gallant child where'er he came
Threw to each fact a tuneful name.
The things whereon he cast his eyes
Could not the nations rebaptize,
Nor Time's snows hide the names he set,
Nor last posterity forget.[1]
Yet every scroll whereon he wrote
In latent fire his secret thought,
Fell unregarded to the ground,
Unseen by such as stood around.
The pious wind took it away,
The reverent darkness hid the lay.[2]
Methought like water-haunting birds
Divers or dippers were his words,
And idle clowns beside the mere
At the new vision gape and jeer.

But when the noisy scorn was past,
Emerge the wingèd words in haste.
New-bathed, new-trimmed, on healthy wing,
Right to the heaven they steer and sing.

A Brother of the world, his song
Sounded like a tempest strong
Which tore from oaks their branches broad,
And stars from the ecliptic road.
Times wore he as his clothing-weeds,
He sowed the sun and moon for seeds.[1]
As melts the iceberg in the seas,
As clouds give rain to the eastern breeze,
As snow-banks thaw in April's beam,
The solid kingdoms like a dream
Resist in vain his motive strain,
They totter now and float amain.[2]
For the Muse gave special charge
His learning should be deep and large,
And his training should not scant
The deepest lore of wealth or want:
His flesh should feel, his eyes should read
Every maxim of dreadful Need;[3]
In its fulness he should taste
Life's honeycomb, but not too fast;
Full fed, but not intoxicated;
He should be loved; he should be hated;
A blooming child to children dear,
His heart should palpitate with fear.

And well he loved to quit his home
And, Calmuck, in his wagon roam
To read new landscapes and old skies;[1] —
But oh, to see his solar eyes
Like meteors which chose their way
And rived the dark like a new day!
Not lazy grazing on all they saw,
Each chimney-pot and cottage door,
Farm-gear and village picket-fence,
But, feeding on magnificence,
They bounded to the horizon's edge
And searched with the sun's privilege.
Landward they reached the mountains old
Where pastoral tribes their flocks infold,
Saw rivers run seaward by cities high
And the seas wash the low-hung sky;
Saw the endless rack of the firmament
And the sailing moon where the cloud was rent,
And through man and woman and sea and star
Saw the dance of Nature forward and far,
Through worlds and races and terms and times
Saw musical order and pairing rhymes.[2]

II

The gods talk in the breath of the woods,
They talk in the shaken pine,
And fill the long reach of the old seashore
With dialogue divine;

And the poet who overhears
Some random word they say
Is the fated man of men
Whom the ages must obey:
One who having nectar drank
Into blissful orgies sank;
He takes no mark of night or day,
He cannot go, he cannot stay,
He would, yet would not, counsel keep,
But, like a walker in his sleep
With staring eye that seeth none,
Ridiculously up and down
Seeks how he may fitly tell
The heart-o'erlading miracle.[1]

Not yet, not yet,
Impatient friend, —
A little while attend;
Not yet I sing: but I must wait,
My hand upon the silent string,
Fully until the end.
I see the coming light,
I see the scattered gleams,
Aloft, beneath, on left and right
The stars' own ether beams;
These are but seeds of days,
Not yet a steadfast morn,
An intermittent blaze,
An embryo god unborn.

How all things sparkle,
The dust is alive,[1]
To the birth they arrive:
I snuff the breath of my morning afar,
I see the pale lustres condense to a star:
The fading colors fix,
The vanishing are seen,
And the world that shall be
Twins the world that has been.
I know the appointed hour,
I greet my office well,
Never faster, never slower
Revolves the fatal wheel!
The Fairest enchants me,
The Mighty commands me,
Saying, 'Stand in thy place;
Up and eastward turn thy face;
As mountains for the morning wait,
Coming early, coming late,
So thou attend the enriching Fate
Which none can stay, and none accelerate.'
I am neither faint nor weary,
Fill thy will, O faultless heart!
Here from youth to age I tarry, —
Count it flight of bird or dart.
My heart at the heart of things
Heeds no longer lapse of time,
Rushing ages moult their wings,
Bathing in thy day sublime.

The sun set, but set not his hope :—
Stars rose, his faith was earlier up :
Fixed on the enormous galaxy,
Deeper and older seemed his eye,
And matched his sufferance sublime
The taciturnity of Time.[1]

Beside his hut and shading oak,
—Thus to himself the poet spoke,
'I have supped to-night with gods,
I will not go under a wooden roof :
As I walked among the hills
In the love which Nature fills,
The great stars did not shine aloof,
They hurried down from their deep abodes
And hemmed me in their glittering troop.[2]

    'Divine Inviters ! I accept
The courtesy ye have shown and kept
From ancient ages for the bard,
To modulate
With finer fate
A fortune harsh and hard.
With aim like yours
I watch your course,
Who never break your lawful dance
By error or intemperance.
O birds of ether without wings !
O heavenly ships without a sail !

O fire of fire! O best of things!
O mariners who never fail!
Sail swiftly through your amber vault,
An animated law, a presence to exalt.'[1]

Ah, happy if a sun or star
Could chain the wheel of Fortune's car,
And give to hold an even state,
Neither dejected nor elate,
That haply man upraised might keep
The height of Fancy's far-eyed steep.
In vain: the stars are glowing wheels,
Giddy with motion Nature reels,
Sun, moon, man, undulate and stream,
The mountains flow, the solids seem,[2]
Change acts, reacts; back, forward hurled,
And pause were palsy to the world. —
The morn is come: the starry crowds
Are hid behind the thrice-piled clouds;
The new day lowers, and equal odds
Have changed not less the guest of gods;
Discrowned and timid, thoughtless, worn,
The child of genius sits forlorn:
Between two sleeps a short day's stealth,
'Mid many ails a brittle health,
A cripple of God, half true, half formed,
And by great sparks Promethean warmed,
Constrained by impotence to adjourn
To infinite time his eager turn,

His lot of action at the urn.
He by false usage pinned about
No breath therein, no passage out,
Cast wishful glances at the stars
And wishful saw the Ocean stream : —
' Merge me in the brute universe,
Or lift to a diviner dream ! ' [1]

Beside him sat enduring love,
Upon him noble eyes did rest,
Which, for the Genius that there strove,
The follies bore that it invest.
They spoke not, for their earnest sense
Outran the craft of eloquence. [2]

He whom God had thus preferred, —
To whom sweet angels ministered,
Saluted him each morn as brother,
And bragged his virtues to each other, —
Alas ! how were they so beguiled,
And they so pure ？ He, foolish child,
A facile, reckless, wandering will,
Eager for good, not hating ill,
Thanked Nature for each stroke she dealt ;
On his tense chords all strokes were felt,
The good, the bad with equal zeal,
He asked, he only asked, to feel.
Timid, self-pleasing, sensitive,
With Gods, with fools, content to live ;

Bended to fops who bent to him;
Surface with surfaces did swim.

'Sorrow, sorrow!' the angels cried,
'Is this dear Nature's manly pride?
Call hither thy mortal enemy,
Make him glad thy fall to see!
Yon waterflag, yon sighing osier,
A drop can shake, a breath can fan;
Maidens laugh and weep; Composure
Is the pudency of man.'[1]

Again by night the poet went
From the lighted halls
Beneath the darkling firmament
To the seashore, to the old seawalls,
Out shone a star beneath the cloud,
The constellation glittered soon, —
'You have no lapse; so have ye glowed
But once in your dominion.
And yet, dear stars, I know ye shine
Only by needs and loves of mine;
Light-loving, light-asking life in me
Feeds those eternal lamps I see.[2]
And I to whom your light has spoken,
I, pining to be one of you,
I fall, my faith is broken,
Ye scorn me from your deeps of blue.

Or if perchance, ye orbs of Fate,
Your ne'er averted glance
Beams with a will compassionate
On sons of time and chance,
Then clothe these hands with power
In just proportion,
Nor plant immense designs
Where equal means are none.'

CHORUS OF SPIRITS

Means, dear brother, ask them not ;
    Soul's desire is means enow,
Pure content is angel's lot,
    Thine own theatre art thou.

Gentler far than falls the snow
In the woodwalks still and low
Fell the lesson on his heart
And woke the fear lest angels part.

POET

I see your forms with deep content,
I know that ye are excellent,
    But will ye stay ?
I hear the rustle of wings,
Ye meditate what to say
Ere ye go to quit me for ever and aye.

SPIRITS

Brother, we are no phantom band ;
Brother, accept this fatal hand.
Aches thine unbelieving heart
With the fear that we must part ?
See, all we are rooted here
By one thought to one same sphere ;
From thyself thou canst not flee, —
From thyself no more can we.[1]

POET

Suns and stars their courses keep,
But not angels of the deep :
Day and night their turn observe,
But the day of day may swerve.
Is there warrant that the waves
Of thought in their mysterious caves
Will heap in me their highest tide,
In me therewith beatified ?
Unsure the ebb and flood of thought,
The moon comes back, — the Spirit not.

SPIRITS

Brother, sweeter is the Law
Than all the grace Love ever saw ;
We are its suppliants. By it, we
Draw the breath of Eternity ;

Serve thou it not for daily bread, —
Serve it for pain and fear and need.
Love it, though it hide its light;
By love behold the sun at night.
If the Law should thee forget,
More enamoured serve it yet;
Though it hate thee, suffer long;
Put the Spirit in the wrong;[1]
Brother, no decrepitude
　　Chills the limbs of Time;
As fleet his feet, his hands as good,
　　His vision as sublime:
On Nature's wheels there is no rust;
Nor less on man's enchanted dust
　　Beauty and Force alight.

FRAGMENTS ON THE POET AND THE POETIC GIFT

I

THERE are beggars in Iran and Araby,
SAID was hungrier than all;
Hafiz said he was a fly
That came to every festival.
He came a pilgrim to the Mosque
On trail of camel and caravan,
Knew every temple and kiosk
Out from Mecca to Ispahan;

Northward he went to the snowy hills,
At court he sat in the grave Divan.
His music was the south-wind's sigh, —
His lamp, the maiden's downcast eye,
And ever the spell of beauty came
And turned the drowsy world to flame. —
By lake and stream and gleaming hall
And modest copse and the forest tall,
Where'er he went, the magic guide
Kept its place by the poet's side. —
Said melted the days like cups of pearl,
Served high and low, the lord and the churl,
Loved harebells nodding on a rock,
A cabin hung with curling smoke,
Ring of axe or hum of wheel
Or gleam which use can paint on steel,
And huts and tents ; nor loved he less
Stately lords in palaces,
Princely women hard to please,
Fenced by form and ceremony,
Decked by courtly rites and dress
And etiquette of gentilesse.
But when the mate of the snow and wind,
He left each civil scale behind :
Him wood-gods fed with honey wild
And of his memory beguiled.
He loved to watch and wake
When the wing of the south-wind whipt the lake
And the glassy surface in ripples brake

IX

And fled in pretty frowns away
Like the flitting boreal lights,
Rippling roses in northern nights,
Or like the thrill of Æolian strings
In which the sudden wind-god rings.[1]
In caves and hollow trees he crept
And near the wolf and panther slept.
He came to the green ocean's brim
And saw the wheeling sea-birds skim,
Summer and winter, o'er the wave,
Like creatures of a skiey mould,
Impassible to heat or cold.
He stood before the tumbling main
With joy too tense for sober brain;
He shared the life of the element,
The tie of blood and home was rent:
As if in him the welkin walked,
The winds took flesh, the mountains talked,
And he the bard, a crystal soul
Sphered and concentric with the whole.

II

The Dervish whined to Said,
" Thou didst not tarry while I prayed.
Beware the fire that Eblis burned."
But Saadi coldly thus returned,
" Once with manlike love and fear
I gave thee for an hour my ear,
I kept the sun and stars at bay,

And love, for words thy tongue could say.
I cannot sell my heaven again
For all that rattles in thy brain." [1]

III

Said Saadi, " When I stood before
Hassan the camel-driver's door,
I scorned the fame of Timour brave;
Timour, to Hassan, was a slave.
In every glance of Hassan's eye
I read great years of victory,
And I, who cower mean and small
In the frequent interval
When wisdom not with me resides,
Worship Toil's wisdom that abides.
I shunned his eyes, that faithful man's,
I shunned the toiling Hassan's glance." [2]

IV

The civil world will much forgive
To bards who from its maxims live,
But if, grown bold, the poet dare
Bend his practice to his prayer
And following his mighty heart
Shame the times and live apart,
Væ solis ! I found this,
That of goods I could not miss
If I fell within the line,
Once a member, all was mine,

Houses, banquets, gardens, fountains,
Fortune's delectable mountains ;
But if I would walk alone,
Was neither cloak nor crumb my own.
And thus the high Muse treated me,
Directly never greeted me,
But when she spread her dearest spells,
Feigned to speak to some one else.
I was free to overhear,
Or I might at will forbear ;
Yet mark me well, that idle word
Thus at random overheard
Was the symphony of spheres,
And proverb of a thousand years,
The light wherewith all planets shone,
The livery all events put on,
It fell in rain, it grew in grain,
It put on flesh in friendly form,
Frowned in my foe and growled in storm,
It spoke in Tullius Cicero,
In Milton and in Angelo :
I travelled and found it at Rome ;
Eastward it filled all Heathendom
And it lay on my hearth when I came home.[1]

v

Mask thy wisdom with delight,
Toy with the bow, yet hit the white,

As Jelaleddin old and gray;
He seemed to bask, to dream and play
Without remoter hope or fear
Than still to entertain his ear
And pass the burning summer-time
In the palm-grove with a rhyme;
Heedless that each cunning word
Tribes and ages overheard:
Those idle catches told the laws
Holding Nature to her cause.

God only knew how Saadi dined;
Roses he ate, and drank the wind;
He freelier breathed beside the pine,
In cities he was low and mean;
The mountain waters washed him clean
And by the sea-waves he was strong;
He heard their medicinal song,
Asked no physician but the wave,
No palace but his sea-beat cave.

Saadi held the Muse in awe,
She was his mistress and his law;
A twelvemonth he could silence hold,
Nor ran to speak till she him told;
He felt the flame, the fanning wings,
Nor offered words till they were things,
Glad when the solid mountain swims
In music and uplifting hymns.

Charmed from fagot and from steel,
Harvests grew upon his tongue,
Past and future must reveal
All their heart when Saadi sung;
Sun and moon must fall amain
Like sower's seeds into his brain,
There quickened to be born again.[1]

The free winds told him what they knew,
Discoursed of fortune as they blew;
Omens and signs that filled the air
To him authentic witness bare;
The birds brought auguries on their wings,
And carolled undeceiving things
Him to beckon, him to warn;
Well might then the poet scorn
To learn of scribe or courier
Things writ in vaster character;
And on his mind at dawn of day
Soft shadows of the evening lay.[2]

PALE genius roves alone,
No scout can track his way,
None credits him till he have shown
His diamonds to the day.

Not his the feaster's wine,
Nor land, nor gold, nor power,
By want and pain God screeneth him
Till his elected hour.

Go, speed the stars of Thought
On to their shining goals : —
The sower scatters broad his seed,
The wheat thou strew'st be souls.[1]

I GRIEVE that better souls than mine
Docile read my measured line :
High destined youths and holy maids
Hallow these my orchard shades ;
Environ me and me baptize
With light that streams from gracious eyes.
I dare not be beloved and known,
I ungrateful, I alone.

Ever find me dim regards,
Love of ladies, love of bards,
Marked forbearance, compliments,
Tokens of benevolence.
What then, can I love myself ?
Fame is profitless as pelf,
A good in Nature not allowed
They love me, as I love a cloud
Sailing falsely in the sphere,
Hated mist if it come near.

For thought, and not praise;
Thought is the wages
For which I sell days,
Will gladly sell ages
And willing grow old
Deaf, and dumb, and blind, and cold,
Melting matter into dreams,
Panoramas which I saw
And whatever glows or seems
Into substance, into Law.[1]

For Fancy's gift
Can mountains lift;
The Muse can knit
What is past, what is done,
With the web that 's just begun;
Making free with time and size,
Dwindles here, there magnifies,
Swells a rain-drop to a tun;
So to repeat
No word or feat
Crowds in a day the sum of ages,
And blushing Love outwits the sages.[2]

TRY the might the Muse affords
And the balm of thoughtful words;
Bring music to the desolate;
Hang roses on the stony fate.

BUT over all his crowning grace,
Wherefor thanks God his daily praise,
Is the purging of his eye
To see the people of the sky:
From blue mount and headland dim
Friendly hands stretch forth to him,
Him they beckon, him advise
Of heavenlier prosperities
And a more excelling grace
And a truer bosom-glow
Than the wine-fed feasters know.
They turn his heart from lovely maids,
And make the darlings of the earth
Swainish, coarse and nothing worth:
Teach him gladly to postpone
Pleasures to another stage
Beyond the scope of human age,
Freely as task at eve undone
Waits unblamed to-morrow's sun.

By thoughts I lead
Bards to say what nations need;
What imports, what irks and what behooves,
Framed afar as Fates and Loves.

AND as the light divides the dark
Through with living swords,
So shall thou pierce the distant age
With adamantine words.

——I FRAMED his tongue to music,
I armed his hand with skill,
I moulded his face to beauty
And his heart the throne of Will.

FOR every God
Obeys the hymn, obeys the ode.

FOR art, for music over-thrilled,
The wine-cup shakes, the wine is spilled.

Hold of the Maker, not the Made;
Sit with the Cause, or grim or glad.[1]

That book is good
Which puts me in a working mood.[2]
   Unless to Thought is added Will,
   Apollo is an imbecile.
What parts, what gems, what colors shine, —
Ah, but I miss the grand design.

Like vaulters in a circus round
Who leap from horse to horse, but never touch the
      ground.

For Genius made his cabin wide,
And Love led Gods therein to bide.

The atom displaces all atoms beside,
And Genius unspheres all souls that abide.

To transmute crime to wisdom, so to stem
The vice of Japhet by the thought of Shem.

HE could condense cerulean ether
Into the very best sole-leather.

FORBORE the ant-hill, shunned to tread,
In mercy, on one little head.

I HAVE no brothers and no peers,
And the dearest interferes :
When I would spend a lonely day,
Sun and moon are in my way.

THE brook sings on, but sings in vain
Wanting the echo in my brain.

HE planted where the deluge ploughed,
His hired hands were wind and cloud ;
His eyes detect the Gods concealed
In the hummock of the field.[1]

For what need I of book or priest,
Or sibyl from the mummied East,
When every star is Bethlehem star?
I count as many as there are
Cinquefoils or violets in the grass,
So many saints and saviors,
So many high behaviors
Salute the bard who is alive
And only sees what he doth give.

Coin the day-dawn into lines
In which its proper splendor shines;
Coin the moonlight into verse
Which all its marvel shall rehearse,

.   .   .   .

Chasing with words fast-flowing things; nor try
To plant thy shrivelled pedantry
On the shoulders of the sky.

Ah, not to me those dreams belong!
A better voice peals through my song.

THE Muse's hill by Fear is guarded,
A bolder foot is still rewarded.

HIS instant thought a poet spoke,
And filled the age his fame;
An inch of ground the lightning strook
But lit the sky with flame.[1]

IF bright the sun, he tarries,
    All day his song is heard;
And when he goes he carries
    No more baggage than a bird.

THE Asmodean feat is mine,
To spin my sand-heap into twine.[2]

SLIGHTED Minerva's learnèd tongue,
But leaped with joy when on the wind
    The shell of Clio rung.

FRAGMENTS ON NATURE AND LIFE

NATURE

THE patient Pan,
Drunken with nectar,
Sleeps or feigns slumber,
Drowsily humming
Music to the march of time.
This poor tooting, creaking cricket,
Pan, half asleep, rolling over
His great body in the grass,
Tooting, creaking,
Feigns to sleep, sleeping never;
'T is his manner,
Well he knows his own affair,
Piling mountain chains of phlegm
On the nervous brain of man,
As he holds down central fires
Under Alps and Andes cold;
Haply else we could not live,
Life would be too wild an ode.[1]

COME search the wood for flowers, —
Wild tea and wild pea,

Grapevine and succory,
Coreopsis
And liatris,
Flaunting in their bowers ;
Grass with green flag half-mast high,
Succory to match the sky,
Columbine with horn of honey,
Scented fern and agrimony ;
Forest full of essences
Fit for fairy presences,
Peppermint and sassafras,
Sweet fern, mint and vernal grass,
Panax, black birch, sugar maple,
Sweet and scent for Dian's table,
Elder-blow, sarsaparilla,
Wild rose, lily, dry vanilla, —
Spices in the plants that run
To bring their first fruits to the sun.
Earliest heats that follow frore
Nervèd leaf of hellebore,
Sweet willow, checkerberry red,
With its savory leaf for bread.
Silver birch and black
With the selfsame spice
Found in polygala root and rind,
Sassafras, fern, benzöine,
Mouse-ear, cowslip, wintergreen,
Which by aroma may compel
The frost to spare, what scents so well.

Where the fungus broad and red
Lifts its head,
Like poisoned loaf of elfin bread,
Where the aster grew
With the social goldenrod,
In a chapel, which the dew
Made beautiful for God : —
O what would Nature say ?
She spared no speech to-day :
The fungus and the bulrush spoke,
Answered the pine-tree and the oak,
The wizard South blew down the glen,
Filled the straits and filled the wide,
Each maple leaf turned up its silver side.
All things shine in his smoky ray,
And all we see are pictures high ;
Many a high hillside,
While oaks of pride
Climb to their tops,
And boys run out upon their leafy ropes.
The maple street
In the houseless wood,
Voices followed after,
Every shrub and grape leaf
Rang with fairy laughter.
I have heard them fall
Like the strain of all
King Oberon's minstrelsy.

IX

Would hear the everlasting
And know the only strong?
You must worship fasting,
You must listen long.
Words of the air
Which birds of the air
Carry aloft, below, around,
To the isles of the deep,
To the snow-capped steep,
To the thundercloud.

For Nature, true and like in every place,
Will hint her secret in a garden patch,
Or in lone corners of a doleful heath,
As in the Andes watched by fleets at sea,
Or the sky-piercing horns of Himmaleh;
And, when I would recall the scenes I dreamed
On Adirondac steeps, I know
Small need have I of Turner or Daguerre,
Assured to find the token once again
In silver lakes that unexhausted gleam
And peaceful woods beside my cottage door.

WHAT all the books of ages paint, I have.
What prayers and dreams of youthful genius feign,
I daily dwell in, and am not so blind
But I can see the elastic tent of day
Belike has wider hospitality
Than my few needs exhaust, and bids me read
The quaint devices on its mornings gay.
Yet Nature will not be in full possessed,
And they who truliest love her, heralds are
And harbingers of a majestic race,
Who, having more absorbed, more largely yield,
And walk on earth as the sun walks in the sphere.

BUT never yet the man was found
Who could the mystery expound,
Though Adam, born when oaks were young,
Endured, the Bible says, as long;
But when at last the patriarch died
The Gordian noose was still untied.
He left, though goodly centuries old,
Meek Nature's secret still untold.

ATOM from atom yawns as far
As moon from earth, or star from star.

When all their blooms the meadows flaunt
 To deck the morning of the year,
Why tinge thy lustres jubilant
 With forecast or with fear?

Teach me your mood, O patient stars!
 Who climb each night the ancient sky,
Leaving on space no shade, no scars,
 No trace of age, no fear to die.

The sun athwart the cloud thought it no sin
To use my land to put his rainbows in.

For joy and beauty planted it,
 With faerie gardens cheered,
And boding Fancy haunted it
 With men and women weird.

What central flowing forces, say,
Make up thy splendor, matchless day?

DAY by day for her darlings to her much she added
    more;
In her hundred-gated Thebes every chamber was a
    door,
A door to something grander, — loftier walls, and
    vaster floor.

SHE paints with white and red the moors
To draw the nations out of doors.

A SCORE of airy miles will smooth
Rough Monadnoc to a gem.

THE EARTH

OUR eyeless bark sails free
    Though with boom and spar
Andes, Alp or Himmalee,
    Strikes never moon or star.

THE HEAVENS

WISP and meteor nightly falling,
But the Stars of God remain.

TRANSITION

SEE yonder leafless trees against the sky,
How they diffuse themselves into the air,
And, ever subdividing, separate
Limbs into branches, branches into twigs,
As if they loved the element, and hasted
To dissipate their being into it.

PARKS and ponds are good by day;
I do not delight
In black acres of the night,
Nor my unseasoned step disturbs
The sleeps of trees or dreams of herbs.

IN Walden wood the chickadee
Runs round the pine and maple tree
Intent on insect slaughter:
O tufted entomologist!
Devour as many as you list,
Then drink in Walden water.

THE low December vault in June be lifted high,
And largest clouds be flakes of down in that enormous
　　　sky.

THE GARDEN

Many things the garden shows,
And pleased I stray
From tree to tree
Watching the white pear-bloom,
Bee-infested quince or plum.
I could walk days, years, away
Till the slow ripening, secular tree
Had reached its fruiting-time,
Nor think it long.

Solar insect on the wing
In the garden murmuring,
Soothing with thy summer horn
Swains by winter pinched and worn.

BIRDS

Darlings of children and of bard,
Perfect kinds by vice unmarred,
All of worth and beauty set
Gems in Nature's cabinet;
These the fables she esteems
Reality most like to dreams.

Welcome back, you little nations,
Far-travelled in the south plantations;
Bring your music and rhythmic flight,
Your colors for our eyes' delight:
Freely nestle in our roof,
Weave your chamber weatherproof;
And your enchanting manners bring
And your autumnal gathering.
Exchange in conclave general
Greetings kind to each and all,
Conscious each of duty done
And unstainèd as the sun.[1]

WATER

THE water understands
Civilization well;
It wets my foot, but prettily
It chills my life, but wittily,
It is not disconcerted,
It is not broken-hearted:
Well used, it decketh joy,
Adorneth, doubleth joy:
Ill used, it will destroy,
In perfect time and measure
With a face of golden pleasure
Elegantly destroy.

NAHANT

ALL day the waves assailed the rock,
   I heard no church-bell chime,
The sea-beat scorns the minster clock
   And breaks the glass of Time.[1]

SUNRISE

WOULD you know what joy is hid
In our green Musketaquid,
And for travelled eyes what charms
Draw us to these meadow farms,
Come and I will show you all
Makes each day a festival.
Stand upon this pasture hill,
Face the eastern star until
The slow eye of heaven shall show
The world above, the world below.

Behold the miracle!
Thou saw'st but now the twilight sad
And stood beneath the firmament,
A watchman in a dark gray tent,
Waiting till God create the earth, —
Behold the new majestic birth!

The mottled clouds, like scraps of wool,
Steeped in the light are beautiful.
What majestic stillness broods
Over these colored solitudes.
Sleeps the vast East in pleasèd peace,
Up the far mountain walls the streams increase
Inundating the heaven
With spouting streams and waves of light
Which round the floating isles unite : —
See the world below
Baptized with the pure element,
A clear and glorious firmament
Touched with life by every beam.
I share the good with every flower,
I drink the nectar of the hour : —
This is not the ancient earth
Whereof old chronicles relate
The tragic tales of crime and fate ;
But rather, like its beads of dew
And dew-bent violets, fresh and new,
An exhalation of the time.[1]

.   .   .   .

NIGHT IN JUNE

I LEFT my dreary page and sallied forth,
Received the fair inscriptions of the night ;

The moon was making amber of the world,
Glittered with silver every cottage pane,
The trees were rich, yet ominous with gloom.
                        The meadows broad
From ferns and grapes and from the folded flowers
Sent a nocturnal fragrance ; harlot flies
Flashed their small fires in air, or held their court
In fairy groves of herds-grass.

HE lives not who can refuse me ;
All my force saith, Come and use me :
A gleam of sun, a summer rain,
And all the zone is green again.

SEEMS, though the soft sheen all enchants,
Cheers the rough crag and mournful dell,
As if on such stern forms and haunts
A wintry storm more fitly fell.

PUT in, drive home the sightless wedges
And split to flakes the crystal ledges.

MAIA

ILLUSION works impenetrable,
Weaving webs innumerable,
Her gay pictures never fail,
Crowds each on other, veil on veil,
Charmer who will be believed
By man who thirsts to be deceived.

ILLUSIONS like the tints of pearl,
Or changing colors of the sky,
Or ribbons of a dancing girl
That mend her beauty to the eye.

THE cold gray down upon the quinces lieth
And the poor spinners weave their webs thereon
To share the sunshine that so spicy is.

SAMSON stark, at Dagon's knee,
Gropes for columns strong as he ;
When his ringlets grew and curled,
Groped for axle of the world.

BUT Nature whistled with all her winds,
Did as she pleased and went her way.[1]

LIFE

A TRAIN of gay and clouded days
Dappled with joy and grief and praise,
Beauty to fire us, saints to save,
Escort us to a little grave.

No fate, save by the victim's fault, is low,
For God hath writ all dooms magnificent,
So guilt not traverses his tender will.

AROUND the man who seeks a noble end,
Not angels but divinities attend.[1]

FROM high to higher forces
      The scale of power uprears,
The heroes on their horses,
      The gods upon their spheres.

LIFE

THIS shining moment is an edifice
Which the Omnipotent cannot rebuild.

ROOMY Eternity
Casts her schemes rarely,
And an æon allows
For each quality and part
Of the multitudinous
And many-chambered heart.

THE beggar begs by God's command,
And gifts awake when givers sleep,
Swords cannot cut the giving hand
Nor stab the love that orphans keep.

IN the chamber, on the stairs,
    Lurking dumb,
    Go and come
Lemurs and Lars.[1]

SUCH another peerless queen
Only could her mirror show.

Easy to match what others do,
Perform the feat as well as they;
Hard to out-do the brave, the true,
And find a loftier way:
The school decays, the learning spoils
Because of the sons of wine;
How snatch the stripling from their toils? —
Yet can one ray of truth divine
The blaze of revellers' feasts outshine.

Of all wit's uses the main one
Is to live well with who has none.

The tongue is prone to lose the way,
Not so the pen, for in a letter
We have not better things to say,
But surely say them better.[1]

She walked in flowers around my field
As June herself around the sphere.

FRIENDS to me are frozen wine;
I wait the sun on them should shine.[1]

You shall not love me for what daily spends;
You shall not know me in the noisy street,
Where I, as others, follow petty ends;
Nor when in fair saloons we chance to meet;
Nor when I'm jaded, sick, anxious or mean.
But love me then and only, when you know
Me for the channel of the rivers of God
From deep ideal fontal heavens that flow.

To and fro the Genius flies,
  A light which plays and hovers
  Over the maiden's head
And dips sometimes as low as to her eyes.
Of her faults I take no note,
  Fault and folly are not mine;
Comes the Genius, — all's forgot,
Replunged again into that upper sphere
He scatters wide and wild its lustres here.[2]

LOVE
Asks nought his brother cannot give;
Asks nothing, but does all receive.
Love calls not to his aid events;
He to his wants can well suffice:
Asks not of others soft consents,
Nor kind occasion without eyes;
Nor plots to ope or bolt a gate,
Nor heeds Condition's iron walls, —
Where he goes, goes before him Fate;
Whom he uniteth, God installs;
Instant and perfect his access
To the dear object of his thought,
Though foes and land and seas between
Himself and his love intervene.[1]

THE brave Empedocles, defying fools,
Pronounced the word that mortals hate to hear —
" I am divine, I am not mortal made;
I am superior to my human weeds."
Not Sense but Reason is the Judge of truth;
Reason 's twofold, part human, part divine;
That human part may be described and taught,
The other portion language cannot speak.[2]

IX

TELL men what they knew before;
Paint the prospect from their door.

HIM strong Genius urged to roam,
Stronger Custom brought him home.

THAT each should in his house abide,
Therefore was the world so wide.

THOU shalt make thy house
The temple of a nation's vows.
Spirits of a higher strain
Who sought thee once shall seek again.
I detected many a god
Forth already on the road,
Ancestors of beauty come
In thy breast to make a home.

THE archangel Hope
Looks to the azure cope,
Waits through dark ages for the morn,
Defeated day by day, but unto victory born.

As the drop feeds its fated flower,
As finds its Alp the snowy shower,
Child of the omnific Need,
Hurled into life to do a deed,
Man drinks the water, drinks the light.

EVER the Rock of Ages melts
    Into the mineral air,
To be the quarry whence to build
    Thought and its mansions fair.

Go if thou wilt, ambrosial flower,
    Go match thee with thy seeming peers;
I will wait Heaven's perfect hour
    Through the innumerable years.

YES, sometimes to the sorrow-stricken
Shall his own sorrow seem impertinent,
A thing that takes no more root in the world
Than doth the traveller's shadow on the rock.

But if thou do thy best,
Without remission, without rest,
And invite the sunbeam,
And abhor to feign or seem
Even to those who thee should love
And thy behavior approve;
If thou go in thine own likeness,
Be it health, or be it sickness;
If thou go as thy father's son,
If thou wear no mask or lie,
Dealing purely and nakedly,—

. . . .

Ascending thorough just degrees
To a consummate holiness,
As angel blind to trespass done,
And bleaching all souls like the sun.

From the stores of eldest matter,
The deep-eyed flame, obedient water,
Transparent air, all-feeding earth,
He took the flower of all their worth,
And, best with best in sweet consent,
Combined a new temperament.

REX

THE bard and mystic held me for their own,
I filled the dream of sad, poetic maids,
I took the friendly noble by the hand,
I was the trustee of the hand-cart man,
The brother of the fisher, porter, swain,
And these from the crowd's edge well pleased
    beheld
The service done to me as done to them.[1]

WITH the key of the secret he marches faster,
    From strength to strength, and for night brings
        day;
While classes or tribes, too weak to master
    The flowing conditions of life, give way.

SUUM CUIQUE

WILT thou seal up the avenues of ill?
Pay every debt as if God wrote the bill.

If curses be the wage of love,
Hide in thy skies, thou fruitless Jove,
    Not to be named:
    It is clear
  Why the gods will not appear;
    They are ashamed.

When wrath and terror changed Jove's regal port,
And the rash-leaping thunderbolt fell short.

Shun passion, fold the hands of thrift,
  Sit still and Truth is near:
Suddenly it will uplift
  Your eyelids to the sphere:
Wait a little, you shall see
The portraiture of things to be.

The rules to men made evident
By Him who built the day,
The columns of the firmament
Not firmer based than they.

On bravely through the sunshine and the showers!
Time hath his work to do and we have ours.

THE BOHEMIAN HYMN

In many forms we try
To utter God's infinity,
But the boundless hath no form,
And the Universal Friend
Doth as far transcend
An angel as a worm.

The great Idea baffles wit,
Language falters under it,
It leaves the learned in the lurch;
Nor art, nor power, nor toil can find
The measure of the eternal Mind,
Nor hymn, nor prayer, nor church.[1]

GRACE

How much, preventing God, how much I owe
To the defences thou hast round me set;
Example, custom, fear, occasion slow, —
These scorned bondmen were my parapet.
I dare not peep over this parapet
To gauge with glance the roaring gulf below,
The depths of sin to which I had descended,
Had not these me against myself defended.[2]

INSIGHT

Power that by obedience grows,
Knowledge which its source not knows,
Wave which severs whom it bears
From the things which he compares,
Adding wings through things to range,
To his own blood harsh and strange.[1]

PAN

O what are heroes, prophets, men,
But pipes through which the breath of Pan doth
      blow
A momentary music. Being's tide
Swells hitherward, and myriads of forms
Live, robed with beauty, painted by the sun;
Their dust, pervaded by the nerves of God,
Throbs with an overmastering energy
Knowing and doing. Ebbs the tide, they lie
White hollow shells upon the desert shore,
But not the less the eternal wave rolls on
To animate new millions, and exhale
Races and planets, its enchanted foam.[2]

MONADNOC FROM AFAR

DARK flower of Cheshire garden,
  Red evening duly dyes
Thy sombre head with rosy hues
  To fix far-gazing eyes.
Well the Planter knew how strongly
  Works thy form on human thought;
I muse what secret purpose had he
  To draw all fancies to this spot.[1]

SEPTEMBER

IN the turbulent beauty
  Of a gusty Autumn day,
Poet on a sunny headland
  Sighed his soul away.

Farms the sunny landscape dappled,
  Swandown clouds dappled the farms,
Cattle lowed in mellow distance
  Where far oaks outstretched their arms.

Sudden gusts came full of meaning,
  All too much to him they said,
Oh, south winds have long memories,
  Of that be none afraid.

I cannot tell rude listeners
    Half the tell-tale South-wind said, —
'T would bring the blushes of yon maples
    To a man and to a maid.[1]

EROS

THEY put their finger on their lip,
    The Powers above:
The seas their islands clip,
The moons in ocean dip,
They love, but name not love.

OCTOBER

OCTOBER woods wherein
The boy's dream comes to pass,
And Nature squanders on the boy her pomp,
And crowns him with a more than royal crown,
And unimagined splendor waits his steps.
The gazing urchin walks through tents of gold,
Through crimson chambers, porphyry and pearl,
Pavilion on pavilion, garlanded,
Incensed and starred with lights and airs and shapes,
Color and sound, music to eye and ear,
Beyond the best conceit of pomp or power.[2]

PETER'S FIELD

[Knows he who tills this lonely field
    To reap its scanty corn,
What mystic fruit his acres yield
    At midnight and at morn ?]

That field by spirits bad and good,
    By Hell and Heaven is haunted,
And every rood in the hemlock wood
    I know is ground enchanted.

[In the long sunny afternoon
    The plain was full of ghosts :
I wandered up, I wandered down,
    Beset by pensive hosts.]

For in those lonely grounds the sun
    Shines not as on the town,
In nearer arcs his journeys run,
    And nearer stoops the moon.

There in a moment I have seen
    The buried Past arise ;
The fields of Thessaly grew green,
    Old gods forsook the skies.

I cannot publish in my rhyme
    What pranks the greenwood played ;
It was the Carnival of time,
    And Ages went or stayed.

To me that spectral nook appeared
    The mustering Day of Doom,
And round me swarmed in shadowy troop
    Things past and things to come.

The darkness haunteth me elsewhere ;
    There I am full of light ;
In every whispering leaf I hear
    More sense than sages write.

Underwoods were full of pleasance,
    All to each in kindness bend,
And every flower made obeisance
    As a man unto his friend.

Far seen, the river glides below,
    Tossing one sparkle to the eyes :
I catch thy meaning, wizard wave ;
    The River of my Life replies.[1]

MUSIC

LET me go where'er I will,
I hear a sky-born music still:
It sounds from all things old,
It sounds from all things young,
From all that's fair, from all that's foul,
Peals out a cheerful song.

It is not only in the rose,
It is not only in the bird,
Not only where the rainbow glows,
Nor in the song of woman heard,
But in the darkest, meanest things
There alway, alway something sings.

'T is not in the high stars alone,
Nor in the cup of budding flowers,
Nor in the redbreast's mellow tone,
Nor in the bow that smiles in showers,
But in the mud and scum of things
There alway, alway something sings.[1]

THE WALK

A QUEEN rejoices in her peers,
And wary Nature knows her own
By court and city, dale and down,
And like a lover volunteers,
And to her son will treasures more
And more to purpose freely pour
In one wood walk, than learned men
Can find with glass in ten times ten.[1]

COSMOS

WHO saw the hid beginnings
   When Chaos and Order strove,
Or who can date the morning,
   The purple flaming of love ?

I saw the hid beginnings
   When Chaos and Order strove,
And I can date the morning prime
   And purple flame of love.

Song breathed from all the forest,
   The total air was fame;
It seemed the world was all torches
   That suddenly caught the flame.

.   .   .   .

Is there never a retroscope mirror
   In the realms and corners of space
That can give us a glimpse of the battle
   And the soldiers face to face?

Sit here on the basalt courses
   Where twisted hills betray
The seat of the world-old Forces
   Who wrestled here on a day.

.   .   .   .

When the purple flame shoots up,
   And Love ascends his throne,
I cannot hear your songs, O birds,
   For the witchery of my own.

And every human heart
   Still keeps that golden day
And rings the bells of jubilee
   On its own First of May.[1]

THE MIRACLE

I HAVE trod this path a hundred times
With idle footsteps, crooning rhymes.
I know each nest and web-worm's tent,
The fox-hole which the woodchucks rent,
Maple and oak, the old Divan
Self-planted twice, like the banian.
I know not why I came again
Unless to learn it ten times ten.
To read the sense the woods impart
You must bring the throbbing heart.
Love is aye the counterforce, —
Terror and Hope and wild Remorse,
Newest knowledge, fiery thought,
Or Duty to grand purpose wrought.

    Wandering yester morn the brake,
I reached this heath beside the lake,
And oh, the wonder of the power,
The deeper secret of the hour !
Nature, the supplement of man,
His hidden sense interpret can ; —
What friend to friend cannot convey
Shall the dumb bird instructed say.
Passing yonder oak, I heard
Sharp accents of my woodland bird ;

I watched the singer with delight, —
But mark what changed my joy to fright, —
When that bird sang, I gave the theme;
That wood-bird sang my last night's dream,
A brown wren was the Daniel
That pierced my trance its drift to tell,
Knew my quarrel, how and why,
Published it to lake and sky,
Told every word and syllable
In his flippant chirping babble,
All my wrath and all my shames,
Nay, God is witness, gave the names.[1]

THE WATERFALL

A PATCH of meadow upland
   Reached by a mile of road,
Soothed by the voice of waters,
   With birds and flowers bestowed.[2]

Hither I come for strength
   Which well it can supply,
For Love draws might from terrene force
   And potencies of sky.

   IX

The tremulous battery Earth
  Responds to the touch of man;
It thrills to the antipodes,
  From Boston to Japan.

The planets' child the planet knows
  And to his joy replies;
To the lark's trill unfolds the rose,
  Clouds flush their gayest dyes.

When Ali prayed and loved
  Where Syrian waters roll,
Upward the ninth heaven thrilled and moved
  At the tread of the jubilant soul.

WALDEN

In my garden three ways meet,
  Thrice the spot is blest;
Hermit-thrush comes there to build,
  Carrier-doves to nest.

There broad-armed oaks, the copses' maze,
  The cold sea-wind detain;
Here sultry Summer overstays
  When Autumn chills the plain.

Self-sown my stately garden grows;
    The winds and wind-blown seed,
Cold April rain and colder snows
    My hedges plant and feed.

From mountains far and valleys near
    The harvests sown to-day
Thrive in all weathers without fear, —
    Wild planters, plant away!

In cities high the careful crowds
    Of woe-worn mortals darkling go,
But in these sunny solitudes
    My quiet roses blow.

Methought the sky looked scornful down
    On all was base in man,
And airy tongues did taunt the town,
    'Achieve our peace who can!'

What need I holier dew
    Than Walden's haunted wave,
Distilled from heaven's alembic blue,
    Steeped in each forest cave?

[If Thought unlock her mysteries,
    If Friendship on me smile,
I walk in marble galleries,
    I talk with kings the while.]

How drearily in College hall
  The Doctor stretched the hours,
But in each pause we heard the call
  Of robins out of doors.

The air is wise, the wind thinks well,
  And all through which it blows,
If plants or brain, if egg or shell,
  Or bird or biped knows;

And oft at home 'mid tasks I heed,
  I heed how wears the day;
We must not halt while fiercely speed
  The spans of life away.

What boots it here of Thebes or Rome
  Or lands of Eastern day?
In forests I am still at home
  And there I cannot stray.

THE ENCHANTER

In the deep heart of man a poet dwells
Who all the day of life his summer story tells;
Scatters on every eye dust of his spells,
Scent, form and color; to the flowers and shells

Wins the believing child with wondrous tales;
Touches a cheek with colors of romance,
And crowds a history into a glance;
Gives beauty to the lake and fountain,
Spies oversea the fires of the mountain;
When thrushes ope their throat, 't is he that
      sings,
And he that paints the oriole's fiery wings.
The little Shakspeare in the maiden's heart
Makes Romeo of a plough-boy on his cart;
Opens the eye to Virtue's starlike meed
And gives persuasion to a gentle deed.[1]

WRITTEN IN A VOLUME OF GOETHE

SIX thankful weeks, — and let it be
A meter of prosperity, —
In my coat I bore this book,
And seldom therein could I look,
For I had too much to think,
Heaven and earth to eat and drink.
Is he hapless who can spare
In his plenty things so rare?[2]

RICHES

HAVE ye seen the caterpillar
  Foully warking in his nest ?
'T is the poor man getting siller,
  Without cleanness, without rest.

Have ye seen the butterfly
  In braw claithing drest ?
'T is the poor man gotten rich,
  In rings and painted vest.

The poor man crawls in web of rags
  And sore bested with woes.
But when he flees on riches' wings,
  He laugheth at his foes.[1]

PHILOSOPHER

PHILOSOPHERS are lined with eyes within,
And, being so, the sage unmakes the man.
In love, he cannot therefore cease his trade ;
Scarce the first blush has overspread his cheek,
He feels it, introverts his learned eye
To catch the unconscious heart in the very act.

His mother died, — the only friend he had, —
Some tears escaped, but his philosophy
Couched like a cat sat watching close behind
And throttled all his passion. Is 't not like
That devil-spider that devours her mate
Scarce freed from her embraces ? [1]

INTELLECT

GRAVELY it broods apart on joy,
And, truth to tell, amused by pain.

LIMITS

WHO knows this or that ?
Hark in the wall to the rat :
Since the world was, he has gnawed ;
Of his wisdom, of his fraud
What dost thou know ?
In the wretched little beast
Is life and heart,
Child and parent,
Not without relation
To fruitful field and sun and moon.
What art thou ? His wicked eye
Is cruel to thy cruelty. [2]

INSCRIPTION FOR A WELL IN MEMORY
OF THE MARTYRS OF THE WAR

FALL, stream, from Heaven to bless; return as well;
So did our sons; Heaven met them as they fell.

THE EXILE

(AFTER TALIESSIN)

THE heavy blue chain
Of the boundless main
Didst thou, just man, endure.

I HAVE an arrow that will find its mark,
A mastiff that will bite without a bark.

VI

POEMS OF
YOUTH AND EARLY MANHOOD

1823–1834

THE BELL

I LOVE thy music, mellow bell,
   I love thine iron chime,
To life or death, to heaven or hell,
   Which calls the sons of Time.

Thy voice upon the deep
   The home-bound sea-boy hails,
It charms his cares to sleep,
   It cheers him as he sails.

To house of God and heavenly joys
   Thy summons called our sires,
And good men thought thy sacred voice
   Disarmed the thunder's fires.

And soon thy music, sad death-bell,
   Shall lift its notes once more,
And mix my requiem with the wind
   That sweeps my native shore.

1823.

THOUGHT

I AM not poor, but I am proud,
    Of one inalienable right,
Above the envy of the crowd, —
    Thought's holy light.

Better it is than gems or gold,
    And oh! it cannot die,
But thought will glow when the sun grows
        cold,
    And mix with Deity.

BOSTON, 1823.

PRAYER

WHEN success exalts thy lot,
God for thy virtue lays a plot:
And all thy life is for thy own,
Then for mankind's instruction shown;
And though thy knees were never bent,
To Heaven thy hourly prayers are sent,
And whether formed for good or ill,
Are registered and answered still.

    1826 [?].

I bear in youth the sad infirmities
That use to undo the limb and sense of age;
It hath pleased Heaven to break the dream of bliss
Which lit my onward way with bright presage,
And my unserviceable limbs forego.
The sweet delight I found in fields and farms,
On windy hills, whose tops with morning glow,
And lakes, smooth mirrors of Aurora's charms.
Yet I think on them in the silent night,
Still breaks that morn, though dim, to Memory's
    eye,
And the firm soul does the pale train defy
Of grim Disease, that would her peace affright.
Please God, I'll wrap me in mine innocence,
And bid each awful Muse drive the damned harpies
    hence.

Cambridge, 1827.

Be of good cheer, brave spirit; steadfastly
Serve that low whisper thou hast served; for know,
God hath a select family of sons
Now scattered wide thro' earth, and each alone,
Who are thy spiritual kindred, and each one
By constant service to that inward law,
Is weaving the sublime proportions
Of a true monarch's soul.   Beauty and strength,

The riches of a spotless memory,
The eloquence of truth, the wisdom got
By searching of a clear and loving eye
That seeth as God seeth. These are their gifts,
And Time, who keeps God's word, brings on the
      day
To seal the marriage of these minds with thine,
Thine everlasting lovers. Ye shall be
The salt of all the elements, world of the world.

TO-DAY

I RAKE no coffined clay, nor publish wide
The resurrection of departed pride.
Safe in their ancient crannies, dark and deep,
Let kings and conquerors, saints and soldiers sleep —
Late in the world, — too late perchance for fame,
Just late enough to reap abundant blame, —
I choose a novel theme, a bold abuse
Of critic charters, an unlaurelled Muse.

Old mouldy men and books and names and lands
Disgust my reason and defile my hands.
I had as lief respect an ancient shoe,
As love old things *for age*, and hate the new.
I spurn the Past, my mind disdains its nod,
Nor kneels in homage to so mean a God.

I laugh at those who, while they gape and gaze,
The bald antiquity of China praise.
Youth is (whatever cynic tubs pretend)
The fault that boys and nations soonest mend.

1824.

FAME

Ah Fate, cannot a man
    Be wise without a beard?
East, West, from Beer to Dan,
    Say, was it never heard
That wisdom might in youth be gotten,
Or wit be ripe before 't was rotten?

He pays too high a price
    For knowledge and for fame
Who sells his sinews to be wise,
    His teeth and bones to buy a name,
And crawls through life a paralytic
To earn the praise of bard and critic.

Were it not better done,
    To dine and sleep through forty years;
Be loved by few; be feared by none;
    Laugh life away; have wine for tears;
And take the mortal leap undaunted,
Content that all we asked was granted?

But Fate will not permit
    The seed of gods to die,
Nor suffer sense to win from wit
    Its guerdon in the sky,
Nor let us hide, whate'er our pleasure,
The world's light underneath a measure.

Go then, sad youth, and shine;
    Go, sacrifice to Fame;
Put youth, joy, health upon the shrine,
    And life to fan the flame;
Being for Seeming bravely barter
And die to Fame a happy martyr.
    1824.

THE SUMMONS

A STERNER errand to the silken troop
Has quenched the uneasy blush that warmed my cheek;
I am commissioned in my day of joy
To leave my woods and streams and the sweet sloth
Of prayer and song that were my dear delight,
To leave the rudeness of my woodland life,
Sweet twilight walks and midnight solitude
And kind acquaintance with the morning stars
And the glad hey-day of my household hours,
The innocent mirth which sweetens daily bread,
Railing in love to those who rail again,

By mind's industry sharpening the love of life —
Books, Muses, Study, fireside, friends and love,
I loved ye with true love, so fare ye well!

I was a boy; boyhood slid gayly by
And the impatient years that trod on it
Taught me new lessons in the lore of life.
I 've learned the sum of that sad history
All woman-born do know, that hoped-for days,
Days that come dancing on fraught with delights,
Dash our blown hopes as they limp heavily by.
But I, the bantling of a country Muse,
Abandon all those toys with speed to obey
The King whose meek ambassador I go.
1826.

THE RIVER

AND I behold once more
My old familiar haunts; here the blue river,
The same blue wonder that my infant eye
Admired, sage doubting whence the traveller came, —
Whence brought his sunny bubbles ere he washed
The fragrant flag-roots in my father's fields,
And where thereafter in the world he went.
Look, here he is, unaltered, save that now
He hath broke his banks and flooded all the vales

IX

With his redundant waves.
Here is the rock where, yet a simple child,
I caught with bended pin my earliest fish,
Much triumphing, — and these the fields
Over whose flowers I chased the butterfly,
A blooming hunter of a fairy fine.
And hark! where overhead the ancient crows
Hold their sour conversation in the sky : —
These are the same, but I am not the same,
But wiser than I was, and wise enough
Not to regret the changes, tho' they cost
Me many a sigh. Oh, call not Nature dumb;
These trees and stones are audible to me,
These idle flowers, that tremble in the wind,
I understand their faery syllables,
And all their sad significance. The wind,
That rustles down the well-known forest road —
It hath a sound more eloquent than speech.
The stream, the trees, the grass, the sighing wind,
All of them utter sounds of 'monishment
And grave parental love.
They are not of our race, they seem to say,
And yet have knowledge of our moral race,
And somewhat of majestic sympathy,
Something of pity for the puny clay,
That holds and boasts the immeasurable mind.
I feel as I were welcome to these trees
After long months of weary wandering,
Acknowledged by their hospitable boughs;

They know me as their son, for side by side,
They were coeval with my ancestors,
Adorned with them my country's primitive times,
And soon may give my dust their funeral shade.

CONCORD, June, 1827.

GOOD HOPE

THE cup of life is not so shallow
That we have drained the best,
That all the wine at once we swallow
And lees make all the rest.

Maids of as soft a bloom shall marry
As Hymen yet hath blessed,
And fairer forms are in the quarry
Than Phidias released.

1827.

LINES TO ELLEN

TELL me, maiden, dost thou use
Thyself thro' Nature to diffuse?
All the angles of the coast
Were tenanted by thy sweet ghost,

Bore thy colors every flower,
Thine each leaf and berry bore;
All wore thy badges and thy favors
In their scent or in their savors,
Every moth with painted wing,
Every bird in carolling,
The wood-boughs with thy manners waved,
The rocks uphold thy name engraved,
The sod throbbed friendly to my feet,
And the sweet air with thee was sweet.
The saffron cloud that floated warm
Studied thy motion, took thy form,
And in his airy road benign
Recalled thy skill in bold design,
Or seemed to use his privilege
To gaze o'er the horizon's edge,
To search where now thy beauty glowed,
Or made what other purlieus proud.

1829.

SECURITY

THOUGH her eye seek other forms
And a glad delight below,
Yet the love the world that warms
Bids for me her bosom glow.

She must love me till she find
Another heart as large and true.
Her soul is frank as the ocean wind,
And the world has only two.

If Nature hold another heart
That knows a purer flame than me,
I too therein could challenge part
And learn of love a new degree.
1829.

A DULL uncertain brain,
But gifted yet to know
That God has cherubim who go
Singing an immortal strain,
Immortal here below.
I know the mighty bards,
I listen when they sing,
And now I know
The secret store
Which these explore
When they with torch of genius pierce
The tenfold clouds that cover
The riches of the universe
From God's adoring lover.

And if to me it is not given
To fetch one ingot thence
Of the unfading gold of Heaven
His merchants may dispense,
Yet well I know the royal mine,
And know the sparkle of its ore,
Know Heaven's truth from lies that shine—
Explored they teach us to explore.

1831.

A MOUNTAIN GRAVE

WHY fear to die
And let thy body lie
Under the flowers of June,
  Thy body food
  For the ground-worms' brood
And thy grave smiled on by the visiting moon.

Amid great Nature's halls
Girt in by mountain walls
And washed with waterfalls
It would please me to die,
  Where every wind that swept my tomb
  Goes loaded with a free perfume
Dealt out with a God's charity.

I should like to die in sweets,
A hill's leaves for winding-sheets,
And the searching sun to see
That I am laid with decency.
And the commissioned wind to sing
His mighty psalm from fall to spring
And annual tunes commemorate
Of Nature's child the common fate.

WILLIAMSTOWN, VERMONT,
   1 June, 1831.

A LETTER

DEAR brother, would you know the life,
Please God, that I would lead?
On the first wheels that quit this weary town
Over yon western bridges I would ride
And with a cheerful benison forsake
Each street and spire and roof, incontinent.
Then would I seek where God might guide my steps,
Deep in a woodland tract, a sunny farm,
Amid the mountain counties, Hants, Franklin, Berks,
Where down the rock ravine a river roars,
Even from a brook, and where old woods
Not tamed and cleared cumber the ground
With their centennial wrecks.
Find me a slope where I can feel the sun

And mark the rising of the early stars.
There will I bring my books, — my household gods,
The reliquaries of my dead saint, and dwell
In the sweet odor of her memory.
Then in the uncouth solitude unlock
My stock of art, plant dials in the grass,
Hang in the air a bright thermometer
And aim a telescope at the inviolate sun.

CHARDON ST., BOSTON, 1831.

DAY by day returns
The everlasting sun,
Replenishing material urns
With God's unspared donation ;
But the day of day,
The orb within the mind,
Creating fair and good alway,
Shines not as once it shined.

. . . . . .

Vast the realm of Being is,
In the waste one nook is his ;
Whatsoever hap befalls
In his vision's narrow walls
He is here to testify.

1831.

HYMN

THERE is in all the sons of men
A love that in the spirit dwells,
That panteth after things unseen,
And tidings of the future tells.

And God hath built his altar here
To keep this fire of faith alive,
And sent his priests in holy fear
To speak the truth — for truth to strive.

And hither come the pensive train
Of rich and poor, of young and old,
Of ardent youth untouched by pain,
Of thoughtful maids and manhood bold.

They seek a friend to speak the word
Already trembling on their tongue,
To touch with prophet's hand the chord
Which God in human hearts hath strung.

To speak the plain reproof of sin
That sounded in the soul before,
And bid you let the angels in
That knock at meek contrition's door.

A friend to lift the curtain up
That hides from man the mortal goal,
And with glad thoughts of faith and hope
Surprise the exulting soul.

Sole source of light and hope assured,
O touch thy servant's lips with power,
So shall he speak to us the word
Thyself dost give forever more.

June, 1831.

SELF–RELIANCE

HENCEFORTH, please God, forever I forego
The yoke of men's opinions.   I will be
Light-hearted as a bird, and live with God.
I find him in the bottom of my heart,
I hear continually his voice therein.

.   .   .   .

The little needle always knows the North,
The little bird remembereth his note,
And this wise Seer within me never errs.
I never taught it what it teaches me;
I only follow, when I act aright.

October 9, 1832.

AND when I am entombèd in my place,
Be it remembered of a single man,
He never, though he dearly loved his race,
For fear of human eyes swerved from his plan.

OH what is Heaven but the fellowship
Of minds that each can stand against the world
By its own meek and incorruptible will?

THE days pass over me
And I am still the same;
The aroma of my life is gone
With the flower with which it came.

1833.

WRITTEN IN NAPLES

WE are what we are made; each following day
Is the Creator of our human mould
Not less than was the first; the all-wise God
Gilds a few points in every several life,
And as each flower upon the fresh hillside,
And every colored petal of each flower,
Is sketched and dyed, each with a new design,
Its spot of purple, and its streak of brown,
So each man's life shall have its proper lights,

And a few joys, a few peculiar charms,
For him round-in the melancholy hours
And reconcile him to the common days.
Not many men see beauty in the fogs
Of close low pine-woods in a river town ;
Yet unto me not morn's magnificence,
Nor the red rainbow of a summer eve,
Nor Rome, nor joyful Paris, nor the halls
Of rich men blazing hospitable light,
Nor wit, nor eloquence, — no, nor even the song
Of any woman that is now alive, —
Hath such a soul, such divine influence,
Such resurrection of the happy past,
As is to me when I behold the morn
Ope in such low moist roadside, and beneath
Peep the blue violets out of the black loam,
Pathetic silent poets that sing to me
Thine elegy, sweet singer, sainted wife.

March, 1833.

WRITTEN AT ROME

ALONE in Rome. Why, Rome is lonely too ; —
Besides, you need not be alone ; the soul
Shall have society of its own rank.
Be great, be true, and all the Scipios,
The Catos, the wise patriots of Rome,

Shall flock to you and tarry by your side,
And comfort you with their high company.
Virtue alone is sweet society,
It keeps the key to all heroic hearts,
And opens you a welcome in them all.
You must be like them if you desire them,
Scorn trifles and embrace a better aim
Than wine or sleep or praise;
Hunt knowledge as the lover wooes a maid,
And ever in the strife of your own thoughts
Obey the nobler impulse; that is Rome:
That shall command a senate to your side;
For there is no might in the universe
That can contend with love. It reigns forever.
Wait then, sad friend, wait in majestic peace
The hour of heaven. Generously trust
Thy fortune's web to the beneficent hand
That until now has put his world in fee
To thee. He watches for thee still. His love
Broods over thee, and as God lives in heaven,
However long thou walkest solitary,
The hour of heaven shall come, the man appear.

1833.

WEBSTER

1831

LET Webster's lofty face
Ever on thousands shine,
A beacon set that Freedom's race
Might gather omens from that radiant sign.

FROM THE PHI BETA KAPPA POEM

1834

ILL fits the abstemious Muse a crown to weave
For living brows; ill fits them to receive:
And yet, if virtue abrogate the law,
One portrait — fact or fancy — we may draw;
A form which Nature cast in the heroic mould
Of them who rescued liberty of old;
He, when the rising storm of party roared,
Brought his great forehead to the council board,
There, while hot heads perplexed with fears the state,
Calm as the morn the manly patriot sate;
Seemed, when at last his clarion accents broke,
As if the conscience of the country spoke.

Not on its base Monadnoc surer stood,
Than he to common sense and common good:
No mimic; from his breast his counsel drew,
Believed the eloquent was aye the true;
He bridged the gulf from th' alway good and wise
To that within the vision of small eyes.
Self-centred; when he launched the genuine word
It shook or captivated all who heard,
Ran from his mouth to mountains and the sea,
And burned in noble hearts proverb and prophecy.

1854

WHY did all manly gifts in Webster fail?
He wrote on Nature's grandest brow, *For Sale.*

NOTES

NOTES

GOOD-BYE. *Page 3.* Not without serious consideration has the editor removed the poem, which his father put at the beginning of his first volume of verse, to a later place. But he has always shared the feeling of regret that Dr. Holmes expressed in his book, that "Emerson saw fit to imitate the Egyptians by placing the Sphinx at the entrance of his temple of song." In the mythology the Sphinx let no man pass who could not solve her riddle; and Emerson's Sphinx has no doubt cut off, in the very portal, readers who would have found good and joyful words for themselves, had not her riddle been beyond their powers.

There is some reason, from a list in the manuscript book in which are found most of the early poems, to think that the author once planned to put "Good-bye" first. It is the earliest of the poems published by him.

Mr. Emerson sent these verses in February, 1839, to his friend Rev. James Freeman Clarke, at his request, to print in *The Western Messenger.* Mr. Clarke then lived in Louisville, Kentucky. Mr. Emerson wrote: "They were written sixteen years ago, when I kept school in Boston, and lived in a corner of Roxbury called Canterbury. They have a slight misanthropy, a shade deeper than belongs to me; and as it seems nowadays I am a philosopher and am grown to have opinions, I think they must have an apologetic date, though I well know that poetry that needs a date is no poetry, and so you will wiselier suppress them. I heartily wish I had any verses which with a clear mind I could send you in lieu of these juvenilities. It is strange, seeing the delight we take in verses, that we can so seldom write them, and so are not ashamed to lay up old ones, say sixteen years, instead of improvising them as freely as the wind blows, whenever we and our brothers are attuned to music. I have heard of a citizen who made an annual joke. I believe I have in April or May an annual poetic *conatus* rather than *afflatus*, experimenting to the length of thirty lines or so, if I may judge from the dates of the rhythmical scraps I detect among my MSS. I look upon this incontinence as merely the redundancy of a susceptibility to poetry which makes all the bards my daily treasures, and I can well run the risk of being ridiculous once a year for the benefit of happy reading all the other days."

Mr. Emerson did not include "Good-bye" in the *Selected Poems*, published in 1876, but it has won its way with readers, and while this boyish utterance does not refer to his retirement to the country twelve years later, to study God in Nature, it seems a prophecy, though written in a different mood. The shy youth of nineteen, assistant in his brother William's school for young ladies in Boston, when the day's lessons were over thankfully fled to the beautiful wilderness in Roxbury (now the "Schoolmaster's Field" in Franklin Park), for his mother established the home in that region for a time.

EACH AND ALL. *Page 4.* The germ of this poem, perhaps, is found in this entry in Mr. Emerson's journal: —

"May 16th, 1834. I remember when I was a boy going upon the beach and being charmed with the colors and forms of the shells. I picked up many and put them in my pocket. When I got home I could find nothing that I gathered — nothing but some dry, ugly mussel and snail shells. Thence I learned that Composition was more important than the beauty of individual forms to Effect. On the shore they lay wet and social, by the sea and under the sky."

This passage he introduced into a lecture called "The Naturalist" given in that month before the Boston Natural History Society. The poem, like "Good-bye," was published in *The Western Messenger* in 1839.

Page 4, note 1. Journal, 1844. "Buonaparte was sensible to the music of bells. Hearing the bell of a parish church, he would pause, and his voice faltered as he said, 'Ah! that reminds me of the first years I spent at Brienne; I was then happy.'"

Page 5, note 1. Mr. Emerson said, "I think sometimes that my lack of musical ear is made good to me through my eyes: that which others hear I see."

THE PROBLEM. *Page 6.* This poem, one of the few that bear a date, — 10 November, 1839, — is better known and more often quoted than any other which Mr. Emerson wrote. It is also remarkable in this, that it would almost seem, like Athene, to have sprung matured and perfect from its author's brain. No fragments, no trials remain; much fewer verbal changes than is usual appear in the manuscript book of poetry, and not one since the poem saw light in the first number of the *Dial* in July, 1840. Mr. Emerson at first called it "The Priest." Here is the thought as recorded in the journal: —

"AUGUST 28, 1838.

"It is very grateful to my feelings to go into a Roman Cathedral, yet I look as my countrymen do at the Roman priesthood. It is very grateful to me to go into an English Church and hear the liturgy read, yet nothing would induce me to be the English priest.

"I find an unpleasant dilemma in this, nearer home. I dislike to be a clergyman and refuse to be one. Yet how rich a music would be to me a holy clergyman in my town. It seems to me he cannot be a man, quite and whole; yet how plain is the need of one, and how high, yes, highest is the function. Here is division of labor that I like not: a man must sacrifice his manhood for the social good. Something is wrong; I see not what.''

Page 6, note 1. The same thought occurs in the essay on Compensation (*Essays, First Series,* p. 108), and this poem is another chapter on the Over-Soul.

Page 7, note 1. Journal, Florence, 1833. ''It is in the soul that architecture exists, and Santa Croce and the Duomo are poor, far-behind imitations.''

In the essays on Art (*Essays, First Series,* and *Society and Solitude*) the inspiration, in its fullest sense, of the best works of man in Art and Architecture is taught.

Page 8, note 1. The gentle, serious and humane priest John of Antioch (347–407) was raised to the bishopric of Constantinople. Because of his Homilies (said to be the best in Christian literature) the name Chrysostom (Golden Mouth) was given him by the Ecumenical Council two hundred years after his death.

In sending to a friend the *Confessions of Saint Augustine,* ''translated two hundred years ago, in the golden time when all translations seemed to have the fire of original works,'' Mr. Emerson said, ''I push this little antiquity toward you merely out of gratitude to some golden words I read in it last summer.''

Of Taylor (1613–1667), the author of *Holy Living and Holy Dying,* Mr. Emerson said in an early journal: —

'' 'T is pity Jeremy Taylor could not always remember 'rien n'est beau que le vrai.' I have been reading the ' Contemplations of the State of Man.' An immense progress in natural and religious knowledge has been made since his death. Even his genius cannot quicken all that stark nonsense about the blessed and the damned. Yet in the 'Life of Christ' I have thought him a Christian Plato; so rich and great was his philosophy. Is it possible the intellect should be so inconsistent with itself? It is singular also that the bishop's morality should sometimes trip, as in his explanation of false witness."

To Rhea. *Page 9.* This poem, probably written in 1843, appeared in the *Dial* in July of that year. It is not to be regarded as personal, but general, — even then as an aspect, from the cold heights of pure intellect, the same that is presented in connection with the discussion of Swedenborg's *Conjugal Love*, in *Representative Men*. But Mr. Emerson recognized the danger of individual detachment. The supremacy of the human, the moral element is recognized in all his thought. Even in the fragmentary essay on the Natural History of Intellect, in the volume thus entitled, he warns of the dangers of pure intellect and gives the other aspect: "Affection blends, intellect disjoins;" and elsewhere he gives this counsel, "The Heart knoweth."

The Visit. *Page 12.* These verses were published in the *Dial* in April, 1844. Great as was Mr. Emerson's hospitality, it was so often overtaxed that he felt that a word of general counsel was due on the subject of visits. For a call he used to say that fifteen minutes was the limit, except in very unusual circumstances.

Journal, 1842. " ' My evening visitors,' said that excellent Professor Fortinbras, ' if they cannot see the clock, should find the time in my face. As soon as it is nine, I begin to curse them with internal execrations that are minute-guns. And yet,' he added, 'the devil take half hospitalities, this self-protecting civility whose invitations to dinner are determined exclusions from the heart of the inviter, as if he said, "I invite you to eat because I will not converse with you." If he dared only say it, that exclusion would be hospitality of angels, an admission to the thought of his heart.' "

URIEL. *Page 13.* From its strange presentation in a celestial parable of the story of a crisis in its author's life, this poem demands especial comment. In his essay on Circles, which sheds light upon it, Emerson said, " Beware when the great God lets loose a thinker on this planet." His letters and journals, even while he was a clergyman, show his belief that religion owed to Copernicus a great emancipation. In a later essay he speaks of the great astronomer's destroying the " pagan fictions of the Church by showing mankind that the earth on which we live was not the centre of the Universe, . . . and thus fitted to be the platform on which the Drama of the Divine Judgment was played before the assembled Angels of Heaven, . . . but a little scrap of a planet, rushing round the sun in our system, which in turn was too minute to be seen at the distance of many stars which we behold." [1] The lapses and perturbations of the planets, as seen from the eccentric earth, which troubled the astrologers under the Ptolemaic system, gave way to the beautiful ordered dance of the heavenly bodies, including the comets, around the sun. From boyhood Emerson was familiar with *Paradise Lost*, and Uriel, the bright Archangel of the Sun, would best see the vast orbits, the returns and compensations, the harmony and utter order of the Universe,

---

[1] " Historical Notes of Life and Letters in New England," *Lectures and Biographical Sketches.*

— God in all. This did away with Original Sin, a separate
principle of Evil, hopeless Condemnation, Mediation, — for
Emerson saw in Nature a symbol. The Law was alike in
matter and spirit. He had shaken off dogma and tradition and
found that the Word

> Still floats upon the morning wind,
> Still whispers to the willing mind.

The earnest young men on the eve of entering the ministry asked him to speak to them. After serious thought he
went to Cambridge (July 15, 1838) to give them the good and
emancipating words which had been given to him in solitude,
well aware, however, that he must shock or pain the older clergy
who were present. The poem, when read with the history of
the Divinity School Address, and its consequences, in mind, is
seen to be an account of that event generalized and sublimed,
— the announcement of an advance in truth, won not without pain and struggle, to hearers not yet ready, resulting in
banishment to the prophet ; yet the spoken word sticks like a
barbed arrow, or works like a leaven.

Page 14, note 1. While the " young deities " (divines)
discuss the Universe, Identity, Illumination, Being and Seeming, one startles them with the doctrine, doing away with
arbitrary bound, of Eternal Return, involving Good out of Evil.
They only see the Circle, not the Spiral which is Advance
combined with Return, adding the element of Progress. They
only see in it Revolution, not Evolution. Perhaps Uriel is not
yet quite clear. In Mr. Henry Walker's fine painting of Emerson's Uriel in the Congressional Library at Washington, clouds
of doubt still hang on the Archangel's brow.

Plotinus said, " The Intellect sees because it is turned back
to its origin, the One; its movement is circular." Professor
Andrews Norton, representing " the stern old war gods,"

said of the Address, "Theories which would overturn society and resolve the world into chaos." Rev. Henry Ware, honored and loved by Mr. Emerson, who had been associated with him as junior pastor, was one of the frowning seraphs, for he could not quite follow his young friend in his new departure. Another honored friend of Mr. Emerson, the Rev. Nathaniel L. Frothingham, soon after, in a sermon to which the Address gave rise, used as a text, "Some said it thundered, others that an angel spake."

Page 14, note 2. The Pythagorean doctrine of transmigration of the soul. "Every partial soul must make periods of ascent from and descent into generation, and this forever and ever." (Proclus.) The next two lines suggest a sentence of Plutarch in the *Morals* : "The Sun is the cause why all men are ignorant of Apollo, by sense withdrawing the rational intellect from that which is to that which appears."

Page 15, note 1. Dr. William T. Harris, in the *Memoir of Bronson Alcott*, apropos of this poem, quotes Plotinus thus : —

"There are two kinds of souls that descend into the world of matter, the higher order, like so many kings, associated with the governor of all things, become his colleagues in the general administration of the world. They descend for the sake of causing the perfection of the universe. The second class of souls descend because they are condemned to suffer punishment." — IV. Ennead, book VIII., chapters 4, 5.

THE WORLD-SOUL. *Page 15.* This poem presents with the freshness of a June morning in New England a doctrine from the ancient East. I quote from Mr. George Willis Cooke's excellent Life of Emerson [1] the following passage : —

[1] *Ralph Waldo Emerson, his Life, Writings, and Philosophy.* Boston : James R. Osgood & Co., 1881.

"Around Plotinus . . . there grew up a distinct school of thought, teaching the philosophic doctrine of the identity of subject and object, mind and matter, and making intuition the method of knowing. One of his disciples was Porphyry, who distinctly taught that matter emanates from . . . the soul. Amelius departed so far from Plotinus as to teach the unity of all souls in the World-Soul, a favorite doctrine of Emerson's."

Page 15, note 2. "But why should you keep your head over your shoulder? . . . It seems to be a rule of wisdom never to rely on your memory alone, but to bring the past for judgment into the thousand-eyed present, and live ever in a new day. . . . A foolish consistency is the hobgoblin of little minds." — "Self-Reliance."

Page 16, note 1. This suggests his words on the effect on the fancy of a horn blown among echoing mountains, "Can a musical note be so lofty, so haughtily beautiful?" — "Nature," *Essays, Second Series.*

Page 17, note 1. In the first few pages of the essay ("ature") quoted in the note above, are passages on the of "these delicately emerging stars, with their private an effable glances, . . . eloquent of secret promises."

Page 17, note 2. Journal, 1851. "There is something — our brothers over the sea do not know it or own it — . . . which is setting them all aside, and the whole world also, and anting itself forever and ever."

Page 18, note 1. September 15, 1842. "I suppose there are secret bands that tie each man to his mark with a mighty force; first, of course, his Dæmon, a beautiful immortal figure, whom the ancients said, though never visible to himself, sometimes to appear shining before him to others." — From *Letters of Emerson to a Friend.*

THE SPHINX. *Page 20.* This poem was published in the

of January, 1841. The only important change it has
gone was the substitution by Mr. Emerson, when he
shed his *Poems*, of two more pleasing lines for grotesque
ones in its first form. The fable is used as an illustration in
Nature, Addresses and Lectures (p. 34) and in " History,"
in *Essays, First Series.*

Mr. Emerson wrote in his note-book in 1859: " I have
often been asked the meaning of the ' Sphinx.' It is this, —
The perception of identity unites all things and explains one
by another, and the most rare and strange is equally facile as
the most common. But if the mind live only in particulars,
and see only differences (wanting the power to see the whole —
all in each), then the world addresses to this mind a question it
cannot answer, and each new fact tears it in pieces, and it is
vanquished by the distracting variety."

Journal, September 3, 1838. " The Egyptian Sphinxes are
observed to have all a countenance expressive of complacency
and tranquillity: an expression of health. There is much history in that fact."

Page 22, note 1. " Let a man then know his worth, and
keep things under his feet. Let him not peep or steal, or
skulk up and down with the air of a charity-boy, a bastard,
or an interloper in the world which exists for him. . . .
Man is timid and apologetic; he is no longer upright; he dares
not say ' I think,' ' I am,' but quotes some saint or sage.
He is ashamed before the blade of grass or the blowing rose."
— " Self-Reliance," *Essays, First Series.*

Page 22, note 2. " Has turned the man-child's head." —
Dial.

Page 24, note 1. " Every man's condition is a solution
in hieroglyphic to those inquiries he would put." — *Nature,
Addresses and Lectures,* p. 4.

Page 25, note 1.

> I am the doubter and the doubt.
>
>   " Brahma."

In the latter part of " Nominalist and Realist," in *Essays, Second Series,* this thought is more fully expressed.

ALPHONSO OF CASTILE. *Page 25.* This poem was written in the summer of 1847.

Alfonso X. of Castile (1252–84), surnamed the Wise, was a monarch of extraordinary gifts and beneficent activity. I quote the following estimate of him from the *History of Spain,* by Ulick Ralph Burke, M. A.: " If his Royal Highness the present heir apparent to the crown of England were a senior wrangler and a double first-class man at our English universities, if he were called upon to fill the place of astronomer royal of England, . . . if he had written a more brilliant history than Macaulay, and a finer poem than Tennyson, if he were fit to teach Wagner music and Cayley mathematics, and if in the intervals of his studies he had found time to codify the entire laws of England into a digest which might endure for six hundred years to come — then and only then could the practical preëminence of his intellectual attainments in modern England represent the practical preëminence of the *sabidura* of Alfonso X. in mediæval Spain."

Alfonso is reported (some say maliciously) to have said, " Had God consulted me in the making of the world, he would have made it differently." Mr. Emerson alludes to King Alfonso in " Nominalist and Realist," in *Essays, Second Series,* p. 238.

Page 26, note 1. " The cosmical debility " in some of the MS. verses.

Page 26, note 2. "To weltering Chaos and old Sleep." — MS.

MITHRIDATES. *Page 28.* Mithridates Eupator, king of Pontus, who gave the Romans so much trouble by his wiles in the first century B.C., was a man of extraordinary and varied learning. Familiar with the lore of other nations, a botanist and skilled in physic, he studied antidotes, and is reputed to have fed on poisons until he rendered himself immune from their noxious effects. Thus his name stands here as symbolic of the wise man who can find virtue in all things and escape the harm.

The poem was written in 1846.

Page 29, note 1. In the first edition the poem ended with these lines: —

> God ! I will not be an owl,
> But sun me in the Capitol.

TO J. W. *Page 29.* The person addressed was Rev. John Weiss, a young clergyman and an able writer, who had seemed to Mr. Emerson to dwell overmuch on Goethe's failings.

DESTINY. *Page 31.* This poem, under the name of "Fate," appeared in the *Dial*, in October, 1841.

Page 32, note 1. Dr. Holmes, in his chapter on Emerson's Poems, says of the passage beginning —

> Alas ! that one is born in blight, —

"If in the flights of his imagination he is like the strong-winged bird of passage, in his exquisite choice of descriptive epithets he reminds me of the *tenui-rostrals*. His subtle selective instinct penetrates the vocabulary for the one word he wants, as the long slender bill of those birds dives deep into the flower for its drop of honey. Here is a passage showing admirably the two different conditions: wings closed and the selective instinct picking out its descriptive expressions; then suddenly wings flashing open and the imagination in the firmament, where it is always at home. Follow the pitiful inventory of insignificances of the forlorn being he describes with a pathetic humor more likely to bring a sigh than a smile, and then mark the grand hyperbole of the last two lines."

Page 32, note 2. "The astronomers are very eager to know whether the moon has an atmosphere: I am only concerned that every man have one." — "Aristocracy," *Lectures and Biographical Sketches.*

Page 32, note 3. In Mr. Emerson's essays or poems a higher note is almost always struck at the end, and here in the last two lines is a good word reserved, if he can but find it, for the "victim of perpetual slight."

GUY. *Page 33.* The balanced soul in harmony with Nature is here described. In one of the earlier verse-books, on the same page with an imperfect form of the six lines beginning "Fearless Guy had never foes," are the following lines, apparently destined for this poem: —

> Fine presentiments controlled him,
> As one who knew a day was great
> And freighted with a friendly fate,
> Ere whispered news or courier told him.
> When first at morn he read the face
> Of Nature from his rising place,
> The coming day inspired his speech,
> And in his bearing and his gait
> Calm expectancy did wait.

Page 33, note 1. The story of Polycrates, tyrant of Samos, is told by Herodotus. Fortune so constantly smiled on him that Amasis, king of Egypt, bade his friend make some great sacrifice to avert the disaster that must come to balance unbroken prosperity. Polycrates flung his wonderful emerald into the sea. It returned to him in a fish on his table next day. Amasis at once broke off his alliance, and soon overthrow and cruel death befel Polycrates.

HAMATREYA. *Page 35.* This poem is a free rendering of a passage in the *Vishnu Purana,* book IV., an everlasting theme which, by changing the imagery to that which surrounded them, Mr. Emerson made striking to his Concord neighbors. The title Hamatreya is evidently some other version of Maitreya, which occurs in this passage copied from the journal of 1845: —

"I have now given you a summary account of the sovereigns of the earth. — These and other kings who with perishable frames have possessed this ever-during world, and who, blinded with deceptive notions of individual occupation, have indulged the feeling that suggests 'This earth is mine, — it is my son's, — it belongs to my dynasty,' — have all passed away. So, many who reigned before them, many who succeeded them, and many who are yet to come, have ceased or will cease to be. Earth laughs, as if smiling with autumnal flowers to behold her kings unable to effect the subjugation of themselves. I will repeat to you, Maitreya, the stanzas that were chanted by Earth, and which the Muni Asita communicated to Janaka, whose banner was virtue.

"'How great is the folly of princes who are endowed with the faculty of reason, to cherish the confidence of ambition when they themselves are but foam upon the wave. Before

they have subdued themselves, they seek to reduce their ministers, their servants, their subjects, under their authority; they
then endeavor to overcome their foes. "Thus," say they,
"will we conquer the ocean-circled Earth;" and intent upon
their project, behold not death, which is not far off. But what
mighty matter is the subjugation of the sea-girt Earth, to one
who can subdue himself? Emancipation from existence is the
fruit of self-control. It is through infatuation that kings desire
to possess me, whom their predecessors have been forced to
leave, whom their fathers have not retained. Beguiled by the
selfish love of sway, fathers contend with their sons, and
brothers with brothers, for my possession. Foolishness has
been the character of every king who has boasted, "All this
earth is mine — everything is mine — it will be in my house
forever;" — for he is dead. How is it possible that such vain
desires should survive in the hearts of his descendants, who
have seen their progenitor, absorbed by the thirst of dominion,
compelled to relinquish me whom he called his own, and
tread the path of dissolution? When I hear a king sending
word to another by his ambassador, "This earth is mine; resign
your pretensions to it," — I am at first moved to violent laughter; but it soon subsides in pity for the infatuated fool.'

"These were the verses, Maitreya, which Earth recited
and by listening to which ambition fades away like snow
before the sun."

Page 35, note 1. Peter Bulkeley, a minister of Odell in
Bedfordshire, a man of learning, piety and substance, was
silenced by Archbishop Laud for non-conformity, and with
many of his flock moved to New England. In company with
Simon Willard, of Kent, a man of experience in trade and in
military affairs, he made the first inland settlement on land
purchased of the Indians, and called it Concord. One of Mr.

IX

Emerson's ancestors married his daughter. The other names in the first line are those of some of the first settlers.

THE RHODORA. *Page 37.* "The Rhodora" was written in 1834 at Newton, where Mr. Emerson was visiting his uncle, Mr. Ladd. Rev. James Freeman Clarke obtained it for publication in his *Western Messenger* in 1839.

Page 38, note 1. "This element [Beauty] I call an ultimate end. No reason can be asked or given why the soul seeks beauty. Beauty, in its largest and profoundest sense, is one expression for the universe." — *Nature, Addresses and Lectures,* p. 24.

THE HUMBLE-BEE. *Page 38.* This entry occurs in Mr. Emerson's journal for 1837: "May 9. Yesterday in the woods I followed the fine humble-bee with rhymes and fancies fine." On the next page he wrote, "The humble-bee and pine-warbler seem to me the proper objects of attention in these disastrous times."

Page 40, note 1. M. René de Poyen Belleisle, in a lecture called *A French View of Emerson,* given before the School of Philosophy in Concord in the summer of 1888, made use of an image drawn from honey-making (which Mr. Emerson borrowed from Montaigne in "Poetry and Imagination," *Letters and Social Aims,* p. 16) to illustrate his method in philosophy: "Comment Emerson se sert-il de ses idées; ou, en autres termes, quelle est sa méthode ? Je prononce là un mot qui sonne étrangement quand on parle d'Emerson. . . . La méthode d'Emerson est toute poétique. Il y a une phrase de Montaigne, que du reste Emerson s'est appropriée, et qui exprime admirablement ce que j'ai dans la pensée. 'Les abeilles,' dit Montaigne, 'qui pillottent de ci, de là, font le miel qui est tout leur; ce n'est plus ni thym ni marjolaine.' Le poëte est cette abeille: tout dans l'homme et dans la Nature l'attire et le miel qu'il en destille est sa pensée.''

BERRYING. *Page 41*. Although Mr. Emerson did not give these verses a place among the *Selected Poems*, they are kept here as giving a pleasant picture of him strolling through the remote pastures on an August afternoon.

Page 41, note 1. In some manuscript copies, the last line has "to our berries went," in others "from," which seems to have been preferred.

THE SNOW-STORM. *Page 41*. "The Snow-Storm" first appeared in the *Dial* for January, 1841.

Journal, November 27, 1832: "Instead of lectures on Architecture, I will make a lecture on God's architecture, one of his beautiful works, a Day. I will draw a sketch of a winter's day. I will trace as I can a rude outline of the far-assembled influences, the contribution of the universe wherein this magical structure rises like an exhalation, the wonder and charm of the immeasurable deep.''

WOODNOTES, I. *Page 43*. Mr. Emerson contributed the first part of the "Woodnotes," in October, 1840, to the second number of the *Dial*. He pruned it to its advantage in the *Poems*, but some of the omitted lines are given, as they may interest readers. It began thus: —

> For this present hard
> Is the fortune of the bard
> Born out of time;
> All his accomplishment

NOTES

From Nature's utmost treasure spent
Booteth not him.

_, _3, note 1. The passage which followed in the *Dial*
was fuller by several lines, with recurrence of the idea: —

With none has he to do,
And none seek him,
Nor men below,
Nor spirits dim.
Sure some god his eye enchants: —
What he knows nobody wants:
In the wood he travels glad
Without better fortune had,
Melancholy without bad.
Planter of celestial plants,
What he knows nobody wants;
What he knows he hides, not vaunts.

Page 44, note 1. Journal, 1835. "Trifles move us more
than laws. Why am I more curious to know the reason why
the star-form is so oft repeated in botany, or why the number
five is such a favorite with Nature, than to understand the
circulation of the sap and the formation of buds?"

Page 45, note 1. The passages about the forest seer fit
Thoreau so well that the general belief that Mr. Emerson
had him in mind may be accepted, but one member of the
family recalls his saying that a part of this picture was drawn
before he knew Thoreau's gifts and experiences.

Page 47, note 1. The opening pages of "Nature," in
Essays, Second Series, describe the "charmed days" and influences that the author found in the woods.

Page 47, note 2. Omitted lines, from the verse-book: —
Hid in adjoining bowers, the birds
Sang their old speech, older than words.

Woodnotes, II. *Page 48.* The second portion of this poem appeared first in the *Dial* for October, 1841.

The stately white pine of New England was Emerson's favorite tree; hence the graceful drawing by Mrs. Alice Stone which adorns the title-page of these volumes. This poem records the actual fact; nearly every day, summer or winter, when at home, he went to listen to its song. The pine grove by Walden, still standing, though injured by time and fire, was one of his most valued possessions. He questioned whether he should not name his book *Forest Essays,* for, he said, "I have scarce a day-dream on which the breath of the pines has not blown and their shadow waved." The great pine on the ridge over Sleepy Hollow was chosen by him as his monument. When a youth, in Newton, he had written, "Here sit Mother and I under the pine-trees, still almost as we shall lie by and by under them."

Page 49, note 1. Here followed, in the original form, these lines: —

> Ancient or curious,
> Who knoweth aught of us ?
> Old as Jove,
> Old as Love,
> Who of me
> Tells the pedigree ?
> Only the mountains old,
> Only the waters cold,
> Only moon and star
> My coævals are.
> Ere the first fowl sung
> My relenting boughs among;
> Ere Adam wived,
> Ere Adam lived,

NOTES

Ere the duck dived,
Ere the bees hived,
Ere the lion roared,
Ere the eagle soared,
Light and heat, land and sea
Spake unto the oldest tree.
Glad in the sweet and secret aid
Which matter unto matter paid,
The water flowed, the breezes fanned,
The tree confined the roving sand,
The sunbeam gave me to the sight,
The tree adorned the formless light;
And once again
O'er the grave of men
We shall talk to each other again
Of the old age behind,
Of the time out of mind,
Which shall come again.

Page 49, note 2. " The city would have died out, rotted and exploded, long ago, but that it was reinforced from the fields. It is only country which came to town day before yesterday that is city and court to-day." — " Manners," *Essays, Second Series.*

Page 50, note 1. " Those that live in solitary places are the saviours of themselves, so far as respects human causes." — Plotinus.

Page 52, note 1. Mr. Emerson's delight in the nebular hypothesis, and evolution, as far as it had then been surmised, appears again and again in his poems. Poetry and the philosophy of the ancient writers had prepared him for the latter belief, and the living Nature in his daily walks confirmed it.

Tyndall spoke of Emerson as " a profoundly religious man who is really and entirely undaunted by the discoveries of science, present, past or prospective; one by whom scientific conceptions are continually transmuted into the finer forms and warmer hues of an ideal world."

Page 52, note 2. The fable of Proteus, Heracleitus's doctrine of the Flowing, and the modern teaching of the correlation and conservation of force, Mr. Emerson saw as versions of Identity in Multiplicity. Among many places where he expresses this thought may be mentioned the first pages of " Circles," and in the *Poems* the end of " Threnody," the lines in the " Ode to Beauty," " Thee gliding through the sea of form," etc., and passages on " The Poet " in the Appendix.

Page 54, note 1. Compare " Merlin," II., celebrating the correspondences and rhymes in Nature.

Page 54, note 2. Journal, 1846. " ' As for beauty, I need not look beyond an oar's length for my fill of it.' I do not know whether he [William Ellery Channing] used the expression with design or no, but my eye rested on the charming play of light on the water which he was striking with his paddle. I fancied I had never seen such color, such transparency, such eddies; it was the hue of Rhine wines, it was jasper and verd-antique, topaz and chalcedony, it was gold and green and chestnut and hazel in bewitching succession and relief, without cloud or confusion." See also " Nature," in *Essays, Second Series*, pp. 172, 173.

Page 56, note 1. Journal, May, 1832. " What has the imagination created to compare with the science of Astronomy ? What is there in *Paradise Lost* to elevate and astonish like Herschell or Somerville ? The contrast between the magnitude and duration of the things, and the animalcule observer.

. . . I hope the time will come when there will be a telescope in every street.''

Page 59, note 1. "The man who shall be born, whose advent men and events prepare and foreshow, . . . shall not take counsel of flesh and blood, but shall rely on the Law alive and beautiful which works over our heads and under our feet." — "New England Reformers," *Essays, Second Series.*

MONADNOC. *Page 60.* In the verse-book of the period between 1833 and 1846 is the half-erased pencilling of an improvisation, the beginning of this poem, very likely written by Mr. Emerson as he sat above the forest waiting for sunrise on the great courses of dark rock, worn by the old glacier; for above the verses is written "1845, 3 May, 4 hours, 10 m., A. M." It is as follows, the introductory passage of the poem evidently having been written later: —

I stand
Upon this uplifted land
Hugely massed to draw the clouds,
Like a banner unrolled
To all the dwellers in the plains
Round about a hundred miles.
In his own loom's garment dressed,
By his own bounty blessed,
Thus constant giver,
Yielding many a cheerful river;
Appearing an aërial isle,
A cheerful and majestic pile,
Which morn and crimson eve shall paint
For bard, for lover and for saint;
The country's core,
Inspirer, prophet evermore;

That which God aloft had set
So that men might it not forget;
It should be their lives' ornament,
And mix itself with each event;
Their almanac and dial,
Painter's palette, sorcerer's phial,

. . . . . .

Mysteries of color duly laid
By the great painter, light and shade;
And sweet varieties of time
And chance
And the mystic seasons' dance;
The soft succession of the hours
Thawed the snow-drift into flowers.

. . . . . .

By million changes skilled to tell
What in the Eternal standeth well.

Page 65, note 1. In the essay in *Conduct of Life*, called "Considerations by the Way," is a passage similar to this.

Page 67, note 1. Mr. Emerson said that the street must be one of the orator's schools. "The speech of the man in the street is invariably strong, nor can you mend it by making it what you call parliamentary. You say, 'If he could only express himself;' but he does already, better than any one can for him, — can always get the ear of an audience to the exclusion of everybody else." — "Eloquence," *Letters and Social Aims.*

Page 69, note 1. "A profound thought will lift Olympus. . . . Go and talk with a man of genius, and the first word he utters sets all your so-called knowledge afloat and at large." — "Literary Ethics," *Nature, Addresses and Lectures.*

Page 71, note 1. To hazard a guess on this riddle, the answer might be, that the berry is the material Universe (whose colors are, — the woods and fields, seen from a mountain, blue and pale yellow, and the heavens, day and night, blue and gold), a symbol of divinity in which all have a share — the Over-Soul. "The poet alone knows astronomy, chemistry, vegetation and animation, for he does not stop at these facts, but employs them as signs." — "The Poet," *Essays, Second Series.*

Page 72, note 1. Here is a note in verse to the same purpose, apparently taken at Monadnoc: —

> Our eyeless bark sails free,
>   Though with boom and spar
> Andes, Alp, or Himmalee,
>   Strikes never moon or star.

Page 73, note 1. "All good and great and happy actions are made up precisely of these blank to-days." — "The Times," *Nature, Addresses and Lectures.*

Page 73, note 2. Dr. Holmes, in his Life of his friend, thus speaks of this poem: —

"How alive he makes Monadnoc! Dinocrates undertook to 'hew Mount Athos to the shape of man' in the likeness of Alexander the Great. Without the help of tools or workmen, Emerson makes 'Cheshire's haughty hill' stand before us an impersonation of kingly humanity, and talk with us as a god from Olympus might have talked."

Page 75, note 1. The concluding lines of the poem are a shorter essay on Immortality.

Before leaving the subject of Monadnoc, the poems of Mr. Emerson's friends and neighbors should be remembered; Thoreau's fine poem, called "Mountains," on the blue eminences on Concord's western horizon, and the part of Mr. Channing's long poem, "The Wanderer," called "The Mountain." This poem, though of most unequal merit, has lines and passages of great beauty and singular descriptive felicity.

There is also a poem by the late Mr. James Nesmith of Lowell, describing with strength and beauty, through all the lights and phases of the changing year, Monadnoc, where it stands

> "Like a huge arrowhead in stone."

Unhappily this poem was only privately printed during the author's life, but it is to be hoped an edition may be published. It seems as if Mr. Nesmith had Mr. Emerson in mind, for he uses for the motto of his "Monadnoc" Shakspeare's line, —

> "Seeing a better spirit doth use thy name."

FABLE. *Page 75.* This little poem was probably written in 1845. Mr. Emerson liked it well enough to include it in the *Selected Poems*.

ODE. INSCRIBED TO W. H. CHANNING. *Page 76.* The circumstance which gave rise to this poem, though not known, can easily be inferred. Rev. William Henry Channing, nephew of the great Unitarian divine, a man most tender in his sympathies, with an apostle's zeal for right, had, no doubt, been urging his friend to join the brave band of men who were dedicating their lives to the destruction of human slavery in the United States. To these men Mr. Emerson gave honor and sympathy and active aid by word and presence on important occasions. He showed his colors from the first, and spoke fearlessly on the subject in his lectures, but his method was the reverse of theirs, affirmative not negative; he knew his office and followed his genius. He said, "I have quite other slaves to free than those negroes, to wit, imprisoned spirits, imprisoned thoughts."

But after the defection of Daniel Webster from the cause of Freedom, when the strife became more earnest, and Slavery more aggressive, he did important service as a free-lance against it. When the Fugitive Slave Act was passed, he spoke of it in public to his hearers as "a law which every one of you will break on the earliest occasion; a law which no man can abet or obey without forfeiting the name of a gentleman."

Page 77, note 1. He was impatient when men false to the cause of Liberty in their own day praised, in Fourth of July orations, the Fathers of the Republic for their sacrifices on her behalf. He wrote in his journal: "The Americans by means of this lust of extending their territory, and through this nefarious means of compromising with Slavery, enlarge the land but dwarf the men."

But when the evil was brought to his own door and by the law of the land any householder who gave help or furtherance to the poor fugitive was a felon, Mr. Emerson felt that men of honor could not leave remedy for this wrong and disgrace to geologic time, but that active help was due from them.

ASTRÆA. *Page 80.* Mr. Emerson's verse-books show that at first he thought of giving this poem for a title ΓΝΩΘΙ ΣΕΑΥΤΟΝ, the Greek maxim signifying *Know thyself;* but considering that this would be intelligible only to the few, he gave it the name Astræa.

Page 80, note 1. "With this prayer on their neck."— First Edition.

Page 81, note 1. " And its lakes reflect all forms."— First Edition.

ÉTIENNE DE LA BOÉCE. *Page 82.* The friendship of Montaigne, as related by himself, with Étienne de la Boéce (or Boetie) has, like that of David and Jonathan, become pro- verbial. Both were educated for the law at Bordeaux, and they later found themselves in the same parliament or court. When they first met, they ran into each other's arms, as if long acquainted. Étienne was a man who seemed made for whatever he undertook. " The happy strength of his genius rejoiced in difficulties." In troublous times he wrote a purely philosophic work, *Discours de la servitude volontaire*, a brave protest against the tyranny of kings. It was widely read, but brought him disfavor at court. He also wrote graceful, imaginative poems. He died in 1563, at the age of thirty- three.

Mr. Emerson used this name to stand for the perfect friend, utterly loyal, yet austere. In this poem is the spirit of the fourth verse of " Give All to Love." Its thought may be found in " Friendship " (*Essays, First Series*, p. 208) and in " New England Reformers " (*Nature, Addresses and Lectures*, p. 273).

It seems probable that the poem was written in 1833. In the journal of that year, opposite the account of his com- ing on Montaigne's *Essays* when a boy, Mr. Emerson writes of friends, " Echo them, and you will see fast enough that you have nothing for them. They came to you for some- what new. A man loves a man."

COMPENSATION. *Page 83.* This poetical word on a favor- ite theme bears the date " New York, 1834."

FORBEARANCE. *Page 83.* In writing this poem it is possible that Mr. Emerson had in mind his friend — later his helper and biographer — James Elliot Cabot. It would even better have fitted his friend Henry Thoreau. The date of its printing in the *Dial* (January, 1842) makes this more likely.

THE PARK. *Page 84.* "The Park" appeared in the same number of the *Dial* with the preceding poem.

The poem describes the bewilderment which the youth with traditions and manners inbred from generations of Puritan ancestors feels when he first meets charming and gracious friends of a wider experience and culture. Yet the beauty of their behavior seems to warrant the quality of its hidden foundations.

Emerson wrote to such a friend in March, 1841: —

"I find myself, maugre all my philosophy, a devout student and admirer of persons. I cannot get used to them: they daunt and dazzle me still. I have just now been at the old wonder again. I see persons whom I think the world would be richer for losing; and I see persons whose existence makes the world rich. But blessed be the Eternal Power for those whom fancy even cannot strip of beauty, and who never for a moment seem to me profane."

FORERUNNERS. *Page 85.* As in the case of "The Problem," almost no trace of work on this poem in honor of the fair Ideals remains. In the book which contains most of the poems included in Mr. Emerson's first collection it appears in but one form, under the name "Guides," with only one word altered and one erased. There is no date, but Mr. Emerson said that it came to him as he walked home from Wachusett.

There is a passage about the promises, never quite fulfilled, by which Nature leads us, in the Essay of that name in the *Second Series* (p. 192).

SURSUM CORDA. *Page 86*. Mr. Emerson had reference in this title to the chanting by the priest, in the introduction to the celebration of the Mass, of the words *Sursum Corda!* (Up, hearts!) to the worshippers.

The thought of this piece — the exaltation that comes with utter humility — did not find quite satisfactory utterance in the poem as printed in early editions, but in its present form he included it in *Selected Poems*.

ODE TO BEAUTY. *Page 87*. The Ode was printed in the *Dial* in October, 1843. In the first stanza, as there printed, the third and fourth line read: —

> To thee who betrayed me
> To be ruined or blest ?

and the thirteenth and fourteenth, —

> Love drinks at thy banquet
> Remediless thirst.

Page 87, note 1. The last four lines of this stanza were a later addition. Mr. Emerson sent the *Dial* to his young friend Henry Thoreau (then teaching Mr. William Emerson's boys in Staten Island), who had contributed "A Winter Walk" to that number. Mr. Thoreau in a letter of just comment on the magazine wrote, "I have a good deal of fault to find with your 'Ode to Beauty.' The tune is altogether unworthy of the thoughts. You slope too quickly to the rhyme, as if that trick should be performed as soon as possible, or as if you stood over the line with a hatchet and chopped off the verses as they came out, some short and some long. But give us a long reel and we'll chop it off to suit ourselves. It sounds like parody. 'Thee knew I of old,' 'Remediless thirst' are some of those stereotyped lines. . . . Yet I love your poetry as I do little else that is near and recent, especially when you get fairly round the end of the line, and are not thrown back upon the rocks.''

Page 89, note 1. Mr. Emerson wrote in October, 1839, to a friend who had lent him a portfolio of engravings, then rare in this country, of the works of the Italian masters: —

"I have your portfolio in my study, and am learning to read in that book too. But there are fewer painters than poets. Ten men can awaken me by words to new hope and fruitful musing, for one that can achieve the miracle by forms. Besides, I think the pleasure of the poem lasts me longer. . . . But the eye is a speedier student than the ear; by a grand or a lovely form it is astonished or delighted once for all, whilst the sense of a verse steals slowly on the mind and suggests a hundred fine fancies before its precise import is finally settled.'' [1]

Margaret Fuller seems also to have sent him a portfolio of reproductions of the drawings of Guercino and Salvator Rosa.

Page 89, note 2. These four lines were used by Mr. Emerson as the motto for "The Poet," in *Essays, Second Series.*

Page 89, note 3. "Nature is a sea of forms. . . . What is common to them all, — that perfectness and harmony, — is Beauty." — *Nature, Addresses and Lectures,* p. 23.

[1] *Letters from Ralph Waldo Emerson to a Friend.* Edited by Charles Eliot Norton. Boston: Houghton, Mifflin & Co., 1899.

Mr. Emerson quotes Proclus as saying that *Beauty swims on the light of forms*.

Page 89, note 4.

> Hollow space and lily-bell

is the expression in the verse-book.

Page 90, note 1. The following scraps from lecture-sheets seem to be appropriate here: —

"Beauty has rightful privilege: may do what none else can, and it shall be blameless. Indeed, all privilege is that of Beauty — of face, of form, of manner, of brain or method."

"How else is a man or woman fascinating to us but because the abode of mystery and meanings never told and that cannot be exhausted? 'T is the fulness of man that runs over into objects, and makes his Bibles and Shakspeares and Homers so great."

GIVE ALL TO LOVE. *Page 90.* For this poem, as for the essays on Love and Friendship and the poems "To Rhea" and "The Initial, Dæmonic and Celestial Love," what Mr. Joel Benton says of Mr. Emerson's verses seems true: —

"Let us admit at the outset, if you will, that the fortitude of his strain — as Matthew Arnold says of the verses of Epictetus — 'is for the strong, for the few; even for them the spiritual atmosphere with which it surrounds them is bleak and gray' — and that

> 'The solemn peaks but to the stars are known,
>   But to the stars and the cold lunar beams;
> Alone the sun arises, and alone
>   Spring the great streams.'" [1]

[1] *Emerson as a Poet.* By Joel Benton. New York: M. L. Holbrook & Co., 1883.

Page 92, note 1. This thought appears in the image at the end of " The Initial Love " : —

> As the wave breaks to foam on shelves,
> Then runs into a wave again,
> So lovers melt their sundered selves,
> Yet melted would be twain.

Page 92, note 2. The last two lines of the poem are used by Kipling in a remarkable manner in his beautiful allegory " The Children of the Zodiac," for which they possibly suggested the theme. Mr. Emerson presents the same idea often in his prose writings, best perhaps in the essay on Compensation: —

" The death of a dear friend, wife, brother, lover, which seemed nothing but privation, somewhat later assumes the aspect of a guide or genius; for it commonly operates revolutions in our way of life, terminates an epoch of infancy or of youth which was waiting to be closed, breaks up a wonted occupation, or a household, or style of living, and allows the formation of new ones more friendly to the growth of character. It permits or constrains the formation of new acquaintances and the reception of new influences that prove of the first importance to the next years ; and the man or woman who would have remained a sunny garden-flower, with no room for its roots and too much sunshine for its head, by the falling of the walls and the neglect of the gardener is made the banian of the forest, yielding shade and fruit to wide neighborhoods of men."

He quotes Hafiz in the journals to this purpose: " Here is the sum, that when one door opens another shuts."

To Ellen at the South. *Page 93.* In December, 1827,

Mr. Emerson first saw Ellen Tucker, while preaching at Concord, New Hampshire. Just a year later they were engaged to one another. She was very young, but a person of great beauty and refinement. A month after their betrothal, signs of consumption appeared, and her family carried her southward in the spring. Mr. Emerson wrote above this poem, "To E. T. E. at Philadelphia, April, 1829," although they were not married until September of that year. So the initials should have been E. L. T. In spite of her delicate health they had great happiness in the year and a half of life together that was granted them.

Mr. Emerson printed this poem in the *Dial* for January, 1843, under the title, "To Eva at the South," but in the first edition of his *Poems* he restored the name of Ellen.

To ELLEN. *Page 94.* These verses, never before printed, only bear the date "December;" probably the year was 1829.

To EVA. *Page 95.* This poem, also to Ellen, was printed by Mr. Emerson in the *Dial*, July, 1843.

LINES. *Page 96.* Besides the preceding poem, Mr. Emerson contributed to the first number of the *Dial* two poems which had sad and tender memories for him. These were his brilliant and loved brother Edward's "Last Farewell" to home and friends when he sailed for Porto Rico, where he died in 1831, and Ellen Tucker's poem written during her engagement. In the *Dial* it bore simply the heading, "Lines."

THE VIOLET. *Page 97.* One other poem by Ellen Tucker, printed by Mr. Emerson in the *Dial* in January, 1841, seems a fitting and a pleasant addition to this group.

THE AMULET. *Page 98.* This poem, with the same subject and date as the two others by Mr. Emerson which precede it, was published by him in the *Dial* in July, 1842.

THINE EYES STILL SHINED. *Page 99.* This poem also was probably written during Mrs. Emerson's absence in the South, either in the Spring before or following her marriage.

Page 99, note 1. Two pleasing verses follow here which Mr. Emerson did not print: —

> With thy high form my sleep is filled,
> Thy blazing eye greets me at morn,
> Thou dost these days with beauty gild,
> Which else were trivial and forlorn.
>
> What arts are thine, dear maiden,
> O tell me what arts are thine,
> To teach thy name to the rippling wave
> And to the singing pine ?

Page 99, note 2. The poem in the manuscript has this ending: —

> Why should I sing of thee ?
> The morning sings of thee;
> Why should I go to seek thy face ?
> No face but thine I see.

EROS. *Page 100.* This poem was printed in the *Dial* for January, 1844.

HERMIONE. *Page 100.* The history of this poem does not appear. It was written at a time when Mr. Emerson was taking pleasure in the study of the poets of Persia and Arabia.

The theme may have been one drawn from them, or it may have been his endeavor, for the consolation of some friend, " to reduce the calamity within the sphere" of the common human experience of disappointment in love. It is the drawing of a great circle around a small one. The poem presents in brief many of the thoughts in the essays on Love and Friendship, and in the poem which serves as motto for the latter.

INITIAL, DÆMONIC AND CELESTIAL LOVE. *Page 103.* In all the editions until Mr. Emerson's revision called *Selected Poems* was published in 1876, the second division had the title " The Dæmonic and Celestial Love," and their treatment was a little confused, — passages really belonging to the " Celestial Love " coming in the second division; the third had no title. The poem as here printed is Mr. Emerson's final arrangement, but the matter, with a few omissions and corrections, is the same as in the first, the ethical confusion having been removed by taking the passage of twenty-six lines, beginning " But God said," from the " Dæmonic Love," as an introduction of the " Celestial Love."

This poem on the loves on ascending planes carries farther the theme of " Hermione," expounded in full in the essay on Love. The imagery is from the *Banquet* of Plato, of which Mr. Emerson says (*Representative Men*, p. 70) that it " is a teaching . . . that the love of the sexes is initial, and symbolizes at a distance the passion of the soul for that immense lake of beauty it exists to seek. . . . Body cannot teach wisdom; — God only." There Plato tells of a plane of Dæmonic life between those of the mortal and celestial. In the chapter on Swedenborg, in *Representative Men*, Mr. Emerson says, " In Nature is no end, but everything at the end of one use is lifted into a superior, and the ascent of these things climbs into dæmonic and celestial natures.''

Page 105, note 1. Mr. Emerson in several copies of the *Poems* corrected this line to

Like leaping lions on their prey,

but did not make the change in *Selected Poems.*

Page 107, note 1. The sentence in the early form was thus finished: —

God-like, — but 't is for his fine pelf,
The social quintessence of self.
Well said I he is hypocrite,
And folly the end of his subtle wit.

Page 108, note 1. Two lines in the first poem are here omitted: —

Arguments, love, poetry,
Action, service, badinage.

Page 109, note 1. A much stronger line than the one for which it was substituted, —

These like strong amulets preferred.

Page 110, note 1. Here followed in the original the passage later rightly placed by Mr. Emerson at the beginning of " The Celestial Love ": —

But God said
There is smoke in the flame, etc.

Page 110, note 2. In the note to the tenth stanza of " The World-Soul," is a reference by Mr. Emerson, quoted from a letter, to the ancient doctrine of Dæmons.

In the passage on the Neo-platonists, in the essay on Books (*Society and Solitude,* p. 203), he said, " The imaginative scholar will find few stimulants to his brain like these writers.

He has entered the Elysian Fields; and the grand and pleasing figures of gods and dæmons and dæmoniacal men, of the 'azonic' and the 'aquatic gods,' dæmons with fulgid eyes, and all the rest of the Platonic rhetoric, exalted a little under the African sun, sail before his eyes.''

Page 110, note 3. The four lines thus ending appear separately in one of Mr. Emerson's verse-books, where they are thus continued: —

> Of her faults I take no note,
> Fault and folly are not mine;
> Comes the genius, — all 's forgot,
> Replunged again into that upper sphere
> Which scatters wide and wild its lustres here.

Page 112, note 1. These four lines here followed in the original, —

> He is an oligarch;
> He prizes number, fame and mark;
> He loveth crowns,
> He scorneth drones.

Page 117, note 1. The doctrine of the blessed fatality of friendship which is found in the essay on the Over-Soul (*Essays, First Series,* p. 294). See also the last lines of the motto of ''Compensation.''

Page 117, note 2. This was so true of his friend Thoreau, who yet had ever tenderness concealed under a stoic exterior, that Mr. Emerson said of him, ''One would as soon think of taking the arm of an elm-tree as Henry's.''

Page 118, note 1. ''Let us not have this childish luxury in our regards, but the austerest worth; let us approach our friend with an audacious trust in the truth of his heart, in the

breadth, impossible to be overturned, of his foundations." —
"Friendship," *Essays, First Series*.

Page 118, note 2. "We owe to man higher success than
food and fire. We owe to man, man."—"Domestic Life,"
Society and Solitude.

THE APOLOGY. *Page 119.* This poem belongs to the early
period of its author's Concord life. "May-Day" and the
other poems of the later period, notably "Two Rivers,"
"Rubies" and "Waldeinsamkeit," show the gain in musical
ear, the lack of which in early days he admitted.

MERLIN. I. *Page 120.* Mr. Emerson, in his recoil from
academic and imitative versifying, found the rude Norse Sagas,
and the no less strong but finer and more imaginative songs of
the Welsh Bards, tonic and inspiring. As a boy he had delighted
in Ossian. Merlin, in the old English metrical romance, but
especially in the *Morte d'Arthur*, stirred his imagination.
Then he read the fragmentary poems, not labored or polished,
but struck out white-hot with enthusiasm or love or grief, that
are attributed to Taliessin, Llewarch Hen and the other great
Cymrian bards. Here and in other later poems (the "Song
of Merlin" and the motto to "Considerations by the Way,"
in *Conduct of Life*) he uses Merlin to typify the haughty,
free and liberating poet, working the magic of thought through
the charm of Art.

Among notes on English poetry in 1853 he wrote: —

"I find or fancy more true poetry, the love of the Vast, in
the Welsh and Bardic fragments of Taliessin and his school,
than in a good many volumes of British classics."

"Merlin" was finished in the summer of 1846, but in the
journal of the year before are its beginnings, which may inter-

est the reader as showing that the finished poem expressed the
author's aspiration: —

> I go discontented thro' the world
> Because I cannot strike
> The harp to please my tyrannous ear:
> Gentle touches are not wanted,
> These the yielding gods had granted.
> It shall not tinkle a guitar,
> But strokes of fate
> Chiming with the ample winds,
> With the pulse of human blood,
> With the voice of mighty men,
> With the din of city arts,
> With the cannonade of war,
> With the footsteps of the brave
> And the sayings of the wise,
> Chiming with the forest's tone
> When they buffet boughs in the windy wood,
> Chiming with the gasp and moan.
> Of the ice-imprisoned flood.
> I will not read a pretty tale
> To pretty people in a nice saloon
> Borrowed from their expectation,
> But I will sing aloud and free
> From the heart of the world.

Page 120, note 1. In his notes for a course of lectures in
the winter of 1835–36, among the sentences on "Ideas that
predominated in the old English," is this: "Their poet is
not a Pope, but a Talliefer, who, whilst he sings, tosses his
sword into the air and catches it as it falls." Alluding, of
course, to the warrior-minstrel who rode out before the Con-

queror's array at Hastings, singing the *Chanson de Roland* and challenging the Saxons.

Page 121, note 1. On a stray lecture-sheet these words occur: " Do not the great always live *extempore*, mounting to heaven by the stairs of surprise ? "

The second part of " Merlin " was omitted by Mr. Emerson in his *Selected Poems*, which is surprising, for it well expressed his favorite idea of correspondence, universal rhyme and harmony in Nature, and compensation in life.

Page 123, note 1. With this passage may be compared that in the " Woodnotes," II., beginning

> Come learn with me the fatal song
> Which knits the world in music strong.

Page 124, note 1. The same thought is to be found in "Clubs," *Society and Solitude*, p. 230.

Page 124, note 2. " All the facts in natural history, taken by themselves, have no value, but are barren, like a single sex. But marry it to human history, and it is full of life," etc. — *Nature, Addresses and Lectures*, p. 28.

Pythagoras taught that " The world subsists by the rhythmical order of its elements. Everywhere in Nature appear the two elements of the finite and the infinite which give rise to the elementary opposites of the universe, the odd and even, one and many, right and left, male and female, fixed and moved, straight and curved, light and darkness, square and oblong, good and bad."

Page 124, note 3. Journal, August, 1838. " As they said that men heard the music of the spheres always and never, so are we drunk with beauty of the whole, and notice no particular."

The building power of music is a very ancient thought;

the walls of Thebes rose to the music of Amphion's harp. Tennyson makes Merlin tell Gareth at the gates of Camelot,

            " A Fairy King

And Fairy Queen have built the city, son;

They came from out a sacred mountain cleft

Towards the sunrise, each with harp in hand,

And built it to the music of their harps."

The idea is used by Mr. Emerson in his poem, "The House."

BACCHUS. *Page 125.* In July, 1846, Mr. Emerson wrote from Philadelphia to Miss Elizabeth Hoar, whom he always considered as a sister, of several poems which he has been writing and is impatient to show her, " especially some verses called Bacchus — not, however, translated from Hafiz."

Mr. Emerson wrote in his own copy of the *Poems* this motto, taken from Plato, to " Bacchus," which sheds light: " *The man who is his own master knocks in vain at the doors of poetry.*"

The chapter on Idealism in Mr. Emerson's first published work *Nature* (see *Nature, Addresses and Lectures,* p. 47), gives a key to this poem on the inspiration which Nature gives, when seen as not final, but a symbol of the Universal Mind.

The poem has affinities with both " Alphonso of Castile " and " Mithridates," which were written about the same time.

The influence of Hafiz is apparent in the poem, though it is no translation, and the wine is more surely symbolic than his.

In a somewhat later verse-book than that which contains " Bacchus " are the beginnings of another poem of the same name, of which a portion is here given: —

Pour the wine ! pour the wine!
As it changes to foam
So Demiourgos
Rushing abroad,
New and unlooked for,
In farthest and smallest,
Comes royally home;
In spider wise
Will again geometrize;
Will in bee and gnat keep time
With the annual solar chime;
Aphides, like emperors,
Sprawl and creep their pair of hours.
Strong Lyæus' rosy gift
Lightly can the mountain lift;
It can knit
What is done
And what's begun;
It can cancel bulk and time;
Crowds and condenses
Into a drop a tun,
So to repeat
No word or feat;
The hour an altar is of ages,
Love, the Socrates of Sages.

  .   .   .   .   .   .

On a brown grape-stone
The wheels of Nature turn,
Out of it the fury comes
Wherewith the spondyls burn,
And because a drop of the Vine

Is Creation's heart,
Wash with wine those eyes of thine.
Nothing is hid, nor whole nor part.
Wine is translated wit,
Wine is the day of day,
Wine from the veilèd secret
Tears the veil away.

In a lecture on Poetry and Imagination Mr. Emerson said: "The poet is a better logician than the anatomist. . . . He sees the fact as an inevitable step in the path of the Creator. . . . Never did any science originate but by a poetic perception. . . . For a wise surrender to the current of Nature, a noble passion which will not let us halt, but hurries us into the stream of things, makes us truly know. Passion is logical, and I note that the vine, symbol of Bacchus, which intoxicates the world, is the most geometrical of all plants."

Page 126, note 1. " Plants are the young of the world, vessels of health and vigor ; but they grope ever upward towards consciousness; the trees are imperfect men, and seem to bemoan their imprisonment, rooted in the ground." — "Nature," *Essays, Second Series*, p. 181.

MEROPS. *Page 127.* The first rhapsody for this poem, from the verse-book (in which a more advanced form bears the title " Rhyme"), shows the writer's longing to express himself in verse, and how patiently he bore the check that his taste, which grew with this desire, put upon it.

What care I, so the things abide,
The heavenly-minded,
The rich and enriching presences,
How long the power to give them form

Stays behind ?
If they remain to me,
I can spare that,
I can wail
Till the stammering fit of life is past,
Till the soul its weed has cast,
And led by desire of these heavenly guides
I have come into the free element
And won a better instrument.
They taught me a new speech
And a thousand silences;
For, as there is but one path for the sun,
So is there ever but one word for me to say.

Merops, in the mythology, was king of Cos, and wedded one of the Oceanides, and hence, but only after his death, was granted a place as a soaring eagle among the constellations.

Professor Charles Eliot Norton, Mr. William Sloane Kennedy says, suggested to him as a reason for the title that Merops in Greek means "articulate speech." This gives further appropriateness to the name of the poem.

THE HOUSE. *Page 128.* "The House," though not restored to the *Poems* by Mr. Cabot in the Riverside Edition, among others that had that fortune, is restored by the present editor for the charm of its last two verses, although it was not included by Mr. Emerson among the *Selected Poems.*

SAADI. *Page 129.* This poem was first published in the *Dial* for October, 1842.

It does not appear in what year Mr. Emerson first read in translation the poems of Saadi, but although in later years he seems to have been strangely stimulated by Hafiz, whom he names " the prince of Persian poets," yet Saadi was his first love; indeed, he adopted his name, in its various modifications, for the ideal poet, and under it describes his own longings and his most intimate experiences.

Saadi, guarding himself from entangling alliances, living apart and simply and in the great sunny Present, recognizing living and pervading Deity, affirming only, and giving freedom and joy to human souls, might be Emerson in Oriental mask.

In whatever form he first came on Saadi's verse, Mr. Emerson's letters show that he did not know the *Gulistan* until 1848, and in that year he wrote in his journal: " In Saadi's *Gulistan* I find many traits which comport with the portrait I drew," evidently referring to this poem, which was first printed in the *Dial* for October, 1842. It pleased him to find that the real Saadi approached his type of what the poet should be. In 1865 Mr. Emerson wrote the preface to the American edition of Gladwin's translation of the *Gulistan*, published by Messrs. Ticknor & Fields, in Boston. This explains the omission of an account of Saadi and his poems in the lecture written soon after on " Persian Poetry," now included in *Letters and Social Aims*.

This paragraph concerning him is from Mr. Emerson's journal of 1843: —

" Saadi was long a Sacayi, or water-drawer, in the Holy Land, ' till found worthy of an introduction to the prophet Khizr (Elias, or the Syrian and Greek Hermes), who moistened his mouth with the water of immortality.' Somebody doubted this, and saw in a dream a host of angels descending with salvers of glory in their hands. On asking one of them for whom those were intended, he answered, ' for Shaikh Saadi of Shiraz, who has written a stanza of poetry that has met the approbation of God Almighty.' Khosraw of Delhi asked Khizr for a mouthful of this inspiring beverage; but he told him that Saadi had got the last of it.

"'It was on the coming of Friday in the month Showal, of the Arabian year 690, that the eagle of the immaterial soul of Shaikh Saadi shook from his plumage the dust of his body.'"

Page 131, note 1. This reference to the sweet wine of Malaga is a youthful reminiscence. In Mr. Emerson's obituary notice of his townsman and classmate, John Cheney, he says, "I remember the Malaga from Warland's" (the Cambridge grocer), which was the Falernian of the Pythologian club, of which he was the Horace, "as more delicious than any wine I have tasted since."

Page 133, note 1. "Life is a bubble and a skepticism. . . . Grant it, and as much more as they will, but thou, God's darling, heed thy private dream; thou wilt not be missed in the scorning and skepticism." — *Essays, Second Series,* p. 65.

Mr. George W. Cooke, in his biography, says that Emerson's Divinity School Address "became the subject of frequent sermons, and the air was full of pamphlets and newspaper articles. The Unitarian ministers debated whether Emerson was a Christian; some said he was not; some that he was an atheist; while others earnestly defended him. By some of the 'Friends of Progress' . . . he was pronounced a pantheist."

Page 135, note 1. Compare the passage in "The Over-Soul," *Essays, First Series,* p. 293.

Page 135, note 2. The image is much like that in the poem "Days."

HOLIDAYS. *Page 136.* This little poem was printed in the *Dial* for July, 1842.

XENOPHANES. *Page 137.* This poem bears the date " Concord, 1834." It is a less agreeable presentation of the ancient doctrine which is happily presented in " Each and All." It represents the sadder mood of Xenophanes of Elea, the rhapsodist and philosopher (570–480 B.C.), who taught the Unity of God and Nature. His doctrine, Ἑν καὶ πᾶν, the One and the All, constantly recurs in Mr. Emerson's writings, and the poem in his verse-book bears the Greek title.

Xenophanes said, " There is one God, the greatest among gods and men, comparable to mortals neither in form nor thought." Mr. Arthur K. Rogers, in his *Student's History of Philosophy,* says that what Xenophanes taught was " that what we name God is the One immutable and comprehensive material universe, which holds within it and determines all those minor phenomena to which an enlightened philosophy will reduce the many deities of the popular faith. The conception is not unlike that of Spinoza in later times."

It is a remarkable fact that after Mr. Emerson's return from Europe, in 1834, his first lectures were upon Natural History. In a lecture called " The Naturalist," given in May, 1834, is a passage similar to the first four lines of this poem.

Page 137, note 1. " So poor is Nature that from the beginning to the end of the universe she has but one stuff, — but one stuff with its two ends, to serve up all her dream-like variety." — " Nature," *Essays, Second Series.*

THE DAY'S RATION. *Page 138.* Among the few entries in Mr. Emerson's autobiographical note-book several relate to his limited strength and, especially, animal spirits, yet the poem expresses but a mood; his days were full and happy. He had only the right proportion of divine discontent. The thought of this poem is also expressed in *Representative Men,* p. 184.

BLIGHT. *Page 139.* This poem was written in midsummer of 1843. Under the name of "The Times" it was printed in the *Dial* for January of the next year. The latter portion of the poem suggests "Alphonso of Castile."

Page 140, note 1. "The poet alone knows astronomy, chemistry, vegetation and animation, for he does not stop at these facts, but employs them as signs." — "The Poet," *Essays, Second Series.*

Page 140, note 2. The teaching of Xenophanes and the Eleatic School.

Page 140, note 3. A similar passage is found in the "Lecture on the Times," *Nature, Addresses and Lectures,* pp. 287, 288.

MUSKETAQUID. *Page 141.* Though born in Boston, Mr. Emerson loved the ancestral village on the Musketaquid. The dear associations of childhood and youth with it are shown in a poem which I have called "At the Old Manse," written when he was twenty-four years old, now for the first time printed, in the Appendix. There also are found the homesick verses written at Naples in 1834. In a letter to his Aunt Mary soon after he settled in Concord, he wrote, "As men say that the apple never falls far from the stem, I shall hope that another year will draw your eyes and steps to this old, dear odious haunt of the race."

Page 142, note 1. A passage in the essay on Experience (*Essays, Second Series,* pp. 82, 83), and also the poem of that name, printed in this volume, which served as its motto, name "The Lords of Life."

Page 143, note 1. Two passages from the journal of 1840 are suggested by these three lines: —

"Cyrus Stow wanted his bog-meadow brought into

grass. He offered Antony Colombe, Sol Wetherbee, and whomsoever else seed and manure and team and the whole crop, which they accepted and went to work, and reduced the tough roots, the tussocks of grass, the uneven surface, and gave the whole field a good rotting and breaking and sunning, and now he finds no longer any difficulty in getting good English grass from the smooth and friable land. What Stow does with his field, what the Creator does with his planet, the Yankees are now doing with America. It will be friable, arable, habitable to men and angels yet!''

'' Over every chimney is a star; in every field is an oaken garland or a wreath of parsley, laurel or wheat-ears. Nature waits to decorate every child.''

Page 144, note 1. Were it not for the passage in his chapter on Swedenborg (*Representative Men*, pp. 113, 114), it would seem unlikely that in this line Mr. Emerson played on the word '' concords;'' but because of his interest at that time in Swedenborg's *Animal World*, with its doctrine of Microcosm and Macrocosm, the possibility may be recognized.

DIRGE. *Page 145.* The explanation of the first two introductory lines, which have a suggestion of Dante about them, is that they were written about the time of Mr. Emerson's thirty-fifth birthday anniversary — when he had completed half of the journey of life allotted to man in Scripture.

Madam Emerson, as she was called in her later years, had six sons: John Clark, William, Ralph Waldo, Edward Bliss, Robert Bulkeley, and Charles Chauncy; and also two daughters, who died in infancy. But John died too early for his brother Waldo to have any clear remembrance of him. William thus became, on graduating from Harvard at the age of seventeen, his mother's main dependence for aid in supporting the family, though all but Bulkeley (who remained childish through life) helped in turn. William, after teaching school successfully, studied theology in Germany, but was obliged by conscientious doubts to abandon divinity for the law, of which he became a successful and respected practitioner in New York. Waldo, Edward and Charles were drawn together by close ties of taste and sympathy, and circumstances allowed them to remain longer together. They eagerly embraced every chance to visit their grandmother, widow of the Rev. William Emerson of Concord, and later wife of Dr. Ezra Ripley, at the Old Manse. This poem and another version of it, printed in the Appendix under the title of " Peter's Field," recall the happy and sad associations with the Great Meadows and Cæsar's Woods. Edward died in 1834, and Charles two years later. Dr. Holmes and Mr. Cabot in their biographies paid a tribute to these brilliant youths, dying before their prime.

Page 146, note 1. " The flower of silken leaf" was the humble lespedeza, which, in after years, Mr. Emerson seldom passed without a tender word for it to his children.

THRENODY. *Page 148.* This " Ode of Tears " was not all written at one time. Little Waldo, the first-born of his parents, died in January, 1842, and the first part of the poem is the expression of his father's great sorrow. The latter portion, beginning

The deep Heart answered, ' Weepest thou ? '

was not written until Time and Thought had brought their healing.

A month after the child's death, his father, in writing to his childless friend, Carlyle, said, " My son, a perfect little boy of five years and three months, has ended his earthly life. You can never sympathize with me; you can never know how much of me such a young child can take away. A few weeks ago I accounted myself a very rich man, and now the poorest of all. . . . From a perfect health and as happy a life and as happy influences as ever child enjoyed, he was hurried out of my arms in three short days by scarlatina. We have two babes yet, one girl of three years, and one girl of three months and a week, but a promise like that Boy's I shall never see. How often I have pleased myself that one day I should send to you this Morning Star of mine, and stay at home so gladly behind such a representative. I dare not fathom the Invisible and Untold to inquire what relations to my Departed ones I yet sustain."

Of the poem Dr. Holmes said, "It has the dignity of Lycidas without its refrigerating classicism, and with all the tenderness of Cowper's lines on the receipt of his mother's picture."

Two days after Waldo's death his father wrote in his journal: —

" 30 Jan. What he looked upon is better, what he looked not upon is insignificant. The morning of Friday I awoke at three o'clock, and every cock in every barn-yard was shrilling with the most unnecessary noise. The sun went up the morning sky with all his light, but the landscape was dishonored by this loss. For this boy, in whose remembrance I have both slept and awaked so oft, decorated for me the morning star and the evening cloud, — how much more all the particulars of daily economy. . . . A boy of early wisdom, of a grave and even majestic deportment, of a perfect gentleness. . . . He gave up his little innocent breath like a bird."

Page 150, note 1. "The boy had his full swing in this

world. Never, I think, did a child enjoy more. He had been thoroughly respected by his parents and those around him, and not interfered with; and he had been the most fortunate in respect to the influences near him, for his Aunt Elizabeth [Hoar] had adopted him from his infancy, and treated him ever with that plain, wise love which belongs to her. . . . Then Henry Thoreau had been one of the family for the last year and charmed Waldo by the variety of toys, whistles, boats, popguns and all kinds of instruments which he could make and mend; and possessed his love and respect by the gentle firmness with which he always treated him. Margaret Fuller and Caroline Sturgis had also marked the boy, and caressed and conversed with him whenever they were here.''

Page 151, note 1. Journal. '' The chrysalis which he brought in with care and tenderness and gave to his mother to keep is still alive, and he, most beautiful of the children of men, is not here.''

Page 158, note 1. The idea of Deity rushing into distribution is treated at length in the first part of the *Timæus* of Plato.

CONCORD HYMN. *Page 158, note 2.* From a copy of this hymn as first printed on slips for distribution among the Concord people at the celebration of the completion of the monument on the battle-ground, I note the differences from the poem here given as finally revised by Mr. Emerson in the *Selected Poems.* In the early editions of the *Poems* the date is given as 1836. This is a mistake. The *Middlesex Yeoman* gives the account of this celebration in 1837, and on the original slip in my possession some one sending it to a friend at that time, has written '' Sung by the people on battle-ground at the completion of the monument, 4th of July, 1837.''

The first two verses retain exactly their original form. In the third, the third line, as sung, was

> We place with joy a votive stone.

The last verse originally began

> O Thou, who made those heroes dare
> To die or leave their children free.

MAY–DAY

In 1867, Mr. Emerson gathered into a new volume the poems of the twenty-one years since the publication of the first, and gave it the name *May-Day* from the happy lyric in honor of Spring with which it opens. His ear had improved, and, though the original vigor remained in the poems, many of them had been kept long by him and had ripened fully. "May-Day," the poem, was probably written in snatches in the woods on his afternoon walks, through many years. Some lines are in journals of 1845. After its publication he saw that the ordering of the different passages to give the advance of Spring was not quite successful, and in the *Selected Poems*, published nine years later, he improved, but did not quite perfect, the arrangement, for at that time he found mental effort of that sort confusing. Therefore in the posthumous edition of the *Poems* in 1883, at the suggestion of the present editor, Mr. Cabot consented to a slight further change made with the same intent.

Page 163, note 1. Of the following six lines in one of the verse-books all but the first were in the first edition: —

Dripping dew-cold daffodillies,
Making drunk with draught of lilies,
Girls are peeling the sweet willow,
Poplar white, and Gilead-tree,
And troops of boys shouting with whoop, and hilloa
And hip, hip, three times three.

Page 163, note 2. This line with a suggestion of English pastoral, found in the first edition, was omitted by the author:—

Or clapping of shepherd's hands.

Page 165, note 1. The stanza had, in the first edition, a different ending:—

The cowslips make the brown brook gay;
A happier hour, a longer day.
Now the sun leads in the May,
Now desire of action wakes,
And the wish to roam.

Page 165, note 2. In the verse-book here followed the couplet—

Her cottage chamber, wall and beam,
Glows with the maid's delicious dream.

Page 165, note 3. It seems as if it must have been by accident that the remarkable lines, concluding this stanza, beginning "The youth sees omens," — six of which, in a different order, served as the motto to the second edition of *Nature*, in 1849, — were omitted in the posthumous edition. They followed immediately in this place.

Page 166, note 1. These last four lines are often quoted to show how early Mr. Emerson accepted the doctrine of evolution. It is not certain in what year they were written, but a sentence in the unpublished lecture on the Humanity of Science, given in Boston in 1836, has exactly the same thought. He alludes to Lamarck as " finding a monad of organic life common to every animal, and becoming a worm, a mastiff, or a man, according to circumstances. He says to the caterpillar, How dost thou, brother ? Please God, you shall yet be a philosopher."

The ancient philosophers, as well as the modern savans, taught Emerson evolution. To the first edition of *Nature* Mr. Emerson prefixed a motto from Plotinus, and Dr. William T. Harris finds the thought of the later motto in these words from the same source: " We might say that all beings, not only the rational ones but even the irrational ones, the plants and even the soil that bears them, aspire to attain conscious knowledge."

In his journal for 1849 Mr. Emerson quotes this sentence from Stallo: " The development of all individual forms will be spiral." — *General Principles of the Philosophy of Nature ;* Boston, 1848.

Page 166, note 2. Mr. Nicholas Longworth, who practised wine-making on a large scale near Cincinnati, was Mr. Emerson's host when he lectured there, and, according to Mr. M. D. Conway, suggested this thought when he showed his wine-cellars to his guest, by telling him of the renewed activity of fermentation in the Spring.

Page 167, note 1. Journal, 1856. "April 5, Walden fired a cannonade yesterday of a hundred guns, but not in honor of the birth of Napoleon."

In Concord, by village comity, the two field-pieces of the Concord Artillery Company were too often lent to political enthusiasts to celebrate the election of their pro-slavery candidate, and the editor thinks that he remembers their firing, on the news of the passage of the Kansas-Nebraska Bill.

Page 169, note 1. It is interesting to see how the association of blessed warmth and life with his favorite South-wind led the author to forget that the southing of the sun meant the coming of winter. Yet "the northing of the sun" would have a comfortless sound.

Page 169, note 2. In his college days the boy must often have gone to the beautiful wooded hills of Mount Auburn, not then a cemetery, above the broad marshes of the Charles River. Journal, 1861. "Ah, the powers of the Spring, and ah, the voice of the bluebird and the witchcraft of the Mount Auburn dell in those days!"

Page 170, note 1. Journal, 10 June, 1838. "Noon. Mercury, 90° in the shade. River of heat, yea, a circumambient sea. Welcome as truly as finer and coarser influences to this mystic solitary 'purple island' that I am! I celebrate the holy hour at church amid these fine Creative deluges of light and heat which evoke so many gentle traits, gentle and bold in man and woman. Man in Summer is Man intensated."

Page 170, note 2. These lines of the original were omitted:

> Boils the world in tepid lakes,
> Burns the world, yet burnt remakes;
> Enveloping heat, enchanted robe,
> Wraps the daisy and the globe.

Page 171, note 1. In one of the verse-books I find the original rhapsody of this part of the poem, which runs thus:

> The Spring comes up from the South
> And Earth and air are overflowed,
> Earth with the melted ice,
> And air with love infusion.
> There is no house or hall
> Can hold her festival.
> We will go to her haughty woods
> Fronting the liberated floods;

We will go to the relenting mountains,
And listen to the uproar of joy,
And see the sparkle of the delivered rivers,
And mark the rivers of sap
Mounting in the pipes of the trees,
And see the colors of love in birds,
And in frogs and lizards,
And in human cheeks,
In the song of birds
And songs of men.

Page 172, note 1. Here are some notes on Nature's spices, from a verse-book: —

Spices in the plants that run
To bring their first fruits to the sun,
Earliest heats that follow frore,
Nerved leaf of hellebore,
Scarlet maple-keys that burn
Above the sassafras and fern,
Frost survivors, berries red,
Checkerberry, — children's bread, —
Silver birch and black
With the selfsame spice to find
In polygala's root and rind;
Mouse-ear, cowslip, wintergreen,
Which by their beauty may repel
The frost from harming what is well.

Page 175, note 1. The divine days in lowly disguise often appear in Mr. Emerson's writings in prose and verse: at best here and in the poem "Days," but also in "Works and Days" (*Society and Solitude*, p. 168) and in the first paragraph of the "Lecture on the Times," in *Nature, Addresses and Lectures*.

Page 177, note 1. This affectionate address to the birds may be found in another version among the "Fragments on Nature," in the Appendix to the *Poems*.

Page 179, note 1. Mr. Emerson was told in 1874, by his brother-in-law, Dr. Charles T. Jackson, that while making a geological survey near Pulpit Rock, on Lake Superior, he heard music like rhythmical organ or vocal chantings, and believed it to come from some singers. He went on a little farther and the music ceased; in another direction, and he heard it again; and by and by perceived that it was the sound of the beating waves on the shore, deprived of its harshness by the atmosphere. This phenomenon, which he called Analyzed Sound, he had never seen treated scientifically, except in a paper by Dr. Wollaston.

I myself, while going across the Plains in an emigrants' caravan in July, 1862, when in the neighborhood of Fort Laramie, strayed alone three or four hundred yards from our camp into a grove of large cottonwoods on the shore of the North Platte River. Suddenly I heard wonderful music not far away, which I could not account for. It seemed loud but rather sad, perhaps suggesting cathedral music, yet was indistinct and seemed unnatural. It was wholly unlike the tom-tom and hideous chanting of the Sioux, and no white settlement or gathering was near except our camp. On my return thither I asked about the music. No one had heard it. The day was cold and cloudy, after great heat, — a brisk norther blowing. We were close by the broad, rushing Platte leaping in short waves in the wind. Only some time after my return did I hear from my uncle of his similar experience.

In "May-Day," as first published, here followed the passage on the Æolian Harp which, in the *Selected Poems,* Mr. Emerson preferred to print as a separate poem. It appears as such in this volume.

Page 180, note 1. From this place was omitted the line,

Nor noon nor eve this music fails.

THE ADIRONDACS. *Page 182.* In August, 1858, Mr. William J. Stillman, an artist by profession, but a man almost of the versatility in accomplishment of The Admirable Crichton, as painter, writer, critic, foreign consul (in which service he showed himself a chivalrous Philhellene), and last, not least, an accomplished woodsman and hunter, led a party of his friends into the then primæval forest of the Adirondac Mountains. The party were, Stillman, Agassiz, Lowell, Judge Hoar, Dr. Jeffries Wyman, the comparative anatomist ; Samuel G. Ward, a near friend of Mr. Emerson's ; Dr. Estes Howe, John Holmes (brother of Dr. Oliver Wendell Holmes), Horatio Woodman, Dr. Amos Binney, and Emerson. Mr. Stillman in his autobiography [1] gives a very interesting account of this company, the region, and their adventures. The following notes of the trip I find in Mr. Emerson's journals. All readers of Lowell will feel pleasure in reading the unexpected postscript to the osprey-nest story.

"Adirondac, August 7th, 1858. Follansbee's Pond. It should be called Stillman's henceforward, from the good camp which this gallant artist has built, and the good party he has led and planted here for the present at the bottom of the little bay which lies near the head of the lake.

"The lake is two miles long, 1 to ½ mile wide, and sur-

[1] *The Autobiography of a Journalist.* Boston : Houghton, Mifflin & Co. 1901.

rounded by low mountains. Norway pine and white pine abound.

"On the top of a large white pine, in a bay, was an osprey's nest, around which the ospreys were screaming, 5 or 6. We thought there were young birds in it, and sent Preston to the top. This looked like an adventure. The tree must be 150 feet high at least; 60 feet clean straight stem, without a single branch, and, as Lowell and I measured it by the tape as high as we could reach, 14 ft. 6 inches in girth. Preston took advantage of a hemlock close by it and climbed till he got on the branches, then went to the top of the pine and found the nest empty, tho' the great birds wheeled and screamed about him. He said he could climb the bare stem of the pine, 'tho' it would be awful hard work.' When he came down, I asked him to go up it a little way, which he did, clinging to the corrugations of the bark. Afterwards Lowell watched for a chance to shoot the osprey, but he soared magnificently and would not alight.

"The pond is totally virgin soil, without a clearing in any point, and covered with primitive woods, rock-maple, beech, spruce, white cedar, arbor vitæ. We have seen bald eagles, loons, ravens, kingfishers, ducks, tatlers. We have killed 2 deer yesterday, both in the lake, and otherwise fed our party with lake-trout and river-trout. The wood-thrush we heard at Stephen Bartlett's carry, but not since, and no other thrush.

"River, lake and brook trout cannot be scientifically discriminated, nor yet male from female.

"Lowell, next morning, was missing at breakfast, and when he came to camp told me he had climbed Preston's pine-tree."

Mr. Stillman painted the forest camp and the company. Mr.

Herbert W. Gleason's remarkably successful photograph of the painting (left to the Concord Library by Judge Hoar) might almost seem a photograph from Nature, so faithfully did Mr. Stillman give the character and the values of the trees. At the left of the picture, Agassiz, helped by the tall Dr. Wyman, is dissecting a fish, while Dr. Estes Howe looks on, and Mr. Holmes, who was lame, sits close by. On the right, Dr. Binney is aiming his rifle at a mark, and a little behind, Lowell and Judge Hoar are waiting their turn to shoot, and Mr. Woodman sits on the ground. The tall, lean figure behind the marksman is the painter himself, hardly distinguishable in the photograph, their tutor in the art of shooting, of which he was master. The guides at the right of the picture critically watch the mark to see the results of the amateurs.

Between the groups, admiring their accomplishments, which are yet foreign to him, but more occupied with Nature in her columned temple, is the poet. The reproduction is too small to do justice to the figure and attitude, which in the picture are given with wonderful success, and but for the unwonted flannel shirt, it might well represent him in his daily commune with the pines.

Page 186, note 1. A remarkable picture, "The Procession of the Pines," was painted of this subject by Mr. Stillman, huge Norway pines on a high promontory standing black against the orange twilight glow, and reflected in the still lake.

Page 186, note 2. This was Mr. Emerson's own experience: paddled noiselessly by the guide, in a boat with torch and reflector in the bow, he was bidden to shoot at the staring " deer " among the lily-pads by the shore. The " square mist " was too much of an illusion, even to the student of

Oriental *Mayas;* he did not fire, and in an instant it was gone.

Page 188, note 1. An Adirondac Club was formed, and Mr. Stillman succeeded in buying for them a lake (Ampersand) and its enclosing mountains, sold for unpaid taxes, at a ridiculously low price. But some people of that part of New York, understanding that Boston capitalists had bought a large tract, could not credit the avowed purpose of the buyers, and, supposing that they knew of some coming railroad and had designs on the lumber, redeemed the land. The camp at Lake Ampersand was, however, occupied by the Club in 1859, but Mr. Emerson did not go there.

Page 189, note 1. Mr. Emerson always held that the introverted eye, and apprehension, had much to do with perverted digestion.

Page 192, note 1. Here is an instance of the interest and pride which this man of the spirit took even in the application of scientific discovery to the convenience of man. It represented an advance and ascent, and this particular discovery was to weld the races together in brotherhood. A prophecy of this event he wrote in his Concord " Ode for the Fourth of July " of the previous year.

Page 192, note 2. The trial for the passage in the verse-book reads thus: —

> To be a brain,
> Or to obey the brain of upstart man,
> And shake the slumbers of a million years.

BRAHMA. *Page 195.* This poem was one of the four which Mr. Emerson contributed to the first number of the *Atlantic Monthly,* in November, 1857. In his note-book for the year before, where it is called " The Song of the Soul," are many pages of extracts from the Hindoo scriptures, yet not those to which the poem gives expression. The first appearance of the doctrine is found in an extract from Parmenides given in the notes on Degerando's *Histoire Comparée des Systèmes de Philosophie*, made by Mr. Emerson in 1830: "Thought and the object of thought are but one."

In the year 1845 he was reading the *Vishnu Purana*, and made these among other extracts: —

"He who eternally restrains this and the other world, and all beings therein, who standing in the earth is other than the earth, whom the earth knows not, whose body the earth is, who interiorly restrains the earth, the same is thy soul, and the Internal Check immortal."

"What living creature slays or is slain ? What living creature preserves or is preserved ? Each is his own destroyer or preserver, as he follows evil or good."

The latter extract he thus rendered in 1845: —

> What creature slayeth or is slain ?
> What creature saves or savèd is ?
> His life will either lose or gain,
> As he shall follow harm or bliss.

Dr. William T. Harris, in his interesting chapter on Emerson's Orientalism,[1] sheds much light on the origin of the poem, quoting various passages in the *Bhagavat-Gita*. The thought of the first verse is thus rendered by Thomson in his translation of the second chapter: —

"He who believes that this spirit can kill, and he who thinks that it can be killed, both of these are wrong in judgment. It neither kills nor is killed. It is not born nor dies at any time. It has no origin, nor will it ever have an origin. Unborn,

[1] *Genius and Character of Emerson; Lectures at the Concord School of Philosophy*. Edited by F. B. Sanborn. Boston : J. R. Osgood & Co., 1885.

changeless, eternal, both as to future and past time, it is not slain when the body is killed.''

Many passages show the independence of Brahma of Time and Space, and the absence in Indian philosophy of the dualism of the Persians, believing in separate principles of Good and Evil; thoughts conveyed in the second verse.

The equivalent of the last line in the third verse Dr. Harris finds in the tenth chapter, where Brahma says, '' Of the Vedas, I am the Sáma-Veda. I am the Vrihatsaman among the hymns.''

The '' Strong Gods '' of the fourth verse are Indra, god of the sky and wielder of the thunderbolt; Agni, the god of fire: and Yama, the god of death and judgment. These shall finally be absorbed into Brahma. The '' Sacred Seven '' are the Maharshis or highest saints.

The last line finds its origin in the eighteenth chapter: — '' Abandoning all religious duties, seek me as thy refuge. I will deliver thee from all sin. Be not anxious.''

The striking passage from the Oriental scriptures with which the essay on Immortality concludes might well be read in connection with this poem.

In '' The Sphinx, '' the line,

> Thou art the unanswered question,

is matched by that in this poem,

> I am the doubter and the doubt.

In a little book in which Mr. Emerson collected quotations concerning Love, he wrote, '' The best word I know on the subject is the motto on a little engraving of the heavenly Cupid, who is represented as turning his head to look down on the towers of Heaven, and underneath is written *Superna respicit Amor*, — He looketh back on Heaven.''

In spite of the difficulties which "Brahma" presented to many minds, and the ridicule which it excited, it presented no difficulty to others who had no Oriental knowledge except that of the New Testament. A little school-girl was bidden by her teacher to learn some verses of Emerson. Next day she recited "Brahma." The astonished teacher asked why she chose that poem. The child answered that she tried several, but could n't understand them at all, so learned this one, "for it was so easy. *It just means ' God everywhere.' "*

Mr. Emerson, much amused when people found "Brahma" puzzling, said to his daughter, "If you tell them to say Jehovah instead of Brahma they will not feel any perplexity."

NEMESIS. *Page 196.* This poem, from *May-Day,* called "Destiny" in the verse-books, is here restored.

FATE. *Page 197, note 1.* "The reason why this or that man is fortunate is not to be told. It lies in the man; that is all anybody can tell you about it." — "Character," *Essays, Second Series.*

"He [man] thinks his fate alien because the copula is hidden. But the soul contains the event that shall befall it." — "Fate," *Conduct of Life.*

FREEDOM. *Page 198.* In the autumn of 1853 Mr. Emerson wrote in his journal the beginnings of this poem expressing his feeling that no muse would help should he attack in song African Slavery, the doleful theme that recurred each morning when he woke. But in life and his private and public speech he was true to Freedom.

In the first form, the lines, after the fourth, ran thus: —

> But the God said, 'Not so;
> Theme not this for lyric flow,
> Keep thy counsel soft and low;
> Name too holy to be said,
> Gift too precious to be prayed,
> Counsel not to be exprest,
> But by will of glowing breast.
> But the power by heaven adored,
> With Truth and Love the Triune Lord,
> When it listed woke again
> Brutish millions into men,' etc.

The last line appears also in the forms,
" Right thou feelest rashly do," or, " instant do."

ODE. *Page 199.* Mr. Emerson was reluctant to mount Pegasus to war against the enemies of Freedom; but when, as he said in his speech on the Fugitive Slave Law (*Miscellanies*), it required him to become a slave-hunter, he was stirred to plead her cause in verse, of which this and the two following poems are examples.

The occasion on which this was sung was a breakfast in the Town Hall, on the holiday morning, to raise money for the improvement of the new cemetery in Sleepy Hollow.

BOSTON HYMN. *Page 201.* In January, 1862, in an address called " American Civilization " given before the Smithsonian Institution in Washington, Mr. Emerson had earnestly urged the emancipation of the slaves. On the first day of the next year, when President Lincoln's Proclamation went into effect, Mr. Emerson read this poem at a great celebration of the event in Boston. It was published in the *Atlantic Monthly* for February, 1863.

Page 204, note 1. In an address before the Anti-Slavery Society in New York in 1855, Mr. Emerson had urged the buying by the people of the whole slave property of the South: —

"I say, Buy! never conceding the right of the planter to own, but acknowledging the calamity of his position, and willing to bear a countryman's share in relieving him, and because it is the only practical course and is innocent. . . . We shall one day bring the States shoulder to shoulder, and the citizens man to man, to exterminate slavery. It was said a little while ago that it would cost a thousand or twelve hundred millions, now it is said it would cost two thousand millions; such is the enhancement of property. Well, was there ever any contribution that was so enthusiastically paid as this will be? The United States will be brought to give every inch of their public lands for a purpose like this. Every State will contribute its surplus revenue. Every man will bear his part. We will have a chimney tax. We will give up our coaches and wine and watches. The church will melt her plate. The father of his country shall wait, well pleased, a little longer for his monument; — Franklin will wait for his; the Pilgrim Fathers for theirs; and the patient Columbus, who waited all his mortality for justice, shall wait a part of immortality also. . . . The rich shall give of their riches; the merchants of their commerce; the mechanics of their strength; the needlewomen will give, and children can have a Cent Society. If, really, the thing could come to a negotiation and a price were named, I do not think that any price, founded upon an estimate that figures could fairly represent, would be unmanageable. Every man in this land would give a week's work to dig away this accursed mountain of slavery, and force it forever out of the world."

VOLUNTARIES. *Page 205.* This poem was printed in the *Atlantic Monthly* for October, 1863.

Page 207, note 1. In July, 1863, Colonel Robert Gould Shaw, who in face of a half-hostile public opinion had given up his commission in a favorite Massachusetts regiment to take command of one of the first enlisted colored regiments, largely made up of ex-slaves, had been killed with many of his officers and men on the slopes of Fort Wagner. This poem may be regarded as their dirge.

Mrs. Ednah Cheney describes a meeting, during the Civil War, presided over by Father Taylor, of the friends of this regiment. She says that, during the meeting, "Mr. Emerson came in from the ante-room with his face on fire with indignation, as I never saw it on any other occasion, and announced to the audience that he had just learned that South Carolina had given out the threat that colored soldiers, if captured, should not be treated as prisoners, but be put to death. 'What answer does Massachusetts send back to South Carolina?' he said. 'Two for one!' shouted voices in the audience. 'Is that the answer that Massachusetts sends?' he asked; and the audience responded with applause. He retired from the platform, it seemed to me a little appalled at the spirit he had raised."

Page 208, note 1. The last four lines of the stanza were added by Mr. Emerson in *Selected Poems.*

Page 209, note 1. The last stanza suggests the following passages, the first being from the journal of January, 1861, three months before the outbreak of war.

"The furious slaveholder does not see that the one thing he is doing by night and by day is to destroy slavery. They who help and they who hinder are all equally diligent in hastening its downfall. Blessed be the inevitabilities."

"The word Fate, or Destiny, expresses the sense of mankind . . . that the laws of the world do not always befriend, but often hurt and crush us. Fate, in the shape of *Kinde* or Nature, grows over us like grass. . . .

" Through the years and the centuries, through evil agents, through toys and atoms, a great and beneficent tendency irresistibly streams." — *Representative Men*, pp. 177, 185, 186.

LOVE AND THOUGHT. *Page 210.* With this poem may be compared the seventh verse in " My Garden," and passages in " Love " (*Essays, First Series*, pp. 175–177) and in " Manners " (*Essays, Second Series*, pp. 150, 151).

UNA. *Page 210.* The solution of the pleasing riddle " Una," restored here to the place it held in the volume *May-Day*, cannot be given with authority. It might be the sense of the general beauty refreshed in a poetical mind by new scenes and friends met in travel — the momentary opening of new vistas of promise.

BOSTON. *Page 212.* Although this poem did not come to its birthday until December 16, 1873, when Mr. Emerson read it in Faneuil Hall, on the Centennial Celebration of the destruction of the tea in Boston Harbor, it was conceived years before. Mr. Emerson wrote in his journal in 1842: —

" I have a kind of promise to write, one of these days, a verse or two to the praise of my native city, which in common days we often rail at, yet which has great merits to usward. That too, like every city, has certain virtues, as a museum of the arts. The parlors of private collectors, the Athenæum Gallery, and the college become the city of the city. Then a city has this praise, that as the bell or band of music is heard outside beyond the din of carts, so the beautiful in architecture, or in political and social institutions, endures; all else comes to nought, so that the antiquities and permanent things in each city are good and fine.''

On his walks with his children on Sunday afternoons Mr. Emerson would often recite poetry to them, and they remember well his telling of his desire to write his Boston poem, and his pleasure in this image, —

> And twice a day the flowing sea
> Takes Boston in its arms.

In his manuscript it opens thus: —

> The land that has no song
> Shall have a song to-day:
> The granite hills are dumb too long,
> The vales have much to say:
> For you can teach the lightning speech,
> And round the globe your voices reach.

Mr. Emerson was never able to finish the poem to his satisfaction. He wished to have a sort of refrain of two rhyming lines at the end of each verse, but after his illness in 1872 his powers of composition failed, and but a portion of his verses were thus rounded out.

The poem appeared first in print in the *Atlantic Monthly* for February, 1876, and in Mr. Emerson's *Selected Poems*, published the same year, it was the concluding poem.

The motto of Boston, which precedes the poem, he translates thus in the last verse, —

GOD WITH THE FATHERS, SO WITH US.

Page 217, note 1. The poem was begun in the sad days preceding the war, when its author blushed for the timidity shown by many of Boston's first citizens, scholars and merchants, and their subservience in the interests of union and commerce to the demands made by the slave-power upon their honor and conscience. When the war had cleared the air, the poem was quite remodelled in a happier day, for the " Boston Tea-Party " celebration.

The following are some of the verses, composed at a sadder time, which, in the early form, followed the lines or Lafayette: —

> O pity that I pause!
>   The song, disdaining, shuns
> To name the noble sires because
>   Of the unworthy sons;
> For what avail the plough or sail,
> Or land or life, if freedom fail ?

> But there was chaff within the flour,
>   And one was false in ten,
> And reckless clerks in lust of power
>   Forgot the rights of men;
> Cruel and blind did file their mind,
> And sell the blood of human kind.

> Your town is full of gentle names
>   By patriots once were watchwords made;
> Those war-cry names are muffled shames
>   On recreant sons mislaid.
> What slave shall dare a name to wear
> Once Freedom's passport everywhere ?

> Oh welaway ! if this be so,
>   And man cannot afford the right,

And if the wage of love be woe,
    And honest dealing yield despite.
For never will die the captive's cry
On the echoes of God till Right draws nigh.

Here is a verse written at another time of patriotic mortification: —

O late to learn, O long betrayed,
    O credulous men of toil,
Who took the traitor to your hearths
    Who came those hearths to spoil.
O much-revering Boston town
    Who let the varlet still
Recite his false, insulting tale
    On haughty Bunker Hill.

The following fragment in lighter vein also occurs in the verse-book: —

O Boston city, lecture-hearing,
O Unitarian, God-fearing,
But more, I fear, bad men revering,
Too civil by half; thine evil guest
Makes thee his byword and his jest,
And scorns the men that honeyed the pest, —
Piso and Atticus with the rest.
Thy fault is much civility,
Thy bane respectability,
And thou hadst been as wise and wiser
Lacking the Daily Advertiser.
Ah, gentlemen — for you are gentle —
And mental maids, not sentimental —

In the volume called *Natural History of Intellect and Other*

Papers, is included Mr. Emerson's lecture "Boston," in which he shows his pride and interest in his native town. Mrs. Ednah Cheney contributed an interesting chapter on "Emerson and Boston" to the book published in 1885 by the Concord School of Philosophy, called *Genius and Character of Emerson.*

LETTERS. *Page 217, note 2.* The poem at first began,

> Every morning brings a ship;
> Every ship brings a word.

Mr. Emerson wrote in his journal, "Hear what the morning says, and believe that."

RUBIES. *Page 218, note 1.* There is another pleasing form of the last verse: —

> But fire to thaw that ruddy snow,
> To break the wine-drop's prison
> And give love's scarlet tides to flow,—
> That sun is yet unrisen.

MERLIN'S SONG. I. *Page 218.* This poem was suggested by the specimens of Welsh Bardic poems which Mr. Emerson took so much pleasure in, and of which he gives specimens in "Poetry and Imagination" (*Letters and Social Aims*, pp. 58, 59), one being not unlike this poem. In the journals are similar passages of which it is hard to tell whether they are from the Bards, or Mr. Emerson cast his own thought in that form, — as the following: —

"I know a song which, though it be sung never so loud, few can hear, — only six or seven or eight persons; yet they who hear it become young again. When it is sung, the stars twinkle gladly, and the moon bends nearer the earth."

MERLIN'S SONG. II. *Page 218.* Although there seems entire fitness in printing this song of Merlin, which Mr. Emerson used for the motto to " Considerations by the Way " in the *Conduct of Life*, in connection with the preceding one, they never appear together in the verse-books.

THE TEST. *Page 220, note 1.* This poem, the author's test of scholars in guessing the five poetic teachers of the race, appeared, with no Solution, in the *Atlantic Monthly* for January, 1861. Mr. Emerson did not prize the poems sufficiently to include them in the *Selected Poems*.

SOLUTION. *Page 220.* I believe the early rhythmic ventures from which this poem grew in time must interest some readers, and therefore give them in part.

The older one (close to a rehearsal for " Alphonso of Castile ") begins thus: —

> Clouds on clouds,
> Thro' clouds of fire and seas of mist
> Burned the globe of amethyst,
> Old forces hardly yet subside
> Within the bounds of time and tide:
> Saurian, snake and dragon can
> Slowly ripen into man.
> Asia spawned its shepherd race,
> Egypt built its granite base;
> Then war and trade and clearest clime
> Precipitate the man of time,
> And forward stepped the perfect Greek
> To fight, to carve, to paint, to speak.
> Will, wisdom, joy had found a tongue
> In the charmed world when Homer sung.

The other beginning runs thus: —

> I am the Muse,
> Memory's daughter,
> I stood by Jove at the first, —
> Take me out, and no world had been
> Or chaos bare and bleak.
> If life has worth, I give it,
> And if all is taken, and I left,
> I make amends for all.
> Long I wrought
> To ripen and refine
> The stagnant, craggy lump
> To a brain
> And shoot it through
> With electric wit.
> At last the snake and dragon
> Shed their scales,
> And man was born.
> Then was Asia,
> Then was Nile,
> And at last
> On the sea-marge bleak
> Forward stepped the perfect Greek;
> That will, wit, joy might find a tongue,
> And earth grow civil, Homer sung.
> Pleased, the planet hummed the tunes, etc.

Page 221, note 1. This phrase from the Vishnu Purana occurs in "Hamatreya."

Page 221, note 2. Mr. Emerson, writing to a friend in 1849, spoke with praise of the translation of the "Inferno" by Dr. John Carlyle, the brother of Thomas Carlyle: "I read it lately by night with wonder and joy at all its parts, and at none more than at the nerve and courage which is as essential to the poet as the soldier. Dante locked the door and put the key in his pocket. I believe we only value those who do so.''

In the verse-book here follow four lines: —

> Silence brooded in my heaven
> For seven times seventy and seven,
> Prelude of the following song
> Well worth such strain to tarry long.

HYMN. *Page 223.* Mr. Emerson wrote this hymn, to be sung at the ordination of his successor, the Rev. Chandler Robbins, as pastor of the Second Church of Boston, in 1831. He justly preferred it to one which he had written before, which, though cast aside, has so much that is pleasing that it is now printed in the Appendix. The accepted version of the hymn was not in the May-Day volume, but was included by Mr. Emerson among the *Selected Poems*.

NATURE. II. *Page 226.* In one of the earlier verse-books the lines called "The Walk," printed in the Appendix, served for the second division of the poem, and there was a third, which Mr. Emerson took for the motto to "Fate," in *Conduct of Life*, beginning, —

> Delicate omens traced in air
> To the lone bard true witness bare.

Page 226, note 1. The thought here expressed is found in the essay "Art," in *Society and Solitude*.

THE ROMANY GIRL. *Page 227.* This poem was one of the group contributed by Mr. Emerson to the opening number of the *Atlantic Monthly*, in November, 1857. It was written nearly three years earlier.

The books of the Englishman George Borrow, who combined in a singular manner love of wild human nature and the missionary zeal of an agent of the Bible Society, were attractive to Mr. Emerson. They gave the motive for this poem, at first in the note-book called " Gypsy Song."

Page 227, note 1. I find in a journal this uncredited line, —

Pâles filles du Nord! vous n'etes pas mes sœurs.

DAYS. *Page 228.* With regard to this poem, which Mr. Emerson once said he thought perhaps his best, the following remarkable entry is from the journal of 1852: —

" I find one state of mind does not remember or conceive of another state. Thus I have written within a twelvemonth verses ('Days') which I do not remember the composition or correction of, and could not write the like to-day, and have only, for proof of their being mine, various external evidences, as the manuscripts in which I find them, and the circumstance that I have sent copies of them to friends, etc. Well, if they had been better, if it had been a noble poem, perhaps it would have only more entirely taken up the ladder into heaven."

To the like purpose in the journal of the following year is this note, headed " The ivory gate " : —

" Poppy leaves are strewn when a generalization is made, for I can never remember the circumstances to which I owe it, so as to repeat the experiment or put myself in the conditions."

[But this image of the disguised divinities recurs again and again in his writings, as in the poem " May-Day," and twice in the " Lecture on the Times " (*Nature, Addresses and*

Lectures, pp. 259, 287), and in "Works and Days" (*Society and Solitude*, p. 168). Dr. Holmes in the interesting chapter on Emerson's Poems, in his Memoir, quotes the latter passage and says: "Now see this thought in full dress, and then ask what is the difference between prose and poetry." He then gives the poem and adds, "Cinderella at the fireside, and Cinderella at the prince's ball!"

"Days" was printed in the first number of the *Atlantic*.

MY GARDEN. *Page 229.* Of his Garden Mr. Emerson wrote to his friend Carlyle on May 14, 1846: —

"I, too, have a new plaything, the best I ever had, — a wood-lot. Last Fall I bought a piece of more than forty acres, on the border of a little lake half a mile wide and more, called Walden Pond; — a place to which my feet have for years been accustomed to bring me once or twice a week at all seasons. My lot, to be sure, is on the farther side of the water, not so familiar to me as the nearer shore. Some of the wood is an old growth, but most of it has been cut off within twenty years and is growing thriftily. In these May days, when maples, poplars, oaks, birches, walnut and pine are in their spring glory, I go thither every afternoon, and cut with my hatchet an Indian path through the thicket all along the bold shore, and open the finest pictures.

"My two little girls know the road now, though it is nearly two miles from my house, and find their way to the spring at the foot of a pine grove, and with some awe to the ruins of a village of shanties, all overgrown with mullein, which the Irish who built the railroad left behind them. At a good distance in from the shore the land rises to a rocky head, perhaps sixty feet above the water. Thereon I think to place a hut; perhaps it will have two stories and be a petty tower, looking out to Monadnoc and other New Hampshire Mountains. There I hope to go with book and pen when good hours come."

" My Garden" is the hill, with a ledge of rock cropping out, these covered by a vigorous growth of oak, on the Lincoln side of Walden, opposite Mr. Emerson's loved pine grove where Thoreau lived for two years. Destructive fires of late years, set by passing railroad trains, have ruined the forest that clothed it.

In his afternoon walks alone in the wood for many years, he strove to " put his woods in song," and to his children, when they went with him, he would often croon a few lines. The resulting verses gradually were separated, and those printed in the Appendix under the title "Walden" are mostly the earlier ones.

" My Garden " was first printed in the *Atlantic Monthly* for December, 1866.

Page 229, note 1. The second verse in the manuscript, here omitted, was: —

> For joy and beauty planted it,
> With faerie gardens cheered,
> And boding Fancy haunted it
> With men and women weird.

Page 230, note 1. The rising and falling of Walden's waters are curiously independent of dry or wet seasons. Its watershed is small; it is fed by springs at its bottom,— its clear water being more than one hundred feet in depth. It has no visible outlet, though it is evident that this must be by filtration through a ridge of sand and boulders one or two hundred yards thick, to a swamp, whence the waters run by the "Sanguinetto Brook," as Mr. Channing named it, to " Fairhaven Bay " on the Musketaquid or Concord River.

Page 230, note 2. This suggests some sentences on the last page of " Nature," in *Essays, Second Series.*

THE CHARTIST'S COMPLAINT. *Page 232.* This poem, also appearing in the *Atlantic* of November, 1857, was in the note-books called " Janus," but Mr. Emerson changed its name because the sad laborer, not the poet who can reconcile the two aspects, speaks. The title was more intelligible fifty years ago, when the Chartist agitation in England against privilege was recent.

THE TITMOUSE. *Page 233.* The chronicle of the poet's adventure with the titmouse was written in verse while it was still fresh in his mind.

The poem appeared in the *Atlantic Monthly* for May, 1862, and here is the story in the journal: —

March 3, 1862. " The snow still lies even with the tops of the walls across the Walden road, and, this afternoon, I waded through the woods to my grove. A chickadee came out to greet me, flew about within reach of my hands, perched on the nearest bough, flew down into the snow, rested there two seconds, then up again just over my head, and busied himself on the dead bark. I whistled to him through my teeth, and (I think, in response) he began at once to whistle. I promised him crumbs, and must not go again to these woods without them. I suppose the best food to carry would be the meat of shagbarks or Castile nuts. Thoreau tells me that they are very sociable with wood-choppers, and will take crumbs from their hands."

On the dangers of the situation, if such there were, Mr. Emerson is silent in the journal, as would be natural with him, and perhaps for Art's sake he magnifies them in the poem, but it is to be remembered how like a lion March often comes in in Massachusetts, that the snow was deep, the woods really remote and the walker approaching his sixtieth year. The American reader will hardly find the poem so obscure as did Matthew Arnold, who said that, after all, one does n't quite get at what the titmouse really did for Emerson.

The titmouse was an old friend. Here is a passage from the journal of 1856: —

" The horse taught me something, the titmouse whispered a secret in my ear, and the lespedeza looked at me, as I passed. Will the academicians, in their Annual Report, please tell me what they said ? "

THE HARP. *Page 237.* " The Harp " formed a part of " May-Day " when that poem first appeared. It followed the passage which tells of the harmonizing by the air of discordant natural sounds at Lake Superior.

The wild wind-harp of the pine, or the artificial one in his study-window played on by the West-wind, gave the music that stirred Emerson.

Page 239, note 1. The story, from the *Morte d' Arthur,* of Merlin hopelessly confined in a chamber of air, from which he speaks to the passing knights, is given in full in " Poetry and Imagination," in *Letters and Social Aims.*

Page 240, note 1. Journal, 1861. " What a joy I found and still can find in the Æolian harp; what a youth find I still in Collins's ' Ode to Evening ' and in Gray's ' Eton College '! What delight I owed to Moore's insignificant but melodious poetry ! That is the merit of Clough's ' Bothie ' that the joy of youth is in it ! "

Page 241, note 1. In a lecture on Italy, which Mr. Emerson gave on his return in 1834, he said: —

" On Ash Wednesday the famous Miserere was sung before the Pope and the Cardinals in the Sistine Chapel. The saying at Rome is that the effect of the piece as performed in the Sistine Chapel cannot be imitated, not only by any other choir, but in any other chapel in the world. . . . Of its merits I am quite unable to speak who know nothing of psalmody. And yet even to me it was sweet music and sounded more like an Æolian harp than anything else."

SEASHORE. *Page 242.* In July, 1857, Mr. Emerson, induced by Dr. Bartol, took his family to spend two weeks at Pigeon Cove, on Cape Ann. The day after our return to Concord, he came into our mother's room, where we were all sitting, with his journal in his hand, and said, " I came in yesterday from walking on the rocks and wrote down what the sea had said to me; and to-day, when I open my book, I find it all reads as blank verse, with scarcely a change."

Here is the passage from that journal, as he read it to us: July 23. " Returned from Pigeon Cove, where we have made acquaintance with the sea, for seven days. 'T is a noble, friendly power, and seemed to say to me, Why so late and slow to come to me? Am I not here always, thy proper summer home? Is not my voice thy needful music; my breath thy healthful climate in the heats; my touch thy cure? Was ever building like my terraces? Was ever couch so magnificent as mine? Lie down on my warm ledges and learn that a very little hut is all you need. I have made this architecture superfluous, and it is paltry beside mine. Here are twenty Romes and Ninevehs and Karnacs in ruins together, obelisk and pyramid and Giant's Causeway; here they all are prostrate or half piled. And behold the sea, the opaline, plentiful and strong, yet beautiful as the rose or the rainbow, full of food, nourisher of men, purger of the world, creating a sweet climate and in its unchangeable ebb and flow, and in its beauty at a few furlongs, giving a hint of that which changes not, and is perfect.''

SONG OF NATURE. *Page 244.* This joyful and eminently characteristic poem seems to have been written by Mr. Emerson in 1859. His belief in the sure advance of life through the ages he had expressed long before, but now, though his belief needed no confirmation, the new and interesting lights on the subject and examples everywhere adduced by Darwin and his followers were inspiring to him, and here found expression.

Page 244, note 1. There are in the manuscript varying expressions in the foregoing poem which are interesting.

In the first, "the gulf of space" originally was "the swallowing space."

In the second, the last line ran, —

> In death new-born and strong.

In the fifth verse, Mr. Emerson hesitated long, as the various trials show, before he changed his line,

> My apples ripened well,

by substituting "gardens" for the more lively image.

Page 246, note 1. Readers who wish nothing unsolved are much troubled by this verse, but Nature is not statistical or immediately intelligible. Like the gods she "says all things by indirection." When the young knight was angered by Merlin's vagueness, Tennyson makes the wise man answer, —

> "Know ye not, then, the riddling of the Bards ?
> Confusion, and illusion, and relation,
> Elusion, and occasion, and evasion.''

Nor can the editor say with authority who was meant in the third line of the next verse. Its very ambiguity was probably intentional and makes it harmonize better with the preceding verse. If it points to Egypt, some readers have suggested Moses, but Mr. Emerson would have been far more likely to refer to one of the great Alexandrian Neo-platonists.

But Italy is more strictly

> Over against the mouths of Nile,

and thus the genius of classic Rome or of the Italian Renaissance, without choosing a representative, might have been indicated. If a choice must be made, the "Solution" would point to Dante. It seems remarkable that in that poem Plato, "the purple ancient . . . of the richest strain," [1] is not named, for the author owed far more to him than to Swedenborg.

Page 247, note 1. In the note-book, "Forces," 1863, is this entry: —

> The sun has lost no beams,
> The earth no virtues,
> Gravity is as adhesive,
> Electricity as swift, heat as expansive, light as joyful,
> Air as virtuous, water as medicinal, as in the beginning.
> And the magazine of thought and the heart of morals
> Are as rich and omnipotent as at the first day.

TWO RIVERS. *Page 248.* This, perhaps the most musical of the poems, gives opportunity to show Mr. Emerson's later method. The thought came on the river-bank, whispered by

---

[1] Mr. Emerson thus named him in his review of Carlyle's *Past and Present.* See "Papers from the Dial," in the volume *Natural History of Intellect.*

the ripples, and very likely was written there; if not, on his
return to his study. It mainly gave the form, for "verse
must be alive and inseparable from its contents." There·
after, when the days came, as Herrick said,

> "That I
> Fitted am to prophesy,"

he repeated or chanted the lines to himself until the right
word was in an instant given to replace the awkward phrase
with redundant syllables, and the polish and the music came
to match the thought. Here is the poem on the day of its
birth, in the early summer of 1856 : —

"Thy voice is sweet, Musketaquid, and repeats the music
of the rain, but sweeter is the silent stream which flows even
through thee, as thou through the land.

"Thou art shut in thy banks, but the stream I love flows
in thy water, and flows through rocks and through the air and
through rays of light as well, and through darkness, and
through men and women.

"I hear and see the inundation and the eternal spending of
the stream in winter and in summer, in men and animals, in
passion and thought. Happy are they who can hear it."

> I see thy brimming, eddying stream
> And thy enchantment,
> For thou changest every rock in thy bed
> Into a gem,
> All is opal and agate,
> And at will thou pavest with diamonds:
> Take them away from the stream
> And they are poor, shreds and flints.
> So is it with me to-day.

This rhapsody does not gain by the attempt to reduce part of
it to rhyme, which occurs later in the same journal: —

> Thy murmuring voice, Musketaquid,
> Repeats the music of the rain,
> But sweeter rivers silent flit
> Through thee as thou through Concord plain.
> Thou in thy banks must dwell,
> But
> The stream I follow freely flows
> Through thee, through rocks, through air as well,
> Through light, through men it gayly goes.

But Mr. Emerson kept the verses by him nearly two years
before, in their perfected form, he gave them to the *Atlantic
Monthly* for January, 1858.

Page 248, note 1. From the first, the image of the stream
applied to thought and life appears in the prose and the poems,
as in the "Over-Soul" (p. 268), in the first series of
Essays, in "Nature" (pp. 178, 179), in the second series,
and in *Nature, Addresses and Lectures* (pp. 26, 27). In the
poem "Peter's Field," in the Appendix, the poet says, —

> Far seen, the river glides below,
>   Tossing one sparkle to the eyes.
> I catch thy meaning, wizard wave;
>   The River of my Life replies.

Page 248, note 2. The words of Jesus when he talked with
the Samaritan woman at the fountain, were, of course, in the
author's mind.

WALDEINSAMKEIT. *Page 249.* Possibly the decision to use
for *Forest Solitude* an equivalent, outlandish in the strict and

respectful sense, may have been influenced by the fact that to woods in the region of Walden more than to others, Mr. Emerson went for communion with Nature, and the German word had a kindred sound. And yet the first two lines tell the story that the poem was begun during a visit to Mr. John M. Forbes at the beautiful island of Naushon, in the summer of 1857. The poem was published in the *Atlantic Monthly* for October of the following year.

Page 249, note 1. " Allah does not count the days spent in the chase " was a favorite quotation, but the sea always suggested to Emerson illimitable time. Mrs. Helen Hunt Jackson relates that when she was a fellow guest with Mr. Emerson at the house of a friend in Newport, he quietly asked, " Are there any clocks in Newport ? " and the meaning did not instantly occur to the hearers.

Page 249, note 2. Journal, 1845. " The wood is soberness with a basis of joy." Immediately under this is written,

Sober with a fund of joy.

TERMINUS. *Page 251.* Terminus was to the Romans the deity presiding over boundaries and landmarks.

In the last days of the year 1866, when I was returning from a long stay in the Western States, I met my father in New York just starting for his usual winter lecturing trip, in those days extending beyond the Mississippi. We spent the night together at the St. Denis Hotel, and as we sat by the fire he read me two or three of his poems for the new May-Day volume, among them " Terminus." It almost startled me. No thought of his ageing had ever come to me, and there he sat, with no apparent abatement of bodily vigor, and young in spirit, recognizing with serene acquiescence his failing forces; I think he smiled as he read. He recognized, as none of us did, that his working days were nearly done. They lasted about five years longer, although he lived, in comfortable health, yet ten years beyond those of his activity. Almost at the time when he wrote " Terminus " he wrote in his journal: —

"Within I do not find wrinkles and used heart, but unspent youth."

Page 252, note 1. Mr. Emerson wrote to his brother William in 1838, —

" All Emersons are slender. There are only two or three sound stocks of that excellent tree."

Journal, 1859. "Shall I blame my mother, whitest of women, because she was not a gypsy and gave me no swarthy ferocity? Or my father because he came of a lettered race and had no porter's shoulders?"

Page 252, note 2. There are in the verse-book lines in the last stanza which Mr. Emerson omitted in the poem. One pair, containing the nautical image, follows the line in the text, —

> Obey the voice at eve obeyed at prime,

with

> ' Is the sky dark?' it saith, ' More near will stand
> The pilot with unerring hand.'

Another pair drop this image, for home surroundings, thus: —

> Obey the voice at eve obeyed at prime,
> And hide myself among my thrifty pears,
> Each fault of mine masked by a growth of theirs.

THE NUN'S ASPIRATION. *Page 253.* This poem is but a metrical rendering of some fine and some touching passages from the journal of Miss Mary Moody Emerson, the sister of Mr.

Emerson's father. She was a person of grea[t]
inspirer, the spur and the constant critic
whom she loved and secretly admired. Mr
account of her remarkable life in the volum
graphical Sketches. In Mr. Cabot's *Memoir of E*
many extracts from the letters that passed between her and
her nephews.

Page 254, note 1. In spite of Miss Emerson's tempera-
mental eccentricities, of which she was aware, and alluded to
them in her journal, she was loved by her nephews, and of
her Mr. Emerson said: "She gave high counsels. It was the
privilege of certain boys to have this immeasurably high stand-
ard indicated to their childhood; a blessing which nothing else
in education could supply."

APRIL. *Page 255.* These verses first appeared among the
Selected Poems which Mr. Emerson published in 1876. A
pleasant little description of the bewitching influences of April,
in a letter written to Margaret Fuller in 1840, was transcribed
by him into a note-book and perhaps was the foundation of the
poem.

MAIDEN SPEECH OF THE ÆOLIAN HARP. *Page 256.* These
lines accompanied Mr. Emerson's New Year's present to his
daughter Edith and her husband, Colonel William H. Forbes,
in 1868.

Page 256, note 1. His own delighted use of the wind-
harp is shown in this fragment of an early lecture: —

"Stretch a few threads over an Æolian harp and put it in
the window, and listen to what it says of the times, and of the
heart of Nature. You shall not believe that the miracle of
Nature is less, the chemical power worn out."

CUPIDO. *Page 257*. This, as well as the three poems which precede it, was first published in *Selected Poems*. It seems to have been written in 1843.

THE PAST. *Page 257*. No trace of the history of this poem remains.

Page 258, note 1. In the first pages of the essay on Memory, in *Natural History of Intellect*, it is said of remorseful recollection of the Past: —

"Well, that is as it should be. That is the police of the Universe: the angels are set to punish you, so long as you are capable of such crime. But . . . the day comes when you are incapable of such crime. Then you suffer no more, you look on it as heaven looks on it, with wonder at the deed, and with applause at the pain it has cost you."

THE LAST FAREWELL. *Page 258*. Mr. Emerson printed his brother Edward's sad farewell to all that was dear to him, six years after his death, in the first number of the *Dial*.

Page 258, note 2. Edward was born in 1805, but though two years younger than Waldo, the latter used to say that they were really very near together, as he was near the foot of his classes, and Edward at the head of his. Those who remembered him said that he was strikingly handsome, a born scholar, more brilliant in his studies and his speech than Waldo, and a favorite in society. All through college he was easily first scholar. Though of delicate constitution, his conscience and his ambition would not allow him to spare himself. Daniel Webster, in whose office he studied law, recognized his powers and his fine character, and committed to him the charge of his two sons. Yet Edward heaped other tasks upon himself, to free himself from debt incurred in the voyage to Europe for his health, until his reason for a time gave way under the strain. This he soon regained, but his mainspring seemed broken. Advised to go to a milder climate, he took a clerkship in a business house in Porto Rico, and worked uncomplainingly there for a few years. Friends who saw his cheerful demeanor reported that he was in the way of recovery of his vigor, but it appears that he himself knew that, as he wrote, "the arrow of the angel had gone too deep." A verse telling of a private grief, which Mr. Emerson omitted, may now be restored.

IN MEMORIAM, E. B. E. *Page 261, note 1.* The Old North Bridge, across which the opening volleys of the Revolutionary War were fired in a battle whose field extended from the Musketaquid to the Charles River, was close behind the Manse built by Rev. William Emerson, the young patriot minister of Concord, and there his grandsons William, Ralph Waldo, Edward and Charles had spent many pleasant days in boyhood. (See the poems "Dirge" and "Peter's Field.") The two British soldiers killed at the first fire lie buried where they fell.

Page 264, note 1. The expression in this line is borrowed from Milton and used by Mr. Emerson more than once in his writings.

ELEMENTS AND MOTTOES

Page 267. The thirteen poems which follow, beginning with "Experience," were selected by Mr. Emerson from the mottoes of the Essays, of which they — all but two — bear the names, for publication in *May-Day and Other Pieces* in 1867. He there called the group "Elements." The motto of the essay on Behavior he called " Manners," the essay of that name having no original motto, but one from Ben Jonson. To the motto of " The Over-Soul " he gave the title " Unity."

It has seemed to the editor that the readers of the Poems would be glad to have the other mottoes which Mr. Emerson gave to his chapters included in this volume. They therefore are printed, with a few exceptions, after the thirteen which the author preferred. The exceptions are as follows: the motto of Self-Reliance is found where Mr. Emerson placed it among the Quatrains as " Power; " the motto to " The Poet," with the exception of its first two lines, is a part of the long poem of that name in the Appendix; most of the lines of " Fate " belong among the fragments on " The Poet," in the Appendix, and the last four lines form the ending of the poem " Fate; " the motto to " Considerations by the Way " seemed better placed with the " Song of Merlin." The second motto of " Charac-ter " and that of " Beauty " are portions respectively of the "Ode to Beauty " and of " In Memoriam, E. B. E." The titles " Promise " and " Caritas " seemed appropriate to the mottoes respectively of "Nominalist and Realist" and "New England Reformers." " Love " had only a verse from the Koran as motto. The Essays in the volumes which followed *Conduct of Life* had no mottoes in Mr. Emerson's life-time, and, with Mr. Cabot's sanction, I supplied these for *Lectures and Biographical Sketches*, in the Riverside Edition, from fragments of verse, never published by Mr. Emerson, which were printed in the Appendix. I have now ventured to do the same for *Society and Solitude* and *Letters and Social Aims*.

Page 271, note 1. Journal, 1840. "I read to-day in Ockley [History of the Saracens] a noble sentence of Ali, son-in-law of Mahomet: 'Thy lot or portion of life is seeking after thee; therefore be at rest from seeking after it.' "

See also " The Over-Soul" (*Essays, First Series*, p. 293).

Page 272, note 1. Compare the quatrain " Northman."

Page 273, note 1. The first six lines of this motto are from " The Poet" (see Appendix).

Page 273, note 2. This poem in the verse-book begins, —

> Ah me! can maxims educate.

There is in " Fate" (*Conduct of Life*, p. 44) a passage on the necessity for the great to be impressionable.

Page 274, note 1. In the notes to " Friendship," *Essays, First Series*, p. 412, are two passages on ideal friendship from letters by Mr. Emerson.

Page 275, note 1. This poem sheds light on " Uriel" and on " Brahma." The essay on Circles, especially pages 317–318, contains much to the same purpose, — the beneficent compensations in Morals, as in Nature. Had Mr. Emerson ever resorted to italics, the use of them in the word " living" would have helped the reader in the first line, which is condensed to the last point. Thy prayers are concerned with a Heaven which is alive, is the meaning. This is shown in the first rhapsody in the verse-book: —

> Heaven is alive;
> Self-built and quarrying itself,
> Upbuilds eternal towers;
> Self-commanded works
> In vital cirque
> By dint of being all;
> Its loss is transmutation.
> Fears not the craft of undermining days,
> Grows by decays,

And, by the famous might that 's lodged
In reaction and recoil,
Makes flames to freeze and ice to boil,
And thro' the arms of all the fiends
Builds the firm seat of Innocence.

Page 276, note 1. Mr. Emerson's note-books are full of verses about the joyful Seyd (or Said) seeking beauty in Nature and man. These may be found in the Appendix, in "Fragments on the Poet." A few of these were taken by him for this motto.

Page 277, note 1. In "Love," *Essays, First Series,* pp. 176, 177, is a passage which these lines recall.

Page 277, note 2. In a letter to a near friend, written in 1841, Mr. Emerson speaks of himself as "an admirer of persons. I cannot get used to them; they daunt and dazzle me still. . . . Blessed be the Eternal Power for those whom fancy even cannot strip of beauty, and who never for a moment seem to me profane." [1]

Page 279, note 1. Mr. Emerson thus changed the title of the motto of "The Over-Soul."

Page 280, note 1. See "Fate" (p. 21 in *Essays, First Series*) and also the poems "Nemesis" and "Voluntaries."

Page 280, note 2. Compare the passage in the Address to the Divinity Students (*Nature, Addresses and Lectures,* p. 121).

[1] *Letters to a Friend,* edited by Charles Eliot Norton. Boston: Houghton, Mifflin & Co., 1899.

QUATRAINS AND TRANSLATIONS

QUATRAINS. *Page 291.* Mr. Emerson's Oriental studies may have given him the taste for this sort of verse. In the essay on Persian Poetry he says: —

"The Persians have epics and tales, but, for the most part, they affect short poems and epigrams. Gnomic verses, rules of life conveyed in a lively image . . . addressed to the eye and contained in a single stanza, were always current in the East."

He gives among other specimens of these gnomic poems this: —

> " 'The secret that should not be blown
> Not one of thy nation must know ;
> You may padlock the gate of a town,
> But never the mouth of a foe.' "

This may have suggested the quatrain "Hush!" Certainly the form of the specimens he gives is suggestive. Most of the Quatrains seem to have been written between 1850 and 1860; one or two much earlier.

Page 291, note 1. In the journal of 1850, Mr. Emerson speaks of the necessity of the great man being highly impressionable, and adds, " He obeys the main current, — that is all his secret, the main current is so feeble a force as can be felt only by bodies delicately poised. He can orient himself. In the woods, I have one guide, namely, to follow the light, — to go where the woods are thinnest; then at last I am sure to come out. So he cannot be betrayed or misguided, for he knows where the north is, knows painfully when he is going in the wrong direction."

Page 292, note 1. Compare *Nature, Addresses and Lectures*, p. 30, and *Conduct of Life*, p. 294.

IX

Page 292, note 2. Journal, July, 1840. "Go to the forest, if God has made thee a poet, and make thy life clean and fragrant as thy office.

> True Brahmin, in the morning meadows wet,
> Expound the Vedas in the violet.

Thy love must be thy art. . . . Nature also must teach thee rhetoric. She can teach thee not only to speak truth, but to speak it truly."

Page 292, note 3. "Frozen leaves or grouse's breast" was the early form.

Page 293, note 1. Journal, 1853. "The Vikings sang, 'the force of the storm is a help to the arm of our rowers; the hurricane is in our service; it carries us the way we would go.'" — Thierry's *Norman Conquest.*

Page 293, note 2. These lines date from May 1, 1838.

Page 293, note 3. This quatrain is Mr. Emerson's tribute to the upright citizen and lawyer, Samuel Hoar, the "Squire" of Concord, and father of his friends, Judge E. R. Hoar and Miss Elizabeth Hoar. Mr. Emerson's sketch of his life is in *Lectures and Biographical Sketches.*

Page 294, note 1. Compare, as to Nature's ever new allurements, *Essays, Second Series,* p. 192.

Page 294, note 2. The last two lines are from an Oriental source, and are also quoted in *Conduct of Life,* p. 10.

Page 295, note 1. The motto of "Self-Reliance."

Page 295, note 2. See *Essays, First Series,* p. 148; also "Demonology," in *Lectures and Biographical Sketches.*

Page 295, note 3. Compare the ending of the verses in the Appendix, beginning, —

> Love
> Asks nought its brother cannot give.

Note-book. "It creeps where it cannot go, it creeps under the snows of Scandinavia, and Lofn is as mighty a divinity in the Norse Edda as Camadeva in the red vault of India."

Page 296, note 1. The last two lines are a rendering of a quotation from a sermon by Caleb Vines, a Puritan, on "Caleb's integrity in following the Lord fully," preached at St. Margaret's, Westminster, before the Honourable House of Commons, November 30, 1642.

Page 296, note 2. A Latin rendering of a Greek saying was spoken of by Mr. Emerson as the source of the quatrain. One asks a neighbor, "But are you not then my friend?" "*Usque ad aras,*" is the reply — *As far as the altars.*

Page 296, note 3. When Dante met his friend Casella, the beautiful singer, in Purgatory, he begged him to sing. When Casella began, *Amor che nella mente mi ragiona,* the souls all flocked to hear.

Page 297, note 1. The title signifies, "They enjoy a tearless age."

Mr. Emerson held the poet to his office of "joy-giver and enjoyer," as he says in the poem "Saadi." It is the more remarkable that he admits Swedenborg as a poet in the "Solution," but it is on the score of his symbolism.

TRANSLATIONS. *Page 298.* Among the poems in his first volume, Mr. Emerson placed two translations from Hafiz, through the German, of course, less pleasing than those here given. These were omitted by him from the *Selected Poems,* and by Mr. Cabot in the Riverside Edition. They are not restored here, because of their length and because the space is needed for restored and early poems, and interesting fragments. In his preface to the American edition of Saadi's *Gulistan,* translated by Gladwin, are some of Mr. Emerson's translations of Persian poetry, and also in the essay on that subject in *Letters and Social Aims*.

Page 300, note 1. Mr. Joel Benton,[1] writing of the quatrains and the translations which follow, and comparing the quatrain " Hafiz " with this rendering, well says, —

" If the translation here seems (as it evidently does) a little more like Emerson than it does like Hafiz, the balance is more than preserved by his steeping his own original quatrain in a little tincture of the wine and spirit of Oriental thought. When he translated Hafiz, he was probably thinking of his own workmanship; when he described him, he was simply absorbed in the *milieu* of the Persian poet."

Mr. Benton says also, " What Goethe says of the Spanish poet Calderon (I quote Lord Houghton's forcible translation) serves equally well if you substitute for his name Emerson's: —

" ' Many a light the Orient throws
O'er the midland waters brought;
He alone who Hafiz knows
Knows what Calderon has thought.' "

This suggests that it very likely was Goethe who drew Emerson's attention to Hafiz.

APPENDIX

THE POET. *Page 309.* This poem, called in its early form " The Discontented Poet, a Masque," was begun as early as 1838, probably earlier. It received additions through several

[1] *Emerson as a Poet.* By Joel Benton. New York : M. L. Holbrook & Co., 1883.

years and was much improved, but Mr. Emerson never completed it.

"The Poet" seems to have been written parallel, so to speak, with the lectures on the same theme which are condensed into the opening essay in the *Second Series*. It was written in the years when Emerson, who saw God and Man and Nature as a poet in the highest sense sees them, was struggling through impediments towards a fitting expression of his vision or thought in verse. He soon discarded the first title and such morbid lines as had been written during a somewhat unrestful period. He felt, as he told a friend, that these desires contained the promise of their fulfilment. The poem truly pictures his own method of seeking inspiration, sitting under the pines in Walden woods by day and walking alone under the stars by night, — listening always. The stanza beginning, —

> The sun set, but set not his hope

(used as the motto for "Character") and that preceding it, show his happy patience, secure that his time would come.

"The Poet" as here printed has a reasonable unity, but around it was a system of satellite pieces on this favorite topic, of a later date and more musical. In these, the poet is called Saadi, or, as often more convenient for metre, Said or Seyd.

Dr. Holmes was greatly interested in these poems. I quote from his Memoir of his friend: —

"If any doubter wishes to test his fitness for reading them, and if the poems already mentioned are not enough to settle the question, let him read the paragraph of 'May-Day,' beginning, —

> 'I saw the bud-crowned Spring go forth,'

'Seashore,' the fine fragments in the Appendix to his published works, called, collectively, 'The Poet,' blocks bearing the mark of poetic genius, but left lying round for want of the structural instinct, and last of all that which is, in many respects, first of all, the 'Threnody.'"

Page 309, note 1. Journal, 1839. "The poet is a namer. His success is a new nomenclature."

"Though the origin of most of our words is forgotten, each word was at first a stroke of genius, and obtained currency because for the moment it symbolized the world to the first speaker and to the hearer." — "The Poet," *Essays, Second Series.*

Page 309, note 2. In his Introduction to Professor W. W. Goodwin's revision of Plutarch's *Morals*, Mr. Emerson quotes Plutarch's sentence: "Were there not a sun, we might, for all the other stars, pass our days in the 'Reverend Dark,' as Heracleitus calls it."

Page 310, note 1. Compare the last sentence in "Man the Reformer," *Nature, Addresses and Lectures.*

Page 310, note 2. Mr. Emerson once spoke of his joy when, as a boy, he "caught the first hint of the Berkeleyan philosophy. I could see that there was a Cause behind every stump and clod, and by the help of some fine words could make every old wagon and wood-pile and stone wall oscillate a little and threaten to dance; nay, give me a fair field, and the selectmen of Concord and the Reverend Pound-me-down himself began to look unstable and vaporous." He said in a lecture, of Shakspeare, "He is the chosen closet companion, who can, at any moment, by incessant surprises, work the miracle of mythologizing every fact of the common life."

Page 310, note 3. In the essay on Domestic Life, *Society and Solitude*, Mr. Emerson dwells on the inestimable advantage of comparative poverty to youth.

Page 311, note 1. Journal, 1838. "The intellectual nomadism is the faculty of Objectiveness or of Eyes which everywhere feed themselves. Who hath such eyes, everywhere falls into true relations with his fellow men. Every man, every object is a prize, a study, a property to him, and this love smooths his brow, joins him to men and makes him beautiful and beloved in their sight. His house is a wagon, he roams through all latitudes as easily as a Calmuc. He must meantime abide by his inward law as the Calmuc by his Khan." — See "History," *Essays, First Series*, pp. 22, 23.

Page 311, note 2. The correspondences and harmonies are dwelt on in other poems, as in "Merlin," II., and in the passage in the second "Woodnotes" —

> Come learn with me the fatal song, etc.

Page 312, note 1. Compare the essay on the Poet, in *Essays, Second Series*, pp. 25 and 39.

Page 313, note 1. See in *Conduct of Life*, "Beauty," p. 304.

Page 314, note 1. This stanza was used by Mr. Emerson as motto for the essay on Character.

Page 314, note 2. Journal, 1837. "To-night I walked under the stars through the snow, and stopped and looked at my far sparklers and heard the voice of the wind, so slight and pure and deep as if it were the sound of the stars themselves revolving."

1841. "Last night a walk to the river . . . and saw the moon in the broken water, interrogating, interrogating."

Page 315, note 1. "1838, 24 June, Sunday. Forever the night addresses the imagination, and the interrogating soul within or behind all its functions, and now in the summer night, which makes the earth more habitable, the more. Strange that forever we do not exhaust the wonder and meaning of these stars, points of light merely, but still they speak and ask and warn, each moment with new mind.''

Page 315, note 2. " The power of music, the power of poetry, to unfix and as it were clap wings to solid nature, interprets the riddle of Orpheus.''— " History,'' *Essays, First Series*, p. 31.

Page 316, note 1. In " The Transcendentalist " (*Nature, Addresses and Lectures*, pp. 341–343) the eager youth who seem to themselves born out of time are described.

Page 316, note 2. Some sentences in the concluding passage of the essay on the Poet recall this stanza picturing the touching loyalty of the family to the man of genius.

Page 317, note 1. Composure is the first virtue of man, as modesty is that of woman.

Page 317, note 2. The opening passage of Mr. Emerson's first book, *Nature*, shows the inspiration which he found in the heavenly bodies, and the lesson to be found in their beauty and their ordered motion. Every astronomical fact interested him.

Page 319, note 1. The doctrine of the Universal Mind.

Page 320, note 1. Compare the passage in Mr. Emerson's Address to the Divinity Students beginning, " The perception of this law of laws awakens in the mind a sentiment,'' etc.

In the journal for 1840, he wrote thoughts which occur in the last two stanzas: " The moon keeps its appointment — will not the good Spirit ? Wherefore have we labored and fasted, say we, and thou takest no note ? Let him not take note, if he please to hide, — then it were sublime beyond a poet's dreams still to labor and abstain and obey, and, if thou canst, to *put the good spirit in the wrong*. That were a feat to sing in Elysium, on Olympus, by the waters of life in the New Jerusalem.''

The last seven lines of the poem were, however, written in 1831.

FRAGMENTS ON THE POET AND THE POETIC GIFT. *Page 320.* What Dr. Holmes says in his chapter on the Poems is especially true of these fragments: "The poet reveals himself under the protection of his imaginative and melodious phrases, — the flowers and jewels of his vocabulary."

The first part of this poem was written in 1845; from it Mr. Emerson took the motto for "Beauty," the first ten lines of which followed

> At court he sat in the grave Divan,

and the rest of the motto followed

> And etiquette of gentilesse.

Page 322, note 1. In the essay on Inspiration, in *Letters and Social Aims*, after quoting what the poet Gray said of the Æolian harp, Mr. Emerson adds: —

"Perhaps you can recall a delight like it, which spoke to the eye, when you have stood by a lake in the woods in summer, and saw where little flaws of wind whip spots or patches of still water into fleets of ripples, — so sudden, so slight, so spiritual, that it was more like the rippling of the Aurora Borealis at night than any spectacle of day."

Page 323, note 1. In his journal of 1842, he wrote under the heading "To-day": —

"But my increasing value of the present moment, to which I gladly abandon myself when I can, is destroying my Sunday respects, which always, no doubt, have some regard to the State and conservatism. But when to-day is great I fling all the world's future into the sea."

Mr. Emerson, from childhood to age, had reverence for

worship, and for public worship, but as he grew in mind and spirit he felt himself cramped by creeds and forms. He found he could worship to more purpose in solitude and in the presence of Nature. He always gladly heard a true preacher, and in his old age, when his critical sense was dulled and the passing Day had fewer gifts for him, he liked to go to the Concord church, were it only for association's sake.

Page 323, note 2. Hassan the camel-driver was, without doubt, Mr. Emerson's sturdy neighbor, Mr. Edmund Hosmer, for whom he had great respect. The camels were the slow oxen, then universally used for farm-work, with which Mr. Hosmer ploughed the poet's fields for him. Compare what is said of manual labor in *Nature, Addresses and Lectures,* pp. 236–238.

Page 324, note 1. Journal, 1855. "What I said in one of my Saadi scraps of verse, I might say in good sooth, that —

Thus the high Muse treated me,

Directly never greeted me, etc.

My best thought came from others. I heard in their words my own meaning, but a deeper sense than they put on them: and could well and best express myself in other people's phrases, but to finer purpose than they knew."

The thought of the last five lines is given more fully in "Art" (*Essays, First Series,* pp. 360, 361).

Page 326, note 1. Sun and moon and everything in Nature are symbols, seeds which quicken in their interpretation, which the poet finds for mankind.

Page 326, note 2. These lines are a more pleasing version of the motto to the essay on Fate, in *Conduct of Life,* with two introductory lines, and without the less poetical ending lines which were used by Mr. Emerson in the poem "*Fate.*"

Page 327, note 1. The last verse is the motto to " Intellect " in *Essays, First Series.*

Page 328, note 1. This in the verse-book is called " Terminus."

Page 328, note 2. These lines appear to have been part of a poem called " Bacchus " that was never completed, referred to in the note to " Bacchus."

Page 331, note 1. This thought is more fully stated in " Fate " (*Conduct of Life,* p. 26) and in " Self-Reliance " (*Essays, First Series,* p. 71).

Page 331, note 2. See " Inspiration," *Letters and Social Aims,* p. 296.

Page 332, note 1. These lines, it is seen in one of the verse-books, describe the true poet; he re-creates, by showing what creation signifies, and thoughts are the seed he sows.

Page 334, note 1. " Every thought which genius and piety throw into the world, alters the world." — " Politics," *Essays, Second Series.*

Page 334, note 2. Asmodeus was an evil spirit. He is mentioned in the Book of Tobit in the Apocrypha. Students of the Black Art held that demons could be kept out of mischief by setting them at hopeless tasks, like making ropes out of sand. The braid-like effect of the wave-markings in shoal water suggested the idea. Mr. Emerson always found it hard to make a tissue out of the thoughts which came to him — he spoke of them once as " infinitely repellent particles."

FRAGMENTS ON NATURE AND LIFE. *Page 335, note 1.* In the leading essay in *Natural History of Intellect* is this passage on the Greek symbolizing of Nature in the god Pan: —

" Pan, that is, All. His habit was to dwell in mountains, lying on the ground, tooting like a cricket in the sun, refusing to speak, clinging to his behemoth ways. He could intoxicate by the strain of his shepherd's pipe, — silent yet to most, for his pipes make the music of the spheres, which, because it sounds eternally, is not heard at all by the dull, but only by the mind. He wears a coat of leopard spots or stars. He could terrify by earth-born fears called *panics*. Yet was he in the secret of Nature and could look both before and after. He was only seen under disguises, and was not represented by any outward image; a terror sometimes, at others a placid omnipotence.''

Page 341, note 1. This was originally in the rough draft of Monadnoc, in which is the image, —

> Of the bullet of the earth
> Whereon ye sail, etc.

Page 344, note 1. Another version of a passage in " May-Day.''

This little note in praise of the animal creation is from one of the verse-books: —

> See how Romance adheres
> To the deer, the lion,
> And every bird,
> Because they are free
> And have no master but Law.
> On the wild ice in depths of sea,
> On Alp or Andes' side,
> In the vast abyss of air,
> The bird, the flying cloud,
> The fire, the wind, the element, —
> These have not manners coarse or cowed,
> And no borrowed will,
> But graceful as cloud and flame
> All eyes with pleasure fill.

Emerson and his brothers walked in youth, must be of earlier date than the "Dirge." It has two verses in common with this, here bracketed.

Here is another account of the brothers' joys,—

> We sauntered amidst miracles,
> We were the fairies of the fells,
> The summer was our quaint bouquet,
> The winter-eve our Milky Way;
> We played in turn with all the slides
> In Nature's lamp of suns and tides;
> We pierced all books with criticism,
> We plied with doubts the catechism,
> The Christian fold,
> The Bible old —

Page 364, note 1. Among the more youthful pieces at end of this volume is another poem on the River and its ciations.

Music. *Page 365, note 1.* The present editor obtained Cabot's permission to include this among the minor ms in the Appendix to the posthumous edition of the ks in 1883, even though Dr. Holmes made some protest st allowing the "mud and scum of things" to have a . At the celebration of the recent centenary of Mr. son's birth, it was pleasant to see that the poem had me a favorite, even with children, and was often quoted.

he Walk. *Page 366, note 1.* Mr. Emerson, after a y walk with Thoreau, wrote in his journal in 1857: Nero advertising for a new pleasure, a walk in the s should have been offered. 'T is one of the secrets for ng old age."

Page 345, note 1. Journal, 1853. "At Nahant the eternal play of the sea seems the anti-clock, or destroyer of the memory of time."

Page 346, note 1. These verses were probably written while Mr. Emerson was visiting Dr. Ezra Ripley (his step-grandfather, always kind and hospitable) at the Manse, after his return from Europe in 1833. Opposite the house is a pasture-hill giving a fine view of the great meadows to the eastward, and, on the western horizon, of some of the mountains on the New Hampshire line.

Page 348, note 1. Journal, 1860. "We can't make half a bow and say, I honor and despise you. But Nature can: she whistles with all her winds and — does as she pleases."

Life. *Page 349, note 1.* See the Address to the Divinity Students (*Nature, Addresses and Lectures,* p. 124).

Page 350, note 1. The Lemures were the household ghosts, and the Lares the household divinities of the Latins.

Page 351, note 1. See "Friendship" (*Essays, First Series,* pp. 191, 211).

Page 352, note 1. The same thought is in the poem "Rubies."

Page 352, note 2. The first four lines are in "The Dæmonic Love."

Page 353, note 1. These verses are written in the older verse-book on the same page with "Eros."

Page 353, note 2. "Statements of the infinite are usually felt to be unjust to the finite, and blasphemous. Empedocles undoubtedly spoke a truth of thought, when he said, 'I am God;' but the moment it was out of his mouth it became a lie to the ear; and the world revenged itself for the seeming arrogance by the good story about his shoe" ("The Method of

Nature," *Nature, Addresses and Lectures*, p. 198). See also *Conduct of Life*, p. 26. Empedocles, the common people believed, threw himself into the crater of Mount Ætna that no trace of his death might appear, and it be supposed that he was translated. Hence, when the volcano cast up his brazen sandal, they were pleased.

Page 357, note 1. In the verse-book, Mr. Emerson gives to these lines the title " Rex," but " The Related Man " might have been better. He delighted in such, as much when he observed them (not, however, filling the dream of high, poetic maids, or consorting with bards and mystics) in the grocery, or insurance-office of the village, as when he saw the master minds of the growing Republic in cities, East or West.

THE BOHEMIAN HYMN. *Page 359, note 1.* This poem appears but once in the verse-books, and no traces of its composition remain, nor is it dated. But from the handwriting it must have been written before 1840, and the internal evidence is convincing that it was written by Mr. Emerson.

Compare a passage in *Representative Men*, pp. 61, 62.

GRACE. *Page 359, note 2.* The *Memoir of Margaret Fuller Ossoli* was written by her friends, Rev. James Freeman Clarke, Rev. William Henry Channing and Mr. Emerson. Mr. Emerson, writing to Mr. Channing about their joint work, referred to this poem thus: —

" For your mottoes to your chapter, I saw that the first had the infinite honor done it of being quoted to Herbert! The verses are mine, — ' Preventing God,' etc., — so I strike them out."

The poem was published in the *Dial* of January, 1842.

INSIGHT. *Page 360, note 1.* This title was given by the editor. The verses have none, and perhaps could be better named. Mr. Emerson wrote the first line also in these forms: —

> Rule that by obedience grows,

and

> Power which by service grows.

PAN. *Page 360, note 2.* Mr. Emerson seems to have considered other titles, as " Pantheos," and " Divine Afflatus." He wrote in the second line " the breath of God," but afterwards decided to use the classical image. By the parables of the divine music played through human pipes, and of the tide of spirit inundating mankind, he teaches the ancient doctrine of Inspiration. In a note-book of 1830 he wrote, " Heracleitus said, ' The senses are canals through which we inhale the divine reason.' " Everywhere in the Essays the *over-soul* is taught, especially in the essay of that name.

MONADNOC FROM AFAR. *Page 361, note 1.* It is strange that Mr. Emerson never printed this little poem. It probably was written not much later than " Monadnoc."

SEPTEMBER. *Page 362, note 1.* These verses have never been printed in full except by Mr. Channing in his *Thoreau the Poet Naturalist*. The text there varies slightly from that here selected as the best version from the journals.

OCTOBER. *Page 362, note 2.* See *Society and Solitude*, p. 298.

PETER'S FIELD. *Page 363.* This poem on the memories and associations of the field by the Concord River, where he

Emerson and his brothers walked in youth, must be of earlier date than the "Dirge." It has two verses in common with this, here bracketed.

Here is another account of the brothers' toys,—

> We sauntered amidst miracles,
> We were the fairies of the fells,
> The summer was our quaint bouquet,
> The winter-eve our Milky Way;
> We played in turn with all the slides
> In Nature's lamp of suns and tides;
> We pierced all books with criticism,
> We plied with doubts the catechism,
> The Christian fold,
> The Bible old —

Page 364, note 1. Among the more youthful pieces at the end of this volume is another poem on the River and its associations.

MUSIC. *Page 365, note 1.* The present editor obtained Mr. Cabot's permission to include this among the minor poems in the Appendix to the posthumous edition of the works in 1883, even though Dr. Holmes made some protest against allowing the "mud and scum of things" to have a voice. At the celebration of the recent centenary of Mr. Emerson's birth, it was pleasant to see that the poem had become a favorite, even with children, and was often quoted.

THE WALK. *Page 366, note 1.* Mr. Emerson, after a day walk with Thoreau, wrote in his journal in 1857: "happy Nero advertising for a new pleasure, a walk in the woods should have been offered. 'T is one of the secrets for dodging old age."

INSIGH *Page 360, note 1.* This title was given by the
editor. T verses have none, and perhaps could be better
named. Mr. Emerson wrote the first line also in these forms: —

and   ͺ le that by obedience grows,

Powe which by service grows.

PAN. *Page 360, note* ₂. Mr. Emerson seems to have considered other titles, as " Pantheos," and " Divine Afflatus."
He wrote in the second line ' the breath of God," but afterwards decided to use the classical image. By the parables of
the divine music played through human pipes, and of the tide
of spirit inundating mankind, he teaches the ancient doctrine
of Inspiration. In a note-book of 1830 he wrote, " Heracleitus
said, ' The senses are canals through which we inhale the divine
reason.' " Everywhere in the Essays the *over-soul* is taught,
especially in the essay of that name.

MONADNOC FROM AFAR. *Page 361, note 1.* It is strange
that Mr. Emerson never printed this little poem. It probably
was written not much later than " Monadnoc."

SEPTEMBER. *Page 362, note 1.* These verses have n
been printed in full except by Mr. Channing in his *Thoreau,*
the Poet Naturalist. The text there varies slightly from ʌau,
here selected as the best version from the journals.   hat

OCTOBER. *Page 362, note 2.* See *Society and Solitu*
p. 298.
                                                          de,

PETER'S FIELD. *Page 363.* This poem on the memo
and associations of the field by the Concord River, where   ries
                                                          Mr.

Page 345, *note 1*. Journal, 1853. " At Nahant the eternal play of the sea seems the anti-clock, or destroyer of the memory of time."

Page 346, *note 1*. These verses were probably written while Mr. Emerson was visiting Dr. Ezra Ripley (his step-grandfather, always kind and hospitable) at the Manse, after his return from Europe in 1833. Opposite the house is a pasture-hill giving a fine view of the great meadows to the eastward, and, on the western horizon, of some of the mountains on the New Hampshire line.

Page 348, *note 1*. Journal, 1860. " We can't make half a bow and say, I honor and despise you. But Nature can: she whistles with all her winds and — does as she pleases."

LIFE. *Page 349*, *note 1*. See the Address to the Divinity Students (*Nature, Addresses and Lectures*, p. 124).

Page 350, *note 1*. The Lemures were the household ghosts, and the Lares the household divinities of the Latins.

Page 351, *note 1*. See " Friendship " (*Essays, First Series*, pp. 191, 211).

Page 352, *note 1*. The same thought is in the poem " Rubies."

Page 352, *note 2*. The first four lines are in " The Dæmonic Love."

Page 353, *note 1*. These verses are written in the older verse-book on the same page with " Eros."

Page 353, *note 2*. " Statements of the infinite are usually felt to be unjust to the finite, and blasphemous. Empedocles undoubtedly spoke a truth of thought, when he said, ' I am God;' but the moment it was out of his mouth it became a lie to the ear; and the world revenged itself for the seeming arrogance by the good story about his shoe" (" The Method of

Nature," *Nature, Addresses and Lectures*, p. 198). See also *Conduct of Life*, p. 26. Empedocles, the common people believed, threw himself into the crater of Mount Ætna that no trace of his death might appear, and it be supposed that he was translated. Hence, when the volcano cast up his brazen sandal, they were pleased.

Page 357, note 1. In the verse-book, Mr. Emerson gives to these lines the title " Rex," but " The Related Man " might have been better. He delighted in such, as much when he observed them (not, however, filling the dream of high, poetic maids, or consorting with bards and mystics) in the grocery, or insurance-office of the village, as when he saw the master minds of the growing Republic in cities, East or West.

THE BOHEMIAN HYMN. *Page 359, note 1.* This poem appears but once in the verse-books, and no traces of its composition remain, nor is it dated. But from the handwriting it must have been written before 1840, and the internal evidence is convincing that it was written by Mr. Emerson.

Compare a passage in *Representative Men*, pp. 61, 62.

GRACE. *Page 359, note 2.* The *Memoir of Margaret Fuller Ossoli* was written by her friends, Rev. James Freeman Clarke, Rev. William Henry Channing and Mr. Emerson. Mr. Emerson, writing to Mr. Channing about their joint work, referred to this poem thus: —

" For your mottoes to your chapter, I saw that the first had the infinite honor done it of being quoted to Herbert! The verses are mine, — ' Preventing God,' etc., — so I strike them out."

The poem was published in the *Dial* of January, 1842.

COSMOS. *Page 367, note 1.* These verses have no title in the verse-books. " Cosmos " is given by the editor. They were originally trials for a " Song of Nature," — Nature is speaking. The May element claimed the later verses, though their sequence was never made out, the first divisions harmonizing fairly, but the last two hopelessly dislocated, though they have a certain charm.

THE MIRACLE. *Page 369, note 1.* This poem was written at about the same period with " My Garden," " Boston " and " Waldeinsamkeit," between 1857 and 1865.

THE WATERFALL. *Page 369, note 2.* In addition to his Walden wood-lots, Mr. Emerson bought one on the edge of Lincoln, for the sake of a miniature waterfall in a little brook, the outlet of Flint's Pond. Mr. Thoreau showed him additional charms, certain shrubs and flowers not plentiful in Concord that grew on its banks, — veratrum with its tropical growth, trillium, jack-in-the-pulpit, yellow violets, and the hornbeam, arrow-wood and a bush of mountain laurel. It was a wonderful resort for the various kinds of thrushes.

WALDEN. *Page 370.* This poem represents the early form of " My Garden." As years went on, verses were added, and at last the groups became distinct.

THE ENCHANTER. *Page 373, note 1.* " Shakspeare is the only biographer of Shakspeare; and even he can tell nothing, except to the Shakspeare in us, that is, to our most apprehensive and sympathetic hour." — *Representative Men*, p. 208.

GOETHE. *Page 373, note 2.* Mr. Emerson read Goethe's works through, largely out of his love for Carlyle, who constantly praised Goethe to him. Writing to his friend, in April, 1840, he said: —

"You asked me if I read German. . . . I have contrived to read almost every volume of Goethe, and I have fifty-five [these were little leather-bound duodecimos], but I have read nothing else [i. e. in German], but I have not now looked even into Goethe, for a long time."

This letter shows approximately the date of the verses.

RICHES. *Page 374, note 1.* There seems to be no question that this is Mr. Emerson's work, in spite of the Scottish garb in which, for his amusement, he clothed the little simile. It has no title in the verse-book.

PHILOSOPHER *and* INTELLECT. *Page 375, note 1.* There is a passage in the journal for 1845, called "Icy light," on the cold-bloodedness of the philosopher, most of which is printed in *Representative Men:* —

"Intellect puts an interval. . . . It is the chief deduction, almost the sole deduction from the merit of Plato (that which is no doubt incidental to this regnancy of the intellect in his work), that his writings have not the vital authority which the screams of prophets and the sermons of unlettered Arabs and Jews possess. There is an interval; and to the cohesion, contact is necessary. Intellect is the king of non-committal: answers with generalities. He gave me wit instead of love."

LIMITS. *Page 375, note 2.* See "History," in *Essays, First Series,* pp. 39, 40.

INSCRIPTION. *Page 376.* This was written at the request of Mrs. John M. Forbes, and is carved on a stone watering-fountain on the top of Milton Hill.

POEMS OF YOUTH AND EARLY MANHOOD

As was said in the Preface, these verses are printed, not for their poetical merit, but as showing the influence, on Mr. Emerson's character, thought and expression, of the sad and the happy events of the third decade of his life. Only a reserve in his strength that could hardly have been expected, together with the serenity of his nature, which was content to wait until the storm blew by, preserved his life during this period with disease ever threatening when it was not actually disabling him. After his establishment of his home in Concord and his second marriage, his health was almost uniformly good, in spite of the very serious exposure involved in his winter lecturing journeys afar, for the remainder of his life.

PRAYER. *Page 380.* The incident of the hayfield where the Methodist haymaker said to Emerson, raking hay beside him on his uncle's farm, that men are always praying, and that all prayers are granted, which gave him the subject of his first sermon, is told in Mr. Cabot's Memoir. It seems to have suggested lines in this poem.

TO-DAY. *Page 382.* Dr. Holmes has named Mr. Emerson's Phi Beta Kappa Address in 1837 as " Our intellectual Declaration of Independence," but this boyish poem, written thirteen years earlier, shows the germ which grew into the " American Scholar."

FAME. *Page 383.* This bit of youthful irony on a theme which, even in college, its author often wrote upon, " Being and Seeming," was very possibly playfully addressed to one of his brothers, or, it may be, to himself.

THE SUMMONS. *Page 384.* In the year 1822, Mr. Emerson wrote to a classmate: "I am (I wish I was otherwise) keeping a school, and assisting my venerable brother to lift the truncheon against the fair-haired daughters of this raw city. . . . Better tug at the oar, . . . or saw wood, . . . better sow hemp, or hang with it, than sow the seeds of instruction ! " Next year matters were worse, for William went abroad, leaving him the school, — a formidable experience for a shy youth, still a minor, and younger than some of his fair and troublesome pupils. The "Good-bye, proud world" was his utterance of relief when he fled from them. They were the "silken troop," skilful in producing his "uneasy blush" alluded to in the present poem. Now he was to have the pulpit for a breastwork, for in 1826 he was approbated to preach.

It is interesting to see that the image of the procession of Days, so often used later, was already in his thought.

THE RIVER. *Page 385.* In the same month in which these lines were written, their author told his brother, in a letter, that he meditated abdicating the profession, for "the lungs in their spiteful lobes sing sexton and sorrow whenever I only ask them to shout a sermon for me."

The poem was evidently written in the beautiful orchard running down to the Concord River behind the Manse.

GOOD HOPE. *Page 387.* These verses show reviving life, and very likely were written when, in December, 1827, the young minister, going to Concord, New Hampshire, to preach, first saw Ellen Tucker, a beautiful girl of seventeen.

LINES TO ELLEN. *Page 387.* A year from the time when he first saw Miss Tucker, Mr. Emerson again went to Concord, New Hampshire, and soon after became engaged to her.

A MOUNTAIN GRAVE. *Page 390.* After the death of his wife, and during the time when the enlargement of his mental horizon made Mr. Emerson regard the forms in use in the church with increasing repugnance, his health again underwent severe strain, and his future became very uncertain, as the next two poems show.

HYMN. *Page 393.* In the main body of this volume is printed the hymn,

> We love the venerable house
> Our fathers built to God,

which was sung at the ordination of Rev. Chandler Robbins, Mr. Emerson's successor. The hymn here printed was probably the first trial for a fit utterance for that occasion.

SELF-RELIANCE. *Page 394.* These lines, without title, however, were written at the time when he resigned his place as pastor of the Second Church.

Mr. Emerson's friend, Mr. Charles Eliot Norton, relates that when they were making the home voyage from England together in 1873, Mr. Emerson showed him his pocket-compass, which he said he carried with him in travelling, and added, " I like to hold the god in my hands."

NAPLES *and* ROME. *Pages 395 and 396.* Journal, Divinity Hall, November, 1827. " Don't you see you are the Universe to yourself? You carry your fortunes in your own hand.

Change of place won't mend the matter. You will weave the same web at Pernambuco as at Boston, if you have only learned how to make *one* texture."

Journal, 1834. "Remember the Sunday morning in Naples when I said, 'This moment is the truest vision, the best spectacle I have seen amid all the wonders; and this moment, this vision, I might have had in my own closet in Boston.' "

" Our first journeys discover to us the indifference of places. At home I dream that at Naples, at Rome, I can be intoxicated with beauty and lose my sadness. I pack my trunk, embrace my friends, embark on the sea and at last wake up in Naples, and there beside me is the stern fact, the sad self, unrelenting, identical, that I fled from. I seek the Vatican and the palaces. I affect to be intoxicated with sights and suggestions, but I am not intoxicated. My giant goes with me wherever I go." — *Self-Reliance.*

WEBSTER. *Page 398.* The first of these fragments on New England's idol — until his apostasy to the cause of human Freedom, in the interests of Union — was the last verse of those beginning,

> Has God on thee conferred
> A bodily presence mean as Paul's,

printed a few pages earlier in this book. The second was the best passage in the Phi Beta Kappa poem, not otherwise remarkable. The third was written sadly after Webster's death.

INDEX OF FIRST LINES

INDEX OF FIRST LINES

INDEX OF TITLES

INDEX OF TITLES

[The titles in small capital letters are those of the principal divisions of the work; those in lower case are of single poems, or the subdivisions of long poems.]

IX

The Riverside Press

CAMBRIDGE · MASSACHUSETTS

U · S · A